Contemporary Kazakh Literature
Poetry Anthology

RÝHANI
JAŃĠYRÝ

The project
«Modern Kazakh Culture in the Global World»
has been realised upon the initiative of the First President of
the Republic of Kazakhstan – Elbasy (Leader of the Nation)
Nursultan Nazarbayev within the framework of the State Programme
Rýhani Jaŋġyrý (Spiritual Rebirth – Modernisation of Kazakhstan's
Identity)

Contemporary
Kazakh
Literature | Poetry

This book is commissioned by the Ministry of Culture and Sport of the Republic of Kazakhstan

©Ұлттық Аударма Бюросы (National Bureau of Translations) 2019

18 Dostyk Street, Office 25, Nur-Sultan, Esil District, The Republic of Kazakhstan

https://100kitap.kz/kz

This book is published by 'Ұлттық Аударма Бюросы' қоғамдық қоры
(Public Foundation National Bureau of Translations) working in partnership with Cambridge University Press.

The publishers would like to acknowledge the support of the Chairman of Rýhani Jańgyrý National Commission Marat Tazhin, and the Secretary of the National Commission Aida Balayeva, and the assistance of the following individuals: Khaliolla Baimen, Zhadyra Baymakhan, Assiya Issemberdiyeva, Narbin Kenzhegulova, Rauan Kenzhekhanuly, Gaukhar Khalyk, Timur Muktarov, Assel Tauekel, Umit Tazhken, Aknur Toleubayeva, Alikhan Tuiebay, Zemfira Yerzhan.

First published in 2019

Printed in the United Kingdom by Latimer Trend

ISBN 978-601-7943-43-1

NATIONAL
BUREAU
OF TRANSLATIONS

If we want to be a nation with a unique place on the global map of the 21st century, we should implement one more project – Modern Kazakh Culture in the Global World. We need the world to know about us not only because of oil resources and major foreign policy initiatives, but because of our cultural achievements as well. First, we need a targeted approach in order to make our domestic culture better known in the six UN languages: English, Russian, Chinese, Spanish, Arabic, and French.

For the first time our culture will be known in all continents and in all main languages.

First President of the Republic of Kazakhstan – Elbasy
Nursultan Nazarbayev

CONTENTS

A NOTE ON TRANSLITERATION

The international *ISO 9 standard of Romanizing the Cyrillic Characters* has been applied while transliterating the Kazakh terms, geographical and personal names. The fact that this norm has been developed by the International Organization for Standardization and adopted by a number of countries in Europe and Asia as a main tool in transliterating the Cyrillic characters into Latin characters has been taken into consideration. Moreover, the Euro-Asian Council for Standardization, Metrology and Certification of 9 CIS countries adopted *The System of Standards on Information, Librarianship and Publishing Rules of Transliteration of Cyrillic Script by Latin Alphabet* in 2000, authentic to the ISO 9 standard.

The Kazakh government has been developing a Latin alphabet for the Kazakh language which, it is planned, will replace the current Cyrillic script in 2025. Although the new version of the alphabet was published in 2018, the grammar is yet to be developed. The current standard of transliteration of Kazakh terms is used in order to avoid any misspellings and discrepancies in the future.

However, while transliterating the names of contemporary Kazakh authors, their own preferred spellings through which they are recognised internationally have been applied.

Russian terms, geographical and personal names have been transliterated according to the *BGN/PCGN Romanization System for Russian* widely used elsewhere.

FOREWORD

Today, Kazakhstan is home to over a hundred ethnic groups, a diversity in national unity reflected by the poets collected in this anthology. More than this, these poets herald First President Nazabayev's programme for Kazakh writers to bring into being *Ruhani Žaṇġyru* or a 'Spiritual Revival', crystallising a distinctive national identity in this vibrant and confident young republic, which is taking its rightful place in the cultural and economic commerce of the modern world. Kazakh poets can draw on the legacy of vivid oral traditions – the poetry contests, *ajtys*, performed by professional bards, as well as rituals (wedding songs, childbirth songs, mourning songs), a colourful panorama of narrative folklore and myth, not forgetting the heroic epics befitting the ancestry of this proud warrior people. These oral traditions took on powerful written form during the nationalist consciousness of the nineteenth century. The senior contributors to this anthology bear witness to the traumas of the twentieth century, the decimation of the Kazakh intelligentsia in Stalin's purges, and those never-to-return fathers and uncles lost in the sacrifice made by the Soviet Union during the Second World War. The younger contributors to this anthology blend this historical consciousness with the technical experimentation of the international avant-garde. Such diverse ingredients give contemporary Kazakh poetry a unique complexion and flavour.

The Nobel-prize winning poet T.S. Eliot once remarked: 'The serious writer of verse must be prepared to cross himself with the best verse of other languages'. Translation has always been the crucial medium for this fruitful cross-pollination. For the first time, this anthology introduces Kazakh poetry to the consciousness of English-language readers. It strikes me that these translations from Kazakh have been highly successful in conveying both the resilience of old traditions and the forging of newer ones. Among the delights to be savoured in these poets are meditations on love, ageing and loss, expressions of pride in region and homeland, celebrations of hospitality and customs, confrontations with the grandeur of mountain, steppe and forest, flights of linguistic wit and verbal play, as well as a nascent concern for ecological issues and, emerging from the traditional framework of Kazakh society, the voices of women poets. To a foreign observer, this constellation of poets offers a rare glimpse not only into the history and geography but, above all, the imagination shaping modern Kazakhstan, initiating a dialogue with the literatures of other nations and languages, and nourishing those pleasures afforded by cross-cultural conversation and exchange.

There is little doubt that the effects of a disintegration of traditional nomadic Kazakh culture have served only to intensify and strengthen a fiercely independent national spirit. Freed of Communist Party compulsion, the modern Kazakh poet enjoys an untrammelled sense of playful reciprocity with their readership. 'Poems are an open letter to the people, / every word carefully chosen' declares the late Kadyr Myrza Ali, the oldest poet in this collection. In his poem 'Mother Tongue', Tumanbay Moldagaliyev bestows the gifts of the Kazakh language and literature to his son with clear pride: 'Understand / my language which is yours and take / my Kazakh heart. The rest is up to you.' The poems of Chinese-born Marfuga Aitkhozha, a keen translator, acutely register the pain of forced migrations – 'Whenever birds fly, whenever they leave, / it always has a meaning' – and, like the Irish legends employed in the poetry of W.B. Yeats, she admires the proud purity of swans, symbols of love and of national renewal. Aitkhozha commits herself to the future of Kazakhstan with a moving, humble, plainspoken simplicity: 'I am a poet at one with her people'. Yesenqul Jaqypbek came to prominence as a skilled improviser, a master of traditional *ajtys*, recognising towards the end of his life that it was the bond with his Kazakh audience that had helped him to mature as a poet: 'I was a tree whose flimsy branches were bent by birds. / People's kindness made me a sturdy tree.' In 'The Man Without a Name' Jaqypbek gregariously welcomes a visitor to his metaphorical feast table; hospitality to outsiders is a feature of the civilisations of Central Asia.

Affection for the rural Kazakh *auyls*, the very heartland of the nation, appears as a symbol of domestic comfort and of durable ties of extended family that survive in modern urban and industrial Kazakhstan beyond their origins in nomadic patterns of life. Fariza Ongarsynova's delightful poem 'Patterns of Grass and Flowers Ran Down onto the Carpets' conjures the thick textures of the interior of the Kazakh yurt, here sipping tea before a smoking hearth, and extolling the moveable pleasures that must be savoured by a people 'born in the saddle and [who] live on the road.' Wild passions are unleashed when Ongarsynova dramatises the 'Thoughts of the Old Kazakh', his sabre and harness flashing on the sunlit steppe. Svetqali Nurjan was a horseman in western Kazakhstan before making his debut as a poet. His 'In Search of Five Weapons' is fuelled by dreams of the swashbuckling life of his predecessors. Nadezhda Chernova is a poet who also revivifies Kazakh folklore, invoking the music of the *dombyra*, a plucked string instrument used by wandering *aḳyns*, to sing of the Žajran Steppe. Nesipbek Aituly has written epic poems dedicated to celebrated Kazakh heroes and events, asserting: 'If I proclaim my country's name, / the spirit of perished heroes will rise.' Each of these poets, in their different ways, demonstrates how it is possible to create links between a legendary past and the new voices of an independent Republic of Kazakhstan.

The immensity of Kazakh geography and its diverse climes has been a source of inspiration for many Kazakh poets. Dreaming of the 'inexhaustible improvisations' – in the words of Kadyr Myrza Ali – of the broad open steppe is a symbol of homeland where the poet can feel the spirit of ancestors. Aituly writes 'Steppe, no time to waste / in drawing your son into / your warm embrace ...'. The English romantic poets were inspired by a leafy countryside constructed on an altogether less epic scale. The sweeping wide angle of vision provided by the flat steppe horizon can be breath taking. Endless forest and steppe enter the imaginative sweep of the poems of Vladimir Gundarev, although at times disciplined by the crisp syllabic forms to be found in Japanese and Korean poetry: 'Earth's head is tired of / rocking on its own slender axis.' Akushtap Bakhtygereyeva views scattered migratory swallows or a lone seagull wandering off-course onto the arid steppe as a trigger for reflections on love, family or the passage of time. Lyubov Shashkova transports us to northern Kazakhstan: 'Erejmentau melting in the haze', claiming the steppe as the heart of the Kazakh poet, 'Only her song / flies in the blink of an eye, / and soars above the ground / rises high into the sky.' In a melancholy mood, Shashkova captures another aspect of her homeland: 'I look at the steppe in the empty gloom. / I recognise it and I weep.'

The love of country entails sensitivity to the impositions of any colonial impact. In the years of the Cold War, Kazakhstan became a site of Soviet nuclear weapons testing, bequeathing a toxic ecological legacy. Olzhas Suleimenov, a trained geologist and anti-nuclear campaigner, conveys a deep affinity with his country through subtle tones and styles, evocative scents and smells, and striking images; for example, in 'August Nights ...' – 'Night fragrant, like tea. / An old carpet thrown down, / fescue on the thick grass, / darkness behind the trunks of / apricot trees / like a crow'. Suleimenov's stylistic control is masterful, his range extraordinary, his poetic voice always warm and inviting. Mukhtar Shakhanov's poems display the worldliness of a prominent public figure who has considered deeply the painful upheavals of Kazakh independence. The virtues of courage and of loyalty, modestly expressed, speak through his poetry, which is shadowed by threats of discord and death. Bakhytzhan Kanapyanov was not afraid to court controversy under Soviet rule, the sort of courage admired by Shakhanov, and yet his poems are notable for the pellucid pristine imagery of the 'clean, cascading wave' of a torrent in a mountain ravine, or the pregnant stillness when 'The forest's heavy silence / is holding the snowflakes in balance.' He is a poet of tender moments – the breath of a sleeping lover rippling the air 'as if she were in the care / of a ghost in a butterfly's shape.'

Tumanbay Moldagaliyev is another recorder of the intricate shifting shades of love, firmly in the Western romantic tradition, but with a modern irony and bathos. The romantic idealist in Moldagaliyev is gently scolded by the wiser yet no less ardent older poetic self: 'Listen, my heart, / don't be fooled any more / by the dream that once opened the door.' In 'Perhaps You Remember the Winter Garden ...' Ulugbek Yesdaulet wistfully recalls embracing his lover in a passionate 'whirlwind of snow' before making a poignant admission: 'Since then, I've had a lot of losses – / desperate ones from those who are insatiable, /

criminally kissing those I don't love ...'. Feelings of nostalgic regret temper the heat of the youthful ardour of these poets.

'I am descended from warriors and hunters' declared Kadyr Myrza Ali with unabashed pride, and yet the reciprocal duties of traditional gender roles have been transfigured rather than rejected by many modern Kazakh poets, engendering some thoughtful reflections. One of the most pleasing aspects of this anthology is the emergence of strong female voices from out of the shadow of the patriarchal family values enshrined in folktale and epic. Kulash Akhmetova has been justly praised for the delicate sensitivity with which she embraces her inheritance from Kazakh culture. In 'A Prayer for My Son and Daughter' each child is given equal hope, a mother's tender blessing, to live a fulfilling life: 'Let each be granted a virtuous partner, / a golden family, a stalwart friend.'

Among a younger generation of female poets, Gulnar Salykbay's work lends a wonderful freshness of vision to her often romantic poetic themes, a defamiliarising inventiveness signalled by her titles 'The Sky Can Capsize Out of the Blue', 'Waiting for You Is Like Adding Pepper to Honey', 'Even the Sky Didn't Suit You', in which a quick wit brings to life the serious drama of her predicament. Tanakoz Tolkynkyzy similarly adds new angles of vision to Kazakh women's writing, daringly exploring the pains of betrayal and vulnerability. Aliya Dauletbayeva's poems express a colloquial lyricism, at times tentative in advancing the ebbs and flows of emotion, mindful of the reproaches of transgression or degradation – 'I conceal my confusion, head well down, / in these days that move along haltingly out of step / with these times where I block out thoughts of eternity / in this restlessly meditative, colourful world.'. In 'The Red Dress', Nazira Berdaly parades an eye-catching colour only to wonder, 'am I like a crimson flower / that no one dares to pick?' Each of these contemporary female poets responds to the presence of modern liberal values in Kazakh society and muses thoughtfully on the changes, complex and variegated, that affect individual lives.

New voices, then, add to the richness of Kazakh literature. Maraltai Raiymbekuly has been an influence on younger poets by creating outlandish images out of everyday material. This transformation of the quotidian is strikingly manifested in the surrealist flights of Akberen Yelgezek, his bourgeois life dispelled by dream-like transformations: 'The suitcase I carry becomes a black dog' precedes an alarming metamorphosis whereby 'I seem insubstantial. / I'm a shirt flapping in the wind.' Bauyrzhan Karagyzuly, in common with Raiymbekuly, combines the piety of Islamic faith with a rapt engagement with the landscape and the people of Kazakhstan. This metaphysical perspective is ultimately both uplifting and life-enhancing. Yerlan Junis, the youngest poet in this anthology, is another contemporary Kazakh poet working out the implications of the unconscious that were mined by Surrealism. 'Don't have many on my wavelength' he disarmingly suggests, although this is more a measure of the shy delicacy of his meditations rather than any inability to capture and express subtle shades of feeling. It is a pleasure to make his poetic acquaintance.

There is an intellectual tenacity in the poems of Tynyshtyqbek Abdikakimuly, who proclaims his study room is crammed with books, some as sweet as wine, others as sour as fermented camel milk: 'There are many books. / Some are like wine, / others taste like *šubat.*' His poems are learned, allusive, elaborate, even cosmic, and daring in execution. The cascading free-verse rhythms of Yessengali Raushanov are a marvel. They possess the sinew and vigour of Ezra Pound's *Cantos*, although this may derive more from his absorption of the oral traditions of Kazakh folklore; after all, in 'The Blast of a Siren ...', Raushanov declares that he is nourished by his homeland: 'I am myself once more / as I return to the source ... / Greetings, *auyl.*'

Several poets in this anthology enjoy, flaunt, their experimental flights. Valery Mikhailov's remarkable poem 'Khlebnikov' pays homage to this Russian Futurist, a revolutionary poet whose radical fractures of morphology and syntax are imagined as volcanic ruptures of solid bedrock: 'magma oozed like leprosy / through the ancient, fragmenting layers.' Iran-Ghayip, a translator of Vladimir Mayakovsky, can adopt the Russian's heroic self-assertion albeit with knowledge of the gun that ended this young life in suicide: 'I'm a gun – / a self-loader. / With a trigger – pulled by itself.' Kazakh poets still wrestle with the creative example of the phase of post-revolutionary Russian poetry, an ambivalent wrestling with the twin inheritance of Soviet idealism and Kazakh nationalism. 'The professor is in a rage. / He has a grudge against us,' writes Serik Aksunkar, a graduate of the Kazakh State University, 'Mayakovsky is his theme'. In 'Monologue of a Wolf' Aksunkar pointedly distinguishes the genealogy of barking dogs from the brave dignity of the Kazakh wolf: 'I am a wild creature / of the wide steppe'.

Descended from horse-riding nomads and warriors, it is perhaps not unexpected to find that horses – swift, sturdy or resilient, galloping in races, battle or in love trysts, prized or stolen, tended to and nursed, as sources of succour, of meat, or even a sweet mead – are a recurrent motif in this anthology. The metaphor of the poet as a skilled steppe horseman is particularly apt. Aksundar's 'Poem of the Nomadic Scythians' bridles the legendary winged stallion ridden by the heroes of myth with his Kazakh nationalism: 'I ran from the steppe into the sky / And a white cloud kissed my wings.' The muse of 'In a Moment of Inspiration' by Temirkhan Medetbek, who can effortlessly combine elemental human passions with an intellectual's self-conscious awareness of our contemporary geopolitical conflict, is equally exalted. His heroic figure of the poet transcends historical trauma and soars above the Great Steppe: 'He's like a whole nation / fighting for its honour.'

Professor Jason Harding, Durham University

KADYR MYRZA ALI
(5.01.1935 – 24.01.2011)

Kadyr Myrza Ali was a poet. He graduated from the Faculty of Philology of Kirov Kazakh State University (now Ǎl-Farabi Kazakh National University) in 1958 before going on to complete a master's degree there. He combined his life as a poet with a career in publishing and politics. His first post was with the children's journal *Baldyrġan* (1958–62), where he went on to be head of poetry and criticism as well as executive secretary for the journal *Žŭldyz* (1962–65). From here he progressed to become head of poetry, initially at the publishing house Žazušy (1968–73) and then at the Writers' Union of the Kazakh SSR (1973–78). In 1992 he was made deputy chairman of the Committee on National Policy, Development of Culture and Language of the Supreme Council of the Republic of Kazakhstan, before finally being elected as a people's deputy in 1994.

His first collection of poems was *Kôktem* (Spring, 1959), followed by *Danyšpan* (The Wise Man, 1961), *Kiškene Ķožanasyr* (A Little Ķožanasyr, 1961), *Oj-Orman* (Thoughts as Thick as Forests, 1965), *Dala Didary* (Face of the Earth, 1966), *Dombyra* (1971), *Žerŭjyķ* (The Promised Land, 1976), *Žazmyš* (Fate, 2001) and *Eņirep ôtken erleraj* (Heroes of the Past, 2001). He also published prose, including a two-volume collection of aphorisims, *Almas žerde ķalmas* (Diamond Cannot Be Ignored, 2004). He wrote plays and historical fiction, and translated foreign literature prolifically into Kazakh. He published a twenty-volume edition of selected works in 2010.

Myrza Ali was the winner of numerous awards: the Lenin Komsomol Prize (1966), the State Prize of the Kazakh SSR for his poem collection *Žerŭjyķ* (1980), the Grand Prix of the Creative and Literary Association of Mongolia (1993), Daryn State Prize for Youth (1993), and the Platinum Tarlan Award (2001). He was the recipient of the Orders of Parasat (2005) and Dostyķ (2010).

Possibilities

They tell you
the snow is melting.
Is the winter just sweating, in fact?
They tell you
that they've seen lightning.
Did the dark just cover a crack?

They tell you
it's barely been raining.
Has the water been squeezed from the clouds?
They tell you
the sky gave a rumble –
or were their whispers that loud?

They tell you
the *Samüryķ* [1] is soaring.
Was a fledgling testing its wings?
They tell you
the nightingale's calling.
Or is somebody sobbing as he sings?

---

[1] *Samüryķ* – in Kazakh folklore, a gigantic, powerful, typically benevolent mythical bird which acts as a mediator between the three worlds: celestial (gods), earthly (man) and underworld (the dead).

The Earth

Now I've found my yurt a place on the globe,
the earth's ordeals are likewise mine.
This means I've broken up with sleep
and forgotten how nightingales hail the dawn.

When moonlight turns the snow to silver,
who wants blood on the earth?
                    Here's Genghis,
together with Batu, Hitler, Attila
skewing their fatal way through the centuries.

More than once they slit the earth's veins,
and more than once stuffed its head in a noose.
But someone whose planet of birth was the same
helped them to walk and worked as their nurse.

Who can enumerate the innumerable tortures,
the civilizations now just ashes?
All of these now
               are the earth's open sores.
And their names are Ravensbrück and Auschwitz.

Earth that I love, you'll need to forgive us
our dreadful fate. You look so defenceless.
If only I could have you sit
on my lap,
            I'd stroke your head and be gentle.

Žigit, Whatever the Storm

Žigit,[2] whatever the storm
that's gathering over our heads,
don't hide your face in fear
but fight for as long as you live.
If victory slips through our fingers,
and we outride death,
what will your boy and mine
then think of us?

Better to go up in flames,
fall into a river of lead,
than lose yourself
and your nerve in battle.
Any *žigit*,
my friend,
can fall on his knees,
but only to kiss
his own, holy earth.

Translated by Alistair Noon

[2.] *Žigit* – generally denoting a 25- to 40-year-old male, the term can also be used as an honorific indicating bravery, endurance, fortitude and being true to one's word.

I Am Descended
from Warriors and Hunters

I am descended from warriors and hunters.
I can walk on thin, unsteady ice.
I can fly to the cheerful starry bonfire.
I can extinguish like a red coal in the ashes of darkness.

Someone's happy, another's sad.
I slip their mind.
I'm bombarded with a chorus of voices.
I'm a river in spate, bursting my banks.
I am safe in my bed, the torrent easing.

In the most precious depths of our soul,
there is frozen ground or a crooked mirror.
I make people laugh, then sink into sadness,
good and evil in a single soul.

On clear days I am both young and old.
My soul gazes at the land, each blade of grass.
A happy thunderstorm
rumbles in the sky,
but inspiration only lasts a moment.

It is a waste of time brooding on my sins.
Better to let honour drive my best efforts in life.
My soul rushes thoughts into the abyss of the sky,
only for them to dash back to earth in a vicious circle.

Translated by Belinda Cooke

Mother, You Were the Start of It All

Mother, you were the start of it all,
the very first word, the very first verse,
as I gurgled, your answer the one that would fall.
It was out of your arms I glimpsed the world first.

Mother, you were the start of it all.
Your eyes are the skies I'm floating through.
Your scolds were sharp when you needed to call
me back. I'm afraid, but only of you.

And whatever you took was always small,
however much it was that you'd give.
This earth, this homeland, what would it all
have come to if you had not even lived?

A Secret of Mine

Each of us has troubles to face.
Take me, cramped, however much space
I've got, and wanting to split my own skull
with a rusted axe: years leave their trace.

There's a wheel my hand is trying to turn,
but my hand is clumsy and less than firm.
I'm not even able to rip out my tongue,
my powerless tongue that resembles a worm.

No, things aren't good, the way they stand.
Sometimes I feel that it's time to hang
from a hook like a ram … Not simple, either,
even when life seems to slip through your hands.

You head for the hills, the ravine is your fate.
The wise strike flag, but the bold will debate.
Whatever, I'm willing to live like you,
at peace with myself, and able to wait.

All I Need Is to See the Fruits
of My Labour

All I need is to see the fruits of my labour.
I don't need silver, I don't need gold.
I'll teach them something, these toddlers who caper
around the sand box, before I'm too old.

The evening is fresh as it follows its course,
but dreams and heat pound away in my head.
As if crossing the steppe, then releasing my horse,
I'd like to lie down on cool grass and rest.

At school I learned my letters and sums,
and must have mastered the art of song.
But I sense an urge, when I see the young,
to swoop through the streets with them now, headlong.

I know what nobody knows about me,
delve into the very last chink of my soul.
I could tell any passing woman how she
looks beautiful out on her evening stroll.

No inheritance, no Qur'an
will save you from tears or ease your mind.
The fact that my enemy is suffering harm,
even his death, leaves nothing behind.

Only a word from the heart, like a leaf
as it falls from a branch, uncovers the truth.
Who knows how to map out my grief?
Who can locate my misery's root?

They freeze, these lines the ice has trapped.
They burn, these lines the fire has charred.
Enough of that now. As if armour-clad,
I walk in thought along these boulevards.

The First Lyric

The jealous give one last cry,
and then their longing ceases.
The dutiful hero will die,
his death in battle a release.

For robbers, a single thrust
from a knife is the fate they face.
It seems the beautiful must
choke inside an embrace.

The steppe-racer leaves behind
the flat-spread dust when he dies.
And no defence was his mind
where the poet's body lies.

Translated by Alistair Noon

Why, in God's Name, Do They Sharpen Their Sword on You …?

Why, in God's name, do they
sharpen their sword on you, so the
blade shines squalidly over the heart
and your heart grows cold?

Trouble still lingers somewhere
over the heart – only the threat is ashes,
it wheezes, caught in a noose,
like an unbridled horse.

The black hearth smokes heavily,
mist hovers about the eyes …
First heart attack – and
death's not cancelled, just on hold.

You might be tougher than diamond,
when that fierce tremor attacks your soul,
but how do you know till it happens,
if you'll make it through next time?

To see life as a nice house,
is an unrealisable dream.
Isn't it really just filled with bile,
nothing else from end to end?

There are words that are harder,
more lethal than a mace,
uttered without pity,
your strength is hard to bear.

Let trouble caution you to take care
of yourself and your heart, my friend.
Hold your anger in check – or you'll end up
breaking someone else's heart for good.

Can You Call Someone Son, if He Fails in His Sacred Duty to His Parents?

Can you call someone son, if he fails
in his sacred duty to his parents?
My job is like the bustle in a
hotel from dawn to dusk.

Day after day, business comes
and goes in an endless routine.
Happiness lights up like a flame.
Sadness comes and shares trouble.

You hurry and rush to and fro.
You see no rest from worries,
like water moving in nature,
a never-ending circle of troubles.

Scarce finished one thing, you must
get to the roots of another. No time
to take a breath, mountains weigh
you down – all that endless work.

Too weak to overcome fatigue,
you can barely move your lips …
It's not just trying to write precisely,
hard even to construct the words.

Sluggish, I can't keep up with
all these affairs, unable to lift the burden.
All these worries drive like a lash,
my shoulders crushed with overwork.

Thoughts circle on all sides,
like a clockwork carousel,
leaving me overwrought and exhausted,
till I fall down in bed half dead.

Yet don't take my gloomy looks
to be a complaint.
If you hold a grudge against life,
you'll never fully know happiness.

A difficult life is worth infinitely more
than an easy death. Happy the person
who can be glad about work, glad about care,
on whose shoulders sweat does not dry.

When Peace Is Given to All Living Things

When peace is given to all living things
I lie down on the sofa,
to remember my best lines.
They keep me like a talisman.

The language of the poet is holy to lovers,
light – for the blind, for the deaf – an alarm.
Poems are an open letter to the people,
every word carefully chosen.

Every line is strong with patience,
and life is equal to its price.
In its last breath, its true testament,
its way lies in other times.

The flow of life is close to my roots,
the rustling leaves of my nights and days.
My poems are lava forced up from the
bowels of the earth – me fast following after.

The poet's gift is not to sing of
beautiful women over some pond.
His heart's stirring should give birth to tears –
sprung as if out of nowhere, and with difficulty.

Translated by Belinda Cooke

The Steppe

O beautiful Kazakh steppe!
Where are you taking me now?
How can I ever draw a line
between the spirit of God and the steppe?

Its vast expanse, filled with music,
has made me a slave to its songs,
its inexhaustible improvisations.
Dear brother, never betray
those timeless words and melodies.

Vigorous and bracing,
this land only sleeps
in the way the leopard does –
half-awake and still alert
to the tiniest of sounds.
Its air is more than air,
its grass not merely grass.
They are both a kind of sorcery.

Who could ever claim he knows
more than a hundredth part
of all that's hidden in this land?
To say that you do is shameless.
Once in a while, your eye
may notice something different.
Your ear will catch a whisper,
your nose a fugitive scent.

Were I even bold enough
to shout across the steppe
I'd share my secrets quietly.
My native land, so many times
I have breathed in your fragrances,
sweeter by far than those you'd buy.
When the sky is draped
in gossamers, climb up to the heights
and take in its beauty.

The spring is like a sketch
on which the ink is barely dry.
The wormwood plant
and the liquorice shimmer
like distant mirages.
The larks are singing blithely,
weaving their nests
inside my head.

What Heaven It Is to See!

What heaven it is to see! How sublime!
As if your eyes were always dazzled
by those, wide open, staring at you.
Spring in the valley is raging,
racing like blood through its veins.

And what mountains they are! How great!
Cast up by God, when he founded the Earth
and built its seven mighty layers?
They are beasts absorbing the Sun's goodness.
They are like sucking calves.
The trees, too, are thirsty
for the Sun's nutritious light.

What a steppe it is! How dazzling!
Sometimes at night, like a cow
that has calved, the Moon
lies at ease licking the stars.

What a desert it is! How alluring!
There are times it seems to point you
to where, far off, the mirage looms,
raising visions of Betpaḳdala.[3]

The hills are wearing haloes,
as if God's blessing rains upon them.
He who gazes with youthful eyes
discovers poetry in a black stone.

[3.] Betpaḳdala – desert region in Kazakhstan. It is located between the lower reaches of the
Sarysu River, the Šu (Chu) River and Lake Balḳaš (Balkhash).

In the Steps of Those Before Us

In the steps of those before us, who walked on burning coals,
good things always go hand in hand with bad.
It's a bad thing to be endlessly driven
but good to have compassion for your native land.

It's bad to be taken in by nonsense
but good to be eloquent in your speech.
It's bad to handle a hoe when you lack all skill,
but good to wield a spear that always hits the mark.

It's bad to wait for years to learn your ABC,
but good if your music's overflowing.
It's bad when brides are sold like cattle,
but good when a groom can steal his darling.

It's bad to be clueless in trade
but good to be upright in your dealings.
It's bad to marry a *žeŋge*,[4]
but good to stop a widow straying.

It's good to be at peace with neighbours,
together they're warm, together their fingers numb.
It's bad to be short of bricks and mortar
but at least in steppe there were no prisons!

Translated by David Cooke

---

[4] *Žeŋge* – wife of an older brother or older relative. The poem refers to an ancient Kazakh custom of levirate marriage, in which the brother of a deceased man is obliged to marry his widow.

TUMANBAY MOLDAGALIYEV
(20.03.1935 – 10.10.2011)

Tumanbay Moldagaliyev was a poet best known for his love lyrics. He graduated from Kirov Kazakh State University (now Ăl-Farabi Kazakh National University), Faculty of Philology, in 1956 and worked for periodicals for fourteen years, becoming executive secretary at *Baldyrġan* journal and editor-in-chief at the *Žalyn* almanac. His debut poetry collection *Student dăpteri* (Student Notebook) was published in 1957, followed by more than forty books, including *Kămila* (1960), *Ķuralaj* (1961), *Kôktem taņy* (Spring Dawn, 1961), *Alatau ķyzy* (Daughter of Alatau, 1963), *Zulajdy kùnder* (Time is Flying, 1966), *Žùregim meniņ saparda* (My Heart Has Taken a Trip, 1966), *Šaķyrady žaz meni* (Summer Calls, 1970), *Žùrek oâu ķašanda* (The Heart Is Always Lit, 1972), *Hattar, Hattar* (Letters, Letters, 1974), *Ķoš, kôktem* (Farewell, Spring, 1971) and many others. He wrote the children's books *Etekbaj atam ùjinde* (At my Granddad Etekbaj's, 1982), and *Balalarġa bazarlyķ* (Gifts for Children, 2011) and numerous popular song lyrics for the composers Nùrġisa Tilendiev, Šăˮmši Ķaldaâķov and Ăset Bejseuov, published as a volume in 2007. He has translated Byron, Mikhail Lermontov, Mahjoor and Rasul Gamzatov into Kazakh, as well as excerpts from the Kyrgyz epic *Manas*. He published three-volume, fourteen-volume and two-volume selected works in 1985, 2004 and 2005 respectively.

Tumanbay Moldagaliyev was named People's Writer of Kazakhstan (1996), and previously won the Lenin Komsomol Prize of the Kazakh SSR for *Žaņa dăpter* (New Notebook, 1968) and the State Prize of the Kazakh SSR for his collection of poems *Žùrektegi žazular* (Inscriptions in My Heart, 1982). He is a laureate of the International Fizuli and Žambyl Žabaev prizes (1992).

Night

The moon is peeping through the leaves,
the soul is enjoying the balmy air.
Cumulus clouds hover over Alatau's peak.[1]
A cool wind blows from the riverbanks.

You can indulge in these fantasies for ages.
Reeds rustle daily when the wind blows
and glittering stars rest above the garden
melted now by moonlight. The voice

of a girl keeps echoing. In the arms
of grieving night, the mountaintop has frozen,
and the leaves are gently whispering
so that the sleeping baby will not wake.

[1.] Alatau – part of the Northern Tien Shan mountain range; the former capital of
Kazakhstan, Almaty, is located at the foot of the range.

Life Sometimes

Life sometimes is like a mountain
whose summit I want to reach.
Or it resembles an enemy
that I want to knock down.

Life sometimes is the base of a mountain
whose flowers I want to pick.
Or it is like a desert
in which I need a drink.

Life sometimes is like a fire
for warming myself up.
Sometimes I can find no happiness
and all I want is to die.

But then life can be a good friend,
one I wish to see every day.
It can be like a big caravan of people
I want to lead,

or like a loyal marriage partner
I would like to pamper.
When I feel happiness waiting for me,
I am eager to get to it quickly.

On occasions life can be a beautiful girl
whom I want to hug and kiss.
And then it can be like you, my mother,
to whom I want to give much joy.

Life is ultimately a joyful feeling.
I want to laugh joyously.
Life is sometimes like me,
and I want to live.

The Birds' Song

The summer is short with its joy.
Birds come, then go.
They fly by like my childhood
which seems to have flashed past
in a moment only. Do the birds
ever get used to our country?
Do they feel they fit in?
They arrive in the spring, singing,
having reluctantly left the land
where they grew up. Their songs,
so tuneful, rock the air.
And people start their day with a smile,
but at their death, they cannot cry.

Witness

Be a witness, Star,
and you, Moon, and my Alatau.
Even when I close my eyes, I see you
and a fresh wind of a dream is blowing.

Be a witness, Alatau, to my happiness,
be a witness, green tree with shadow.
I have long searched and found it today.
Hear me start my song of love,
and you, birch tree, cherishing my dream,

witness it. Blue river too as you smile –
also the twinkling stars and white Moon
in the expanse of sky. Listen, my heart,
don't be fooled any more
by the dream that once opened the door.

Spring Night

If a cool breeze blows from the hills,
the surface of the lake will shimmer,
and apple trees will sing
as they put on their white dresses.

The flowers are whispering,
mocking the girl at her ballet.
They are tired of dancing and dancing,
their petals about to drop.

If a girl tells secrets to her boyfriend,
parting her graceful lips –
even if as a couple they are sad –
it means they love each other.

The picture of a girl and boy
embracing, arms around one another,
laughing, joking and chatting
makes the lake glimmer and glisten

as if it can see everything
and hear even hushed secrets.
The moon looks down benevolently
on two joined shadows leaving.

Orphan Lamb

I am grazing a flock of lambs,
humming the song of my grandfather,
a shepherd. As if the whole pasture
is singing amidst countless melodies.

An orphaned lamb, more timid
than the rest, beads of tears in his eyes,
runs to the *auyl*[2] – as if chased by a dog –
where all the lambs are bleating their alarms.

Pitying him for being an outsider,
I cannot keep my eyes off him as he jumps
in the air. The lambs and sheep are baa-ing.
as if they haven't seen each other for years.

No one feels sorry for him or calls
for him as he runs along, bleating, at times
looking in my direction. Occasionally
he grabs a nipple, then runs forward again,

making me want to be a mother to him.
At sunset the whole barn goes quiet,
stars are streaming from the sky
and only his bleating voice resounds.

Many a night, I felt I was a white lamb
looking for its mother, frantic with fear.
Plunged in deep thoughts, as a child,
I wanted to roam the world.

---

[2] *Auyl* – social-economical formation considered to constitute the heartland of the nation
and a basis for an ethnic and cultural union of the nomadic community. Consisting of
50–70 yurts in the eighteenth century, it developed into its current permanent state of
'rural settlement' (of a minimum of 100 dwellers) when Kazakhs adopted a settled mode
of life in the nineteenth and twentieth centuries. *Auyl* can also be used as a synonym for
'native land' and 'homeland', concepts revered by the Kazakhs.

Boots

Childhood's wheel was racing onwards
and enemies shot holes in my dreams.
Hungry, I slept on a floor in a cold house.
I do not know how I survived.

My mother worried herself sick about me.
We had one pair of boots that we wore
in turns. Enraptured, I listened to the stories
and poems my beloved mother told me.

I went to school in her boots while she stayed
at home by the stove. Many laughed at me,
an orphaned son. And I sat quiet, isolated
in the playground where gangs hooted and yelled.

I wept when the boots became too small for me,
my face streaked and dirty with tears.
'You will wear your father's boots when he returns',
my mother said as she bypassed the house.

We had enough flour to last until the summer.
Happiness for us was someone's help.
My childhood passed by while I kept saying
'I will wear my Daddy's boots when he returns.'

Snowdrop

When you say, 'The earth is warming up
and you will get warm too', a snowdrop
peeks out from under the snow. She climbs up
from a gorge filled with melody and dreams.

After a beam from the sun, she smiles
in her dress of white snow. Her chest
smells of spring. Her body, open, excited,
searching for a dream, is visible to poets

far and wide. She looks just like a girl
in a white dress rushing to spring after winter.

Men Who Pamper Women
Are Blessed

Men who pamper women are blessed,
for what can this world do without women?
If there is no hostess to give warnings,
the man will faint and wither.
After all, a woman is a cook and nurse.
After all, with a woman you are flame and fire.
Without a woman you are a streak of smoke.
A woman is your counsellor and strength,
and with her you will never hear sad songs.
She is your protector, guard, your holiday and joy.
Only in her there are dreams, hopes –
an inquisitive look from her eyes conquers you.
Having absorbed the scent of flowers,
she is created from sunlight. Remember –
you loved a woman and a woman loved you.
Man to woman, woman to man: respect shown.
And if you want to be called a son of the people,
then learn to be a servant to women.
O woman, woman, you are the song
of a dream, you are a song on the road,
you are the universe's gentle evening wind.
Honour a woman and you will respect your daughter,
and to your mother give eternal reverence.

Red-Green Butterfly

Red-green butterfly,
listen to my wish.
Sit on a flower
and let its head sway.

We admire, butterfly,
your wings, beauty.
But we do not catch you.
You do not give in to my will.

Along the river
there is tumbleweed,
young bolly cottons and
the butterfly I'm chasing down.

O butterfly, butterfly,
You cheat when not caught.
Stop flying and circling.
And take a break.

If I do catch you,
I won't torture or hit you.
I won't remove your eyes,
or tear off your wings.

Freeing yourself from my hands,
you are flying far away.
I'm chasing you –
which is a joy for me.

If I catch you again,
I'll release you to play
so you will know, butterfly,
you have a *kôke*.[3]

[3.] *Kôke* – respectful form of address to an older patron or protector; it can be applied to both males and females.

My Heart

Ah, my heart, my young heart,
you were once a spring, a flood,
inquisitive and adventurous.
When I think of my youth, I cannot sleep.

My youth, you are looking back
at me in vain. How to reach you
now? One day my heart will stop
and age will have passed me by.

Ah, my heart as an eagle,
how can you not fly with wings?
You sob alone into yourself,
unknown, unheard.

I do not regret the days flying by.
My heart, let followers see you.
My verses will let me live forever.
My song will lead me far away.

Father

It seems to me that my father is still alive
in this wide land, driving away the enemy,
even if the enemy's bell of victory has rung.

I was six years old when we said goodbye
on the black road. I didn't show my tears
to look like a hero. We hugged,

said goodbye and he vanished into the crowd.
He hid his tears too so as not to upset me.
A paper came announcing my father's death.

I had to pull myself together and ignore
the transparent tears rolling from my eyes.
For the first time ever I cried. Many years later,

my mother still has not come to terms with it.
In my mind I still see my father and hug
the young man he was, like I am now.

There are nights when I look for my father,
for his courage and dignity. I am waiting always
for him, waiting, waiting. If I stop waiting

then he may never come back. I don't want to believe
that his bones lie at the foot of a birch.
But maybe he is still alive
and even if he did die, in his very last breath

I know he thought about me and wanted to see me
just once more. I carry the weight of life on my back,
perhaps my lot is waiting for my father day and night.

Mother Tongue

My child, today you have learnt
one word in my mother tongue.
And since you were born a Kazakh,
it is important you die a Kazakh.

As an intelligent person, you will learn
many languages. You must not forget
your own country wherever you are,
and raise high your national flag.

I'm proud that I understood my mother,
that I learned the language and its songs.
Those who do not respect their mothers
have little respect for their homeland.

My son, listen to my words. When you burn,
you yourself will burn as fire. Understand
my language which is yours and take
my Kazakh heart. The rest is up to you.

Two Stars

And who knew what time of night it was?
The stars were going out, one by one.
Everything was being extinguished
along with my hope. My soul was burning
as I stood, hugging the fire.
Time went by without stopping,
without being noticed by us.
It seemed there were only two stars
in the sky, two stars we couldn't let go of,
two happinesses in the sky that stayed
above us and did not disappear.
We saw only those two stars in the sky
because there were two of us, also.
It was beginning to dawn,
the Sun was rising from the horizon smiling.
Silently, two stars were going out,
leaving a bright light in me.
Days and years will pass by, and we will change.
Don't write me letters then.
Just look up, to the sky
To see if two stars still hold together.

Translated by Patricia McCarthy

OLZHAS SULEIMENOV
(b. 18.05.1936)

Olzhas Suleimenov is a poet, literary scholar, politician and anti-nuclear activist. He graduated in Geological Sciences from Kirov Kazakh State University (now Āl-Farabi Kazakh National University) in 1959 and went on to study at the Maxim Gorky Institute of Literature in 1961. He was editor-in-chief of the film studio Ķazaķfil'm (Kazakhfilm), newspaper *Kazakhstanskaya Pravda* and journal *Prostor* (1962–71), before being appointed the secretary of the Writers' Union of the Kazakh SSR (1971–81), and subsequently the chairman of the Kazakh SSR State Committee on Cinematography (1981–83). His political activities include: a leading role in the 1989 Nevada–Semej (Semipalatinsk) campaign to close nuclear sites in the United States and Kazakhstan; establishment of the Peoples' Congress Party in 1991 and being deputy to the Supreme Council of Kazakh SSR/USSR/Kazakhstan between 1980 and 1995. Suleimenov served as the ambassador of the Republic of Kazakhstan to Rome (1995–2001) and to UNESCO (2001–14). In December 2018, he was appointed the director of the Centre for the Rapprochement of Cultures in Nur-Sultan (formerly Astana). His most influential work, *AZ-i-Ya*, was published in 1975. Suleimenov's other major works include *Argamaki* (Stallions, 1961), *Zemlya poklonis' cheloveku* (Earth, Bow Down before Man, 1961), *Solnechnye nochi* (Sunlit Nights, 1962), *God obez'iany* (Monkey Year, 1967), *Glinianaya kniga* (The Clay Book, 1969), *Yazyk pis'ma* (Language of Writing, 1995), *Ulybka Boga* (The Smile of God, 1998), *Turki doistorii: o proiskhzhdenii drevnetiurkskikh yazykov i pis'mennostei* (Turks in Prehistory: On the Origin of Ancient Turkic Languages and Writing, 2002), *Kod Slova* (The Code of the Word, 2013). He was awarded the Kazakh SSR Komsomol Prize (1961, 1963), State Prize of the Kazakh SSR (1967), USSR Komsomol Prize (1967), and a number of other state and international prizes, orders and medals. Suleimenov is People's Writer of the Kazakh SSR (1990) and Hero of Labour of Kazakhstan (2016).

August Nights …

August nights,
walk away, but remember –
there are no blacker nights.
Apple tree bough over my head,
night fragrant, like tea.
Open your mouth,
and invisibly
a stream will run in your throat,
flowing through the green city,
at this hour.
The apple tree bough
is slightly raised like a veil,
in the black sky there is a fire.
Screwing up my brow, I try to recall
the name of this star.
Mars. It is probably Mars.
A horse responds in the barn,
my raven-coloured *Žolbarys*
softly tinkles his iron bridle.
Weariness from the dusty road –
Coolness. Sleep.
Starry sky like a cone,
a pierced helmet,
as if the brightest star
had flared up and hung over his face –
Mars, it's probably Mars.
Overripe, transparent fruit,
drags and weighs down
the bough –
bends it
breaks it.
August nights,
walk away, but remember –
there are no brighter nights.
Still so much
I don't understand.

Night fragrant, like tea.
An old carpet thrown down,
fescue on the thick grass,
darkness behind the trunks of
apricot trees
like a crow –
I lay my head against the saddle …
the saddle smells
of sweat and dust …
the straight stems toss and turn
beneath me.

The Outskirts

The hour when it is warm
without heat
and lamps are bent beneath the weight,
like a weak denial of the darkness
light truly serves the Asiatic night.
I go to the glow of cigarettes,
where lamps are smashed by eligible young men,
where in May the frost is on my back,
where life is not worth a penny,
unless you are pushy.

Here it smells sweetly of ancient theft,
thrown on the saddle with the cry of a girl.
Pride in one's roots is a soul on the margins,
with a low, wild *Slobodian*[1] cry.

It is dark. White movements are visible,
the bench is busy, she is
practising witchcraft on him –
the woman is blowing into the man's collar,
tearing his shirt off his back.
My own kin, stretch out your palms,
touch the acacia, take your time silently,
now walk towards me.
Your face
floats in the shadows
like a ball of lightning.

The moon has risen.
In the silence the water murmurs.
The dog is sleeping. The watchman with the halberd sleeps.
In the outskirts under the apple tree there is a shovel.
And the vegetable stall is closed forever.

---

[1] *Slobodian* – another word for Ukrainian. Here it suggests a liberating cry.

Actor and the Night City after the Premiere

The bridge is pretending
to be a black rainbow.
The rain is pretending to be
London rain.
They clap their hands,
but he is not happy:
a slapping of wet soles.
The disease is pretending to be flu.
This woman is playing hard to get.
The door opens with a creak.
The door closes with a knock.
The man is pretending to be
an ordinary person –
but he's not very good at it …
just a bit too much
of a ne'er-do-well …
I wish I was able
to pretend to be the Prince of Denmark …
You, there, what would you advise?
You agree that talent is to be able to pretend …
So how can you pretend
to be sad
if you already are?
See these faces.
They have a desperate resilience.
Surely they will be sad.
But these people won't retreat.
They hug you till they crack your ribs,
and sit on a chair with a bang.
We are unhappy, and you like it.
How condescending and evil is that.
We are sullen so you can be happy.
We are sad so you can be lucky.
Tired to death of acting,
you open your door
like a thief.

You sleep
and dream of applause.
… In the courtyard, someone is beating a blanket
with a stick.

Asian Bonfires

We remember that
         which equalises all,
there are many examples in history,
one night shamans came to us
from noble motives and meaningful exchange.
They lit a fire and taught us
to preserve and
         respect fire,
to treat certain illnesses with fire.
They taught us how to approach the horse,
and base their beliefs on the Sun,
         and read the stars –
They have brought you:
your dance and song,
your honouring of the spring,
how to plough, grow and bake,
carpets and planes, and
prospecting for diamonds.
Then the Samoyeds[2] massacred them.
Yet even then as they burned on the fire,
they continued to teach you.
The shamans drew the light out of your blindness.
They found you Beethovens for your deafness.
They smelted Homer out of the darkness,
still not knowing what lay ahead of them.
From ore they mined
in carats,
Talmuds and Qur'ans,
panning for nuggets, revealing mountains
from the midst of their deep learning.
But in your eyes
         it was just flowing honey,
For you it was opium dens –
diamond words, golden names,
platinum hopes, that all paid for the smoke.
You hung out on your warm bunks
         with your pipes in your mouths,

[2.] Samoyeds – tribal group who lived on the Yenisey River.

down and out, off your face,
till it starts again,
thief, Asian, slave,
dog among other dogs.
When you were told
                to pay,
pool, *tangi* and *mana*,[3]
were all in short supply,
so you burned
                the shamans on fires
                                to pay for the smoke.
They who had
                                invented the fires
                for warmth.
Is it about suffering?
No. It's about efforts of the great.
My strange world,
                we are born into it as prospectors.
O Asia, you have wasted without end …
                Again the fires have been lit
for smoke.

[3.] *Pool, tangi, mana* – different terms denoting money.

Mama!

What can we make of this village
love … life … endlessly here
beneath this spacious sky?
As if for the first time
the leisureliness of sunsets
leads me far into a field of meditation –
like the spring rook or autumn goose,
whose wing, already half circling the world,
dips its feather in the Limpopo River,
drunk with the spicy winds of Ceylon.
What can we make of this road?
Be proud. Give as good as you get
when you're right –
they are not your prophet's father.
With the shy, though, be gentle
they are not your slave, not anyone's …
I really tried to do this, road, but I'm not God,
I couldn't help everyone in the queue.
One lone poet doesn't have all the answers,
but I never lied,
even though I could have …

Wolf Cubs

A man was walking the steppe.
On and on he walked.
Where was he going and why?
It is not for us to know.
Deep in the hollow he saw a wolf,
a she-wolf, a mother to be precise …
She lay there panting and trembling
in the thicket of wormwood,
paws thrown back and teeth bared,
blood thick as dirt streaming from her throat.
Who could possibly have done this –
A wolf? A pack of hounds?
No way her blind wolf cubs could know,
jostling and growling there as they sucked
from this immense intractable mother.
The hungry wolf cubs forgot
how powerfully the dill smelt in the undergrowth.
They nestled up to their mother,
her thick blood growing cold,
yet greedily they drank it
doing all they could to ease their thirst.
And with the mother's blood they sucked revenge,
as blind as the cubs themselves.
They must find someone to hate.
Who? Anyone.
Only they must be sure not to forgive,
but they must do it alone,
and together –
though when they meet up
they will take vengeance on each other …
The man walked his road.
We will never know where or why.
He was a hunter of wolves,
but he didn't touch the wolf cubs –

The mother no longer protected them.

On Pushkin Square

The poet should be beautiful as God.
Who has seen a god? Anyone who saw Pushkin –
stunted and black as jackboots,
with heavy blackamoor lips.
Whereas d'Anthès[4] was devilishly tall,
white-lipped and pale as memory …
The poet's wife – the divine Natalia.
No one called her Natasha.
Well, she lived on his reputation,
as if on the glittering parquet of a ballroom,
gentlemen gliding lightly about her,
while he, like a slave, gazed through the portières
firmly grasping a knife in his hand:
'Tell me sir,
why are you hanging about here?
Do you find it hard to believe that I could also fall in love?
Can't you see she has drugged us all like hashish!'
Well what do you expect?
Her pale throat and shoulders,
breasts huge as a scaffold.
This slave went out in the snow
on that January night.
This god went out and died,
clutching his stomach …
But he got his revenge in the end,
in a way neither the duellist, nor the Tsar, nor bandits could.
His revenge was godly.
He fell silent.
That was all.
Silent like the bullet that flies.
And all evil strength lay in that silence.
Pushkin alone wasn't enough for the bullet that flew …
but it found many targets all across Russia.
We don't know them, but the bullet managed to find them.

[4.] d'Anthès – Baron Georges-Charles de Heeckeren d'Anthès: he was the lover of Pushkin's
wife, Natasha, who killed Pushkin in a duel.

In Konyushennaya[5] the crowds stood
in the squares of yellow light from the windows in the snow.
And all through the ages generations
stood beneath other windows in the snow,
in order to find the right words
for those they love and cherish.
They always save the best words
for speeches over the grave …
while a mourning Pushkin
stooped and broken, hat in his hand,
just looks down examining us intensely.

---

[5] Konyushennaya Square – one of the central squares in Saint Petersburg, where people gathered to pay their last respects to Pushkin.

Women Up to My Shoulders

Women up to my shoulders.
Women up to my chest.
But only one
reached my heart.
I knew her off by heart.
Everything goes well together –
that longing in her eyes,
and little bits of fluff in her hair,
and that fickle look she always had,
the icy way she bared her teeth –
even the cracking of her knuckles,
and the fact she was too short,
and all her thirty-four years.
Everything goes well together –
yes, just like everything that goes!

Mountains, You Love Me

Mountains, you love me.
You love me pines
and the years dressed in blue and white
were flying over me,
wearing the name of grasses,
so precious
in their gaudy colours
          absorbed
in all shades of silence.
As with a mountain journey
I was the ruler of the plain.
I walked along the slopes of the avalanche,
and the snowy dust
dropped down on the long winding
of my years,
with a flourish of meteors,
years of illusion.
Do you love me, mountains?
You love,
people.

They will never put you right.
They won't transform you to flatness,
your peaks,
mountains
are impossible to smooth out.
You are so misshapen,
mountains –
but correctness is banality.
They won't put you right, mountains.
There is nothing compared to you.
You don't care, mountains
if they love you
          or not.

Language of Our Fathers, Ancient Language

Language of our fathers, ancient language,
time has transformed you to fired clay.
The blow of your sword, the whistle of your lash,
you contain male pride and female passion.

You express the forgotten dialects of
Sumerians and Huns, the wheeze of Mongolian words.
Where were you born? In the fires of seven languages?
You travel to us through our veins.

And you can be heard filling your body
with a blow to the heart, a ringing of souls.
I wouldn't exchange one word of my fate.
I swear I will come to you.

Thus from distant, happy travels,
this son returns to his forgotten father,
all dressed up in bright expensive attire,
if not at the start of his life then the end.

Rišad Son of the Steppes

I give you a *tûbetejka*,[6]
woven all over in gold,
your father silently turned away,
probably reminded of his youth.

The beautiful mother flaps her arms about,
prattling on, going into raptures.
Rišad looks like a Spaniard,
the son of a French woman,
or an Adaj![7]
'Are you heading to the state of Nebraska?
There, there are such fine prairies,
such cacti, such hills, such heat,
as for the horses and dust – amazing!
Are you going to go there?'
His face is full of desire,
as he fashions a picture with his hands.
In the summer people head off to the sea,
but he is drawn to the dry steppe,
and hops on his horse!
He flings away his sombrero.
The wind is all black hair and wisps.
With his *tûbetejka* on his head.
Full gallop, off he goes,
heading out along the wolf trail.

Breathe in and shout out, my boy,
a poet's passion – is both weeping and laughter.
Your father finally then weeps himself,
and in my veins I feel something cold.

[6.] *Tûbetejka* – Russian for *taķiâ*, a short, round skullcap for men, typically worn in the summer or under the *tymaķ* (winter cap) in winter.

[7.] Adaj – tribe of the junior *žùz* (a tribal and territorial division in Kazakhstan; there are senior, middle and junior *žùzes*). They reside in western Kazakhstan and are famous for their bravery as well as musical and literary talent.

I would travel to the state of Nebraska,
but I need to hurry to my homeland.
There the landscape is nothing special.
I will travel to my own homeland.

I will travel to the Adaj prairies,
there there is cacti, heat and frost,
dust and such horses! Amazing –
I will travel to my own homeland.

Song of the Cumans[8]

Ancestors,
in battle support me under the arms.

I will not walk past a single tree.
I will hang a lasso
at each crooked bough.
Not at the first,
but at the last battle I will fall.
Who won't recognise my golden Sakian[9] armour?

Away the star collapsed.
My head bowed down lower.
Having made a loyal oath to a woman,
I kissed her palm.
I will not offend
neither the owl, crow, or swan.
Aruak![10]
Show me the road to Lake Balaton.[11]
I will gallop forever and ever.
Who knows from where.
Only I will leave deep tracks
for people,
so that after rain
the whole of my journey will be visible to my enemies
as a series of *pialas*[12]
so that they do not burn from thirst like me.

---

8. Cumans – Turkic nomadic people, part of the Cuman–Ķypšaķ confederation. After the Mongol invasion in 1237, many of them sought asylum in the Kingdom of Hungary.
9. Sakian – Saka, also Scythians, were a group of nomadic and semi-nomadic tribes who around 1000 BC lived in the northern and eastern Eurasian Steppe and the Tarim Basin.
10. *Aruak* – ancestral spirit. It is believed that *aruaks* protect the living descendants, thus they are treated with deep reverence. Kazakhs visit their ancestral graves to ask for guidance; they make vows in the name of *aruaks* and call their ancestors' names in a battle cry.
11. Lake Balaton – lake in western Hungary.
12. *Piala* – Russian word for *kese*, a traditional Kazakh bowl for drinking tea.

Elm

In a hollow there are aspens,
      a spring and herbs,
and shadow is thick, like poison.
Here the roots aren't deep,
and autumn is right,
so the year is growing with mould.

Look –
at the mound,
where the wind sings,
where wolf cries can be heard.
Having seized the roots
in my heart,
swaying,
the elm stands.

Neither heat, nor snowstorms
smash it –
nor the thirst of peaceful days.
It stands,
opened to meet the winds,
shoulders of black branches.
And the horseman, who was lucky to see,
having seen, starts to weep,
and gallops.
In the lowlands, he gives the horse to drink
and without words
the elm will be grateful.

In Our *Auyl* There Was a Shoemaker

The shoemaker made all his shoes
to fit his feet.
He thought this would make all people equal,
the fanatic.
He was Bonaparte's height,
so for us big guys,
it wasn't easy to wear such shoes.

And each thought that shoes
have been made by God,
in order that Muslims would pray
more frequently.
(You see, you take your shoes off to pray.)
Prayer is the songs of numb feet.

Off to the mosque they ran,
old and young,
shouting on the run
(foot in a vice).
'Allah is great!'
Praise the prophet –
the boot orders.
Only the barefoot don't believe in God.
Even the shoemaker doesn't believe in God.
But his shoes fit perfectly.

Allah is great! But he is far from us. And the cursed shoemaker
here is grinning. We now pray with the whole *auyl*,[13] so that the
shoemaker's feet get larger, that tailors aren't so paunchy, and
hatmakers not too narrow-faced.

Translated by Belinda Cooke

[13.] *Auyl* – social-economical formation considered to constitute the heartland of the nation
and a basis for an ethnic and cultural union of the nomadic community. Consisting of
50–70 yurts in the eighteenth century, it developed into its current permanent state of
'rural settlement' (of a minimum of 100 dwellers) when Kazakhs adopted a settled mode
of life in the nineteenth and twentieth centuries. *Auyl* can also be used as a synonym for
'native land' and 'homeland', concepts revered by the Kazakhs.

MARFUGA AITKHOZHA
(b. 25.08.1936)

Marfuga Aitkhozha is a Kazakh poet, composer and translator. She graduated in journalism from Kirov Kazakh State University (now Ăl-Farabi Kazakh National University) in 1965 before going on to advanced literature courses at the Maxim Gorky Institute of Literature in Moscow in 1971. She worked for the newspapers *Ķazaķ ădebieti* and *Uchitel' Kazakhstana* (1961–85).

Aitkhozha is the author of more than 30 poetry volumes, including *Balķuraķ* (Youth, 1962), *Šyņdaġy žazu* (Inscriptions at the Peak, 1964), *Aķķuym meniņ* (My Swan, 1971), *Kôzimniņ ķarasy* (The Apple of My Eye, 1975), *Aķ besigim* (My Sacred Cradle 1978), *Žarķyra, meniņ žŭldyzym* (Shine, My Star, 1980), *Aķķu žùrek* (Swan-Heart, 2001) and *Alataudyņ aķ batasy* (Blessing of Alatau, 2005). Many of her poems reflect on the issues of memory and longing for her native parts left in China, although striving for national unity in the Greater Homeland, Kazakhstan. She has been translated into more than forty languages and is widely published in foreign publications, including *Molodaya Gvardiya* (Moscow, 1983), *Anthologie de la Poésie* (Paris, 1987) and *Lotos* (Cairo, 1973) and a range of foreign anthologies, including in German, French and Arabic languages. She has translated works by Mongolian, Russian, Arabic, Kyrgyz, Tatar, Hungarian and Ukrainian poets into Kazakh.

Aitkhozha is an Honoured Worker of the Repubic of Kazakhstan, a recipient of the orders Ķùrmet Belgisi (1986) and Parasat (1998), and many other awards, as well as the Certificate of Honour of Pakistan for the romantic verse cycle *Islamabad aspany* (Islamabad's Sky, 1998). She was awarded the Cambridge University International Professional of 2007 award for her outstanding contribution to Kazakh literature.

When Birds Arrive

When seasonal birds are soaring,
the heart breaks out from its nest.
My dear mother used to tell me
that when the migrant birds return
our lives are one year shorter.
When birds flap their wings
or ruffle their feathers,
it never fails to stir your heart.
Whenever birds fly, whenever they leave,
it always has a meaning
for the poet in love with verses and life.
Each year I wait for spring to arrive,
my eyes alert to its signs
as if I were waiting for one I love.
Then out of the blue my birds arrive.
They have travelled over countless peaks,
endowing the sky with splendour.
As if they were touched
by the nightingale's song,
beads of tears drop from the leaves.
When I see the uplands
embracing each other,
so patient and splendid,
it banishes sleep.
Gazing up at the mountains,
I found it hard to shut my eyes,
dozing as fitfully as a bird.
Oh birds!
Soaring!
Gliding!
You revealed your secrets to me.
Gathering around the shores of the lake
the birds will start their feast.
Be safe and secure, wherever you go.
And though I love the ways you fly,
I'm jealous too.

I love and long each year for spring –
glorious spring and the feast of *Nauryz*[1] –
as out of the blue
the birds arrive,
flying from the far.

[1.] *Nauryz* – Kazakh annual holiday. In Kazakhstan, spring arrives fully on 21 March – the day when *Nauryz* is celebrated, signifying not only the spring equinox, but also renewal of nature.

Forgive Me

Beloved mountains of Talky!
How proudly you stand.
You are my inner pain.
As I gaze up at you now,
You seem to have grown loftier.
Beloved mountains of Talky!
How proudly you stand.
You are my land's cornucopia
overflowing with wealth.
Take me up to your shimmering peaks,
There's nothing else I'd wish for,
even if you burned me in your heat.
Beloved mountains of Talky!
How proudly you stand.
But ever since I left you
I haven't heard your melodies.
Please, play them again for me
from your soul full of music.
I feel that I could burst
like a stormy rain cloud.
Beloved mountains of Talky!
How proudly you stand.
Your breeze is soothing.
You are kissing my face.
Like a child I had no sense
of how much you meant to me.
My beautiful mountains,
forgive me,
should I forsake you again!

At the Graveyard

My dearest mother, will you
still worry when I tell you
that the time has come
for me to see my homeland.
After thirty years away,
your child is visiting your grave.
Yes, I am visiting your grave,
sensing your patience
has worn you out.
Did any others like you
bear the pains of absence?
I exhausted the wings of longing,
preparing myself for this journey.
Waiting so long to meet you again,
my heart was ready to burst.
My nights were sleepless,
so far away that I couldn't see
your Ķosaġaš.[2]
How should I not weep?
My eyes were misty
as I approached my homeland
and saw so many familiar faces.
My dear mother, my white dawn,
who can say,
when I'll be back again?
So let me take now
take some soil from your grave.

[2.] Ķosaġaš – Kazakh *auyl* in the Ili Kazakh Autonomous Prefecture in Xinjiang region,
China, a native *auyl* of the poet's mother.

Žajḳoŋyr

'Žajḳoŋyr'.[3] It's the name of a cheerful song,
And yet, my life, where has it gone?
How did the years pass so quickly?
The singer Estaj, the poet of the steppes,
left his burnished song behind him.
He lived in Bajti in Ḳaraôtkel.
When I came on a visit
it took my breath away.
His songs are as deep as the ocean,
his wisdom is great.
Throughout his life
he held his head up high.
All those who inhabit the steppes are great,
the elderly and the young –
Žaâu Mùsa,[4]
and the singer Majra[5] as well.
These great people were of your stock.
They were born here, these great people.
Though I am not as powerful
as Isa,[6]
I come from the land
where the great Sara[7] was born,
I am not dull as rust on the ground.
I am not dull as rust on the ground.
I am a poet,
a native of this land,
I am in love with poetry
and the people acknowledge my skill.
With tears in my eyes, I write my verses.
I come from afar,
from East Turkestan,

[3.] 'Žajḳoŋyr' – song by the famous Kazakh poet, singer and folk composer Estaj Berkimbajùly (1874–1946).
[4.] Žaâu Mùsa Bajžanùly (1835–1929) – prominent Kazakh poet, singer and composer.
[5.] Majra Uǎliḳydy Šamsutdinova (1861–1927) – Kazakh singer and composer.
[6.] Isa Bajzaḳov (Baizakov; 1900–46) – Kazakh aḳyn (poet-improvisator) and composer.
[7.] Sara Tastambekḳyzy (1853–1907) – prominent Kazakh poet.

I gaze at the sky through clouds of longing.
I have drunk from the depths
of the ocean of art.
I have been in love with poetry
since the day that I was born.
My voice is authentic,
though I'm far from knowing all things …
It wasn't me who decided
to leave my homeland behind.
A mystical dream impelled me,
a dream like a dark storm,
a dream like a youth,
a dream that sings
and soothes my woes.
When louring clouds covered our sky,
a fair prospect beckoned me.
I'll never forget that time.
There is a river in the east called Ìle,
Its current ripples with verses.
When I was leaving Ìle
It asked me to wish its best to the poets.
It asked me to wish the best to my land.
Have you ever spoken to Ìle?
I carry its amulet on my neck,
that's why poetry is always with me.
That's why poetry is always with me.
It never leaves me alone.
I'm never poor or sad
when I travel new lands
so long as their people
have poetry in their hearts.
There's a city in the east called Ķùlža.[8]
My heart will draw breath and rest there.
How proud Ķùlža will be
when the two nations live in peace.

[8.] Ķùlža (Ghulja) – the most populous city in the Ili Kazakh Autonomous Prefecture in China.

There's a mountain there called Tǎŋir.[9]
When my soul wept,
its dawns soothed me.
The children of Tǎŋir are kind-hearted.
They clutch the *šaŋyraḳ*[10] in their hands.
Memorialising our difficult past,
my music pours forth
like rain from clouds. Estaj!
Your daughter has come to see you,
may your homeland enlighten us all!
I am not merely a pilgrim,
but greet you with my songs.
My venerable, honoured poet,
you should know
that you are still alive to us.
Your fame will live for generations.
Though people build memories
out of stones, there's no statue
for you in Ḳaraôtkel.
Yet still your songs are known by all.
They are written on the sky.
Although I am patient
and tolerant, enduring all,
my emotions are streaming through my blood.
A sacred spirit among the Kazakh people,
you wrote that mighty song 'Ḳorlan'.
A grand song,
You are a sacred spirit
among Kazakhs!

---

[9] Tǎŋirtau – (lit. 'divine mountains'; also Khan Tengri/Khan Tǎŋir); Kazakh name of Tien Shan, a major system of mountain ranges located in Central Asia. Tengri (Tǎŋir) is also considered to be the primary god of early Turkic peoples. The name now also denotes 'God' or 'Allah'.

[10] *Šaŋyraḳ* – upper dome of a yurt; its image is considered to be a symbol of unity.

When My Thoughts Were Dark

I am a poet at one with her people,
who never wanted a life without verses,
when my thoughts were dark.
So what made you so sad?
When did it happen?
It seemed your heart pulsed with song.
There was never a day,
when you thought of your land,
that did not find you heaving a sigh,
as if a tempestuous black steed
had borne you away.
A traveller buffeted by the wind,
and burned by the sun,
I took my chances on the road.
Whether my road was long or short,
I've been travelling ever since,
trying to reach my dreams.

I may not reach the birds in the sky.
But still I embraced this road
as if it were my spouse, my brother.
And did not embrace the storms of life vainly.
Even if you find yourself
in the ancestral homeland
it is not the same as living
in your birthplace.
There are wonderful days behind me
that I'm unable to describe in full!
Longing for those days
is a pain deep in my heart,
cold as ice on mountain peak.
But if I'm sad,
who else will care about my woes?
My tears are like a lake.
No steed will get across it.
I was brought up like a leaf that grew in the shade,
one who longed for the sunlight.
Though life is good now,

I long for other days
when I drank spring water, crystal clear.
My life! I didn't weep for you in my twenties,
but now in my fifties, I do.
My homeland,
I'm weeping …
Forgive me,
my homeland,
forgive me, my mother!
People are wiser as they grow older.
I have striven to conquer the peaks
with the clouds of verses!
I am a poet at one with her people,
who never wanted a life without verses,
when my thoughts were dark.
Why are they sad like an autumn sky?

The Northern Breeze

The chilling northern breeze
blows relentlessly
across the steppes.
The green firs are drowsing on the shore.
They have seen
the ancient and more recent days.
The green fir trees,
rearing up to the skies,
have earned the right
to grow and think,
having witnessed grief.
They have seen
so many of our people
exiled to the camps of *Itžekken*.[11]
I have come here to sing of you
in weighty songs
that seek to tell the truth.
In the distant past
the waves flowed against us,
but now our boats
can sail on serenely.
Having so often
witnessed hard times,
I am the child of the high mountains.
The scattering
leaves of a birch tree
are they responding also to that past?
The chilling northern breeze
blows relentlessly
across the steppes.
The green firs are drowsing on the shore,
they have seen
the ancient and more recent days.

[11.] *Itžekken* – Kazakh term for Siberian prison camps.

Pebbles

How beautiful and rounded the pebbles are.
The water hides them beneath its waves.
Cast up on the shores of the lake
they hold out against the storms.
They are so persistent, so ancient,
their faces washed and polished by years.
Sajram's[12] pebbles are my favourite,
their surfaces striped.
The endless waves wash over them.
They are trusting in their persistence.
Embracing the shore in a stony circle,
no man can vie with you in strength.
Though I am free to do what I want
and live in the circle of verses,
I long for Sajram's ringing pebbles
to grant me their favour.
Sleeplessly, you keep guard.
Your feelings are like tender plants.
I couldn't help but gather you up,
so many, into my hands.
Don't ask me why. I cannot say.
How beautiful and rounded the pebbles are.
The water hides them beneath its waves.
Cast up on the shores of the lake,
you hold out against the storms.

[12.] Sajram – lake located in the Ili Kazakh Autonomous Prefecture in Xinjang region, China.

Let My Voice Remain

I am not the slave of my time,
God protects every slave.
If rushing rivers do not rise
high up in the mountains
they will not roar,
they will not rage,
they will not overflow!

I am not a spring
or a stream
I am a river,
I pour down steep rock
in a torrent of lyrical verses.
My shining poems
wind their way
into the hearts of those
attuned to their sincerity.

Not born to weep, I will not cry.
Let no man abuse another
though humans too often
are cruel rather than kind
and this is what perturbs me.

I am a simple person
who has her strengths
and weaknesses.
To whom should I reveal
my countless griefs?
Buried in my heart
let my poems
be whispered.
Let my voice be heard!

At the Waterfall

How capricious is the waterfall,
against the backdrop
of the proud Talķy Mountains!
The eagles soar above its blue
like one they are enamoured of.
Bursting out of the highest rocks,
how I envy the water's mysterious course,
streaming down in winter
like one who wishes to share
its abundant feelings,
and, like a pure angel,
has waited years for me to arrive.
Though my hand couldn't reach you,
my heart like a bird longed for you.
Did my verses attain
the heights I couldn't reach?
Perhaps I was ignorant,
although I dreamed of seeing you
flowing down from the rocks.
My soul was with you here.
I wished you all success.
I also look down your lower reaches,
and can see there are difficulties.
My soul resembles yours.
So give me a song!

I grieve at the thought of you.
What else would make me grieve?
As I grew up in the mountains
I learned to be proud by looking at you.

Although the high peaks
rise up beyond me,
I came to you to bow my head.
If I do not overflow in streams like you
I am not that child in tears.
I am not that child in tears,
but I am your sacred deer,

the one who has abandoned you.
Wait, I'll be back when fortune smiles,
when the land wears
its green coat.
When I visited you in the winter,
I lost so much with little gain.

In the freezing winter time,
the waterfall
did not reveal its mysteries.
Deep in thought,
our ancestors named the stones.
There were poets then
who were like the mountains.
Inured to the vanities of life,
I am unabashed, devoid of envy.
Nothing means more to me than my poems.
My mind is free.
It masters my sense.
I'm your lost swan.
Your waters are wings
that lift me up towards my dreams.
Wings make me fly with dreams.
I have so often wished to see you,
but you are so far away.
Táṇirtau![13]
The only thing I can do,
is to be as proud as you.

[13.] Táṇirtau – also Khan Taniri (lit. 'celestial mountains' or 'divine mountains'); Kazakh
name of Tien Shan.

Appassionata

Like a boy walking contentedly
down the street,
as if his arms were full of lilies,
Beethoven's majestic music,
is leading the traveller home.
Allaying past fears
and creating a sense of truth,
the piano
reveals a sorrow,
subduing your soul with awe.
It is a music
that captures the essence of being.
It is a music evoking
the power of the past eras.
In this music you'll find
the power of imagination,
the mind's
cohesive thought.
This music expresses
that we all breathe and sigh.
In this music you'll find
a silver summer garden.
It is a music
depicting reflections.
It is a music
inspiring great deeds.
This music
depicts natural phenomena.
In it you will find
the convoluted ways of the world.
It speaks
with the voices of men
who raise the banner of justice.
In this music
you'll hear Time's caravan,
and the voices
of subtle people who've gone,
when a new era

shook itself free
from the unbearable yoke of meanness.
Like a boy walking contentedly
down the street,
as if his arms were full of lilies,
Beethoven's majestic music,
is leading the traveller home.

Swan Island

Although they lived through hard times,
crossing fords and bridges,
our ancestors were marksmen
who never missed their target.
But they never sought an easy prey.
There's a deer more beautiful
than any other deer, but the wise man leaves it,
knowing what's right and wrong.
The poet Estaj loved a swan
among so many other girls,
the one he chose
among so many other beauties.
Though stricken mad with true love
he did not shoot his swan
but melted her heart
with his songs and music.
He spelled out his love in verses
and did not lose his pride and honour –
his music still revered
by youths,
who love the true art.

A Swan Heart

In spite of the hardships I've endured
a swan's heart has coloured my poems.
When the dawn arrives
and peaks are bathed in light,
life will never be sad again!

A swan's dream, a pure swan's heart,
taught me how to bear my grief.
When it is May in the mountains,
like Alatau[14] reaching the skies,
let my passion be reborn,
my innocent hopes blossom!

The swans' cries resounding across the lakes,
touched the emotions of flowers.
Moved by their proud destinies,
how many people
were startled by fate?

Having been freed from life's pains,
many dreams have nested
in my soul.
From the blue tops of the mountains,
the sun descends, pensive,
till it sinks beneath the horizon.

Dawn appears, then once again
the flaming sun goes down.
But who has found his dream in it?
The one thing I ask
is to let my verses
be as pure as the swan.

Translated by David Cooke

---

14. Alatau – part of the Northern Tien Shan mountain range; the former capital of
Kazakhstan, Almaty, is located at the foot of the range.

FARIZA ONGARSYNOVA
(25.12.1939 – 23.01.2014)

Fariza Ongarsynova was a poet and public figure. She graduated from Guryev Teacher Training College (renamed Atyrau in 1991) and subsequently worked as a teacher in rural schools of the region (1966–68). She began her career in journalism in the local newspapers *Kommunistik eṇbek* and *Leninšil žas* (later renamed *Žas alaš*) and was a special correspondent in the Guryev, Aḵtôbe and Oral areas. Later she was editor-in-chief at the *Ḵazaḵstan pioneri* (later renamed *Ũlan*) newspaper and *Pioner* journal (subsequently renamed *Baldyrġan*) (1960–2000) in Almaty, then capital of the Kazakh SSR. From 2000 to 2004 she was elected a deputy for Mǎžilis (Mazhilis), the lower chamber of the Parliament of Kazakhstan.

Fariza Ongarsynova's first collection was *Sanduġaš* (Nightingale, 1966), followed by *Maṇġystau maržandary* (Monologues of Manghystau, 1970), *Mazasyz šaḵ* (Uneasy Time, 1972), *Asau tolḵyn* (Proud Generation, 1973), *Kôgeršinderim* (My Pigeons, 1974), *Šilde* (July, 1978), *Žùrek kùndeligi* (Diary of the Heart, 1984) and *Daua* (Remedy, 1985). She published a two-volume edition of selected poems in 1987 and a ten-volume collection of poetry in 2004. Her poetry has been highly regarded by the literary community and wider audiences for the strong and clear leading female voice. She also published a collection of essays, *Biiktik* (Height, 1976), and brought out a documentary of her life, *Kǎmšat*, also in 1976. She has had six of her books translated into Russian and translated numerous poets into Kazakh, notably Alexander Blok, Evgeny Evetushenko and Pablo Neruda. She was the People's Writer of Kazakhstan (1991), poet laureate of the State Prize of the Kazakh SSR (1984), and the recipient of the Orders of Ḵùrmet Belgisi (1976) and Parasat (1996).

Patterns of Grass and Flowers Ran Down onto the Carpets ...

Patterns of grass and flowers ran down onto
the carpets, across the white yurts, which lay
like porcelain bowls – smoking hearths
and quiet conversation till nightfall.

When in spring you see the yurts
protruding from the hills, in green *žajlau*,[1]
you will sing warmly with a single voice
of earthly glory, without music and words.

Dawn has risen. It still seems early.
Boys rush around – the day is not enough,
to chase the rams, hard at their heels,
to round them up like horses.

Each is jealous of a future glory,
selflessly biting back his lip,
visualising himself first in the *bǎjge*,[2]
the wind his only rival.

Tea more delicious because of the ritual,
traveller and host drink it slowly...
The heavy weight of years now offloaded
from the soul – the new ways are already calling.

---

[1] *Žajlau* – summer pastures, one of the four seasonal pastures traditionally used by nomadic peoples.
[2] *Bǎjge* – traditional type of horse race popular in Kazakhstan; the distance can be from six to one hundred kilometres.

We were born in the saddle and live on the road.
The time of stopping places has quickly passed –
sadly and endlessly the scarecrow's sleeves,
wave from the outskirts of the *auyl*.[3]

---

[3] *Auyl* – social-economical formation considered to constitute the heartland of the nation and a basis for an ethnic and cultural union of the nomadic community. Consisting of 50–70 yurts in the eighteenth century, it developed into its current permanent state of 'rural settlement' (of a minimum of 100 dwellers) when Kazakhs adopted a settled mode of life in the nineteenth and twentieth centuries. *Auyl* can also be used as a synonym for 'native land' and 'homeland', concepts revered by the Kazakhs.

The Train Approaches.
Heartbeats Outstrip …

The train approaches. Heartbeats
outstrip the wagons' knock
on rail-junctions, the pink sky's smoke
mixing with the engine's steam –
lump in the throat, hair standing on end,
we don't know where are we going,
or who is saying farewell to whom.

So soon? Rehearsing farewell
until it finally sinks in –
the timid flight of the second hand.
The sad siren alerts us
that our lives are divided in two.
We parted for a month –
but it seemed like forever.

Goodbye and remember me.
Over hell the sign:
'Exit to the town'.
But madness has already
grabbed him by the throat,
leaving them both
grappling in anguish.

We acted out our parting like a play.
When the moment came,
I forgot how to say my lines –
sadly and wordlessly,
the conductress made a sign of the cross:
the few words remaining were
dissolving … fading …

Suddenly the train shouts:
'It did happen ... it did happen.

'Return –
        return –
                return –
                        return ...'

Thoughts of the Old Kazakh

Mounting your horse at full gallop ... (Beats walking
covered in dust, tongue parched as *saxaul*[4])
The *žigit*[5] skilfully rides the steppe's feather grass –
the harness sparkles, the sabre sings.

Galloping, we ripped open the belly of the dawn.
Having grabbed the Sun, hot and huge,
we rolled into the *auyl*, all misfortunes forgotten,
charmed with the whole world.

How wild are the passions of the young ...
Having bridled his horse, the unrestrained horseman
releases his trained falcon on the fox,
and with a sacred anger,
                            and a heartrending scream

tramples on the foul spirit of his forefathers,
yet, he remains meek
before the elder, eyes downcast,
face illuminated by meditation.

Yes, youth captivates the beautiful women of the steppe:
no need to pray – you can be reckless in passion.
Anyone with a *žigit*'s heart will die from the power
of a single embrace. Will that moment ever return?

Lord, will there ever be such an evening, night,
or dawn, with my loved one when, half asleep,
I again hear her sigh beneath my tender caress,
to the birdsong, in the early morning light?

[4.] *Saxaul* – dry, prickly tree growing in the desert and semi-desert; a symbol of endurance.
[5.] *Žigit* – generally denoting a 25- to 40-year-old male, the term can also be used as an
honorific indicating bravery, endurance, fortitude and being true to one's word.

To be gone, not to return, not to forget these days ...
I have all the memories of generous will and passion.
I am an eagle seeing clearly into the distance –
What do I see? A doddery old peasant, called Old Age.

***

I was wrong to think
I could live my life
through the young –
I couldn't ...

My soul became clouded,
my mind confused,
my brain gone soft ...

But – I *was* a falcon –
my son cannot fail me
I know – he cannot ...

Heat

The only sunset where we have the right to admire the heat,
is where it is so hot that it feels like hell.
We sail along the waves of the sand like a homeless Noah,
in the company of a bird, a beast, a spider and a reptile –
by the will of the waves and unpredictable wind.

We are strong before the solstice.
A star that melts in the heat cannot resound.
Sunset solemnly enters its zenith.
The herd rattles their hoofs like gold,
and the withered stalks whisper.

The shelter is a wretched hillside.
An old man stretches out his hand.
The world glows,
young and many-sided,
a young pup
racing downhill at full speed.

Primordial world.
You appeared, plain and simple.
We are descended from *žajlau*.
We drive herds on the grass.
We greedily inhale the air of melted lava,
as if for the first time.

The light is tumbling over the edge,
bursting from the horizon into the open.
Heat spreads its power that
spreads over the eternal steppe …
There is still a camp fire at the white yurts –
the smoke that hovers there props up the sky.

Romanticism

A chopped syllable, and a cry –
guttural tunes
captivate the spirit.
Keep silent poet,
in this network of names.
Don't cause the trunk of the song
to collapse –
so that it supports the tree we have:
Baratashvili,[6] Lermontov[7] and Mahambet.[8]

My three demons,
three cheeky cherubs,
   cast down to dust,
     but you came back up –

so in my voice
    wistful, eternal,
your three longings burst like leopards.

To merge my life with poetry and song,
I often sit awake all night – a desolate owl,
and the 'Evil Spirit' trembles,
and the 'Colour of Heaven' grows dim,
something stirs … but
     not the slightest ripple of sound …

---

[6] Prince Nikoloz 'Tato' Baratashvili (1817–45) – Georgian poet who fused modern Georgian nationalism with European Romanticism.

[7] Mikhail Lermontov (1814–41) – Russian poet, the greatest figure of Russian Romanticism.

[8] Mahambet Ôtemisùly (1804–46) – Kazakh poet, a major figure of Kazakh Romanticism, also known for his leadership roles in rebellions against Russian colonialism. This activity is believed to have resulted in his treacherous murder.

Whether our language be Georgian, Russian or Kazakh –
    we are all people,
and we are only unified in grief,
and even if Elysium provides a blessedness
from which there is no waking,
my three demons will rise from their sleep.

When deep inside me,
my soul clutches at my chest,
so as not to interrupt the three conversations that have started
–
it's useless, there's nothing but sick flesh,
    we have been guests,
at sordid everyday affairs
    idling time on holidays,
      our hectic social life.

I don't have enough time –
I will really have to hurry
if I want to translate
what they reveal of love
into my own words,
    these our own …
      native faces they float
       and call to us in the haze …

And who is Christ?
And who is Allah?

When taste tells me –
I am eating some
awful stale cake,
or lets me know a star-filled hour has passed,
or takes me along the earthly path,
I will stand before them transparent and say:
I wasn't poor –
I had the poet –
who is three Gods in one above me.

Camel Thorn

You can be sure to meet a camel thorn tree in the desert,
while in search of your future you need to be up in the clouds.
The shepherd and wandering pilgrim admire her beauty,
Just like the poet and philosopher admire a higher life.

The desert flows in time's hourglass, in never-ending
circles, with transport roads just passing through.
There is a little life here – a dozen prickly bushes,
spread needles sticking out on the path like a warning.

Even a torch won't find a palm tree in these parts,
only the unmerciful stalks of camel feed.
Let's look more closely and revive them,
reminding ourselves of their pale extensive roots.

Indolently and full of the stars, idly sprawled above us,
the deserted sky will look down indifferently.
A soul that is suddenly perturbed will cling to the stem of the
                                                                living –
given the thirst for flowering, it inflicts *takyr*[9] on the soil.

I stand with this flowering thorn before the winds in my path.
Like a rough stalk I cling with my roots to the earth.
I also want to grow from the depths of the stranded,
like the immortal greenery of these miserable eternal sands.

---

[9] *Takyr* – lit. 'smooth, even or bare'; a type of relief occurring in the deserts of Central
Asia and Kazakhstan, particularly in Maṇġystau and Ùstirt.

Weeping About a Stolen Horse

O, radiant brow –
my cuckoo –
my horse!
A curse on you –
horse thief!

From childhood I thought that the saddle
of a camel inherits a foal,
but thieves spat on the law.
Stolen!
At this time –
during autumn I'd gone to catch falcons.
I thought I'd finish up.
Yes, I'll sort my clothes,
for winter.
But no, my tied up horse
has been untied and taken away –
to hell with it!
To which end of the earth?
In someone else's herd!
Where should I go?
And I'm on foot –
It is death without a horse on the steppe.

Go there where the Sun does not shine,
and I even believe that I deserve
to be lashed with a whip.
The law says:
death to anyone who steals a horse –

D-e-a-t-h!
Why did you choose me?

Paper Clouds, Like Cotton in a Linen Sky

Paper clouds like cotton in a linen sky.
Branches like wings, are ready to soar in the sky.
Spring grasses do magic on the young wine,
dew ringing out
        with its unique song.
The valleys are like fluffy coloured bedspreads,
with their decorated border of shaggy tamarisk,
caressing, kissing and luxuriating –
        a flock of birds
makes a great racket heading back home,
after wandering from afar.

And the udder of the Earth is filled with milk,
and the Sun looks down amiably at
        the low-horned steer.
Life is celebrated by all –
there on the Earth in its various patterns:
valleys, ravines, roads, peaks and spurs.

Everything, everything, is all the more amazing this spring.
The silent sands, lost in *saxaul*,
embarrassed and timidly blushing, numbed from sleep,
not at all like
        the winter sands of the Ķaraķùm Desert.[10]

[10.] Ķaraķùm Desert – desert in Kazakhstan lying to the north-east of the Caspian Sea. It spreads over the Żylyoj district of the Atyrau region and the Bejneu district of the Maṇġystau region. (Not to be confused with the larger Karakum Desert in Turkmenistan. – Ed.)

And suddenly beyond a jagged hill,
                    among other signs
another cries out
                    from the meadow throat:
the camel tosses about,
                    and hunchbacked was born
into the world, as if the hill,
                    was a
blueish-white camel.

Light of the Native Hearth

– Is there anyone to compete with?
Answer me hills.
They reply: 'Hurry up.
Winter is not far away.
This is not the first time we have stayed here.
The wind is just happy to try –
it wore down the minds of travellers.'

The wind also responds:
'I don't go out at night –
here I've got a lot on my plate:
stars light up billions of candles
every night …
I just take my mouth and blow.
The steppe gets burned by them …'
But the star laughs at it,
burning with a blue flame
and has a lot to say for itself:

'We are in infinite space –
jewellery does not play with fire.
We shine, but we do not ignite.
We do not close our eyes at night.
We live the century as insomniacs.
We are not like the plain …'

Here, the plain lifted up its clay
like a lion raising a mane
says to me: 'Judge!
Call the star to answer.
Everything is subject to the poet here.
Who do you need on the journey?'

I say: 'Poets are circling
and wander from afar.
Most of the way we need
the light of the hearth.'

And the hills parted, and presented
a red haze with pure crystal.
Memory protected me from trouble,
from the stars and plains, hills and winds.
If only they could carry out frail legs –
here it is, an old shelter.

Grandma's voice, untouched by decay,
heard: 'Do not cool the hearth!'
It has already served three generations –
we left, and it did not wither.

Coal is warm under rough ash.
A raging steppe whirlwind whines in a pipe.
The door swings open, the biting wind flies in,
in come neighbours, each with a cast iron pot.

Since that time there hasn't been a winter
that we haven't dropped the tongs from our hands,
as if, closely related to Prometheus,
mother distributes coals in the pot.

Even the fire of the infinite universe
cannot overpower the fragments from the fire,
taken on the road from the essence of the imperishable,
and it does not turn me away from the house.

Yurt

As if I had gone back to other ages,
as if I have never been here before,
I cannot calm the avalanche in my heart.
The Sun is looking at me from the ceiling.

Here, I still remember, I was swaddled.
I thought the whole world was filled
with the smell of that swaddling –
wormwood that drives away sadness.

I will throw off the cover for that reason.
Healing wormwood tinctures –
like a harsh spirit, public and persistent,
the lungs are full – breathe out.

Who is it here who has tied his horse?
The horse is real, but as if from a picture.
every cavity here and part,
I know from top to the bottom.

The horse is impatient with trembling legs …
In an instant I will cover this area like a bird,
and if I was destined to be killed here –
it is more honourable than being afraid.

'Ours?' – asked the gust of wind.
Ribs made of wood, felt on the roof,
all hemispheres that move, breathe,
the head's crown is covered with the yurt's hat.

Oģlandy

I had heard about Mount Oģlandy[11] since childhood,
when it was almost my neighbour,
but childhood flew away with adolescence.
and here I wandered at night
before winter, looking for a corner,
to the mountain, where the ancient relics decayed.

Under the watchful eyes of strict stars,
swallowing bitter-salt tears,
I went to the top under the guidance of Beket,[12]
and since that time I have been too busy:
an external sound hampered this calling,
while my summer didn't pass.

Beyond the pass is a new pass.
From afar it rose invisible.
So it is only for youngsters to risk.
I wandered, stumbling and sliding,
and I remembered that you can't turn back.
Whoever retreats stagnates without light.

It seemed the night never passed.
By sentence of the Last Judgment
I was tormented by memory or conscience.
A hundred pilgrims walked alongside,
some not known among the living,
and each carried a tattered tale.

---

[11] Oģlandy – Mount Oģlandy, located in western Kazkhstan, is considered to be a sacred place, a mosque and a resting place of Beket *ata* (see footnote 12).

[12] Beket Myrzaģùlùly (1750–1813) – Sufi religious figure known as Beket *ata*. He is seen as a patron (*pir*) and a teacher by the Kazakhs and is a cult figure particularly popular in western Kazakhstan, where he is called upon in times of trouble and asked for spiritual guidance.

From all over the tormented land
they went here to sleep forever;
I, for the blessing of the night.
I'll be back, pay off debts, finish the path,
to live with dignity, not just anyhow,
and speak up before moving on.

Beket, I only ask for courage.
I never bowed to money –
only to one star, and now she has fallen.
I wander among the dead lights,
O help me out of the sands
O, help me start the day over again.

Poems Do Not Age – Only Poets Do

Poems do not age – only poets do,
but did the poets regret it?
From the wrinkled cage like a golden dream,
the firebird of immortal love flies out.

O, eternal youth possessing hard frost –
snow on the temples, and burning souls,
the poet's soul does not know how to grow old.
It is capable of burning just as it did, at twenty.

And sometimes it is lonely,
like a grey-haired boy with a young soul.
The clock fell apart, spun like worsted.
What was measured, got dark peacefully.

Spaciousness is dazzled from galloping.
Old age introduces its cunning labyrinth.
Modernity and antiquity
have become a tightened knot.

Bestial jealousy triggered insomnia,
death dug up under the cliff of all years
has been maddened with songs –
and the poet has become eternal.

Translated by Belinda Cooke

MUKHTAR SHAKHANOV
(b. 2.07.1942)

 **Mukhtar Shakhanov** is a poet and public figure. He is well known for leading the commission on the Željtoķsan Tragedy (December '86), the rigidly suppressed Kazakh youth upheaval against Soviet rulers in 1986, and for raising awareness on the need to protect the Aral Sea. After graduation from Šymkent Pedagogical Institute, he worked at local newspapers, subsequently becoming editor-in-chief of the major literary journal *Žalyn* in Almaty (1984–86). He has had numerous prominent roles as a political figure. He was elected deputy of the Supreme Council of the USSR (1986–90) and Kazakhstan (1991), chairman of the Committee on the Ecology of Kazakhstan (1992), ambassador to Kyrgyzstan (1993–2004), deputy of the Mäžilis (Mazhilis) of Kazakhstan (2004–07). Today he is editor-in-chief of *Žalyn* and the leader of the Täuelsizdikti ķorġau People's Movement.

He has published almost twenty books, including *Baķyt* (Happiness, 1966), *Balladalar* (Ballads, 1968), *Aj tuyp keledi* (New Moon, 1970), *Sejhundariâ* (Seihun Darya, 1975), *Senim patšalyġy* (Kingdom of Trust, 1979) and *Mahabbatty ķorġau* (Protecting Love, 1982). His prose includes the essay-dialogue *Ķūz basyndaġy aņšyņyņ zary* (Cry of a Hunter Over the Abyss, 1997) in collaboration with Chingiz Aitmatov and the documentary novel *Željtoķsan èpopeâsy* (The Epic of Željtoķsan, 2004). Shakhanov also wrote plays, such as *Sokratty eskeru tùni* (The Night of Paying Respects to Socrates, 1997) and *Šyņġys hannyņ pendelik ķūpiâsy* (The Human Frailty of Genghis Khan, 2001). His works have been translated into some sixty foreign languages.

He is the People's Writer of Kazakhstan (1996), People's Poet of Kyrgyzstan (1999) and the recipient of a number of national and international awards.

The Fickleness of Himalayan Tigers
or the Ballad of Human Courage

Terrible to admit:
almost all of us
should be afraid
of ourselves above everything …
I remember
how a few years ago,
staying in the Himalayas
I once met
a tiger hunter:
          'Just imagine
you are walking
along the side of a mountain
deep in the forest
and suddenly unexpectedly
out of nowhere
right in front of you
there is a striped tiger
with terrible predatory eyes.
What are you going to do?'
he asked me.
Somewhat taken aback,
I shrugged my shoulders.
'The main thing,' –
he continued,
'is to stand firm
and to look him
straight in the eyes
and not to bend.
That's your only chance.
For if you go on all fours
like an animal,
then that's your lot –
you've had it!
He'll be on you in a trice
like a coiled spring

with one powerful leap ...'
And scientists are puzzled.
Why does the tiger hate it
when a man
takes on the look
of an animal?
Even God
created tigers
in such a noble form
to inspire humans
to be like them.
So when I see some
individual bowed down
and fawning,
I see red –
I want to jump on him
like a tiger.
In Almaty,
where I spent
my youth,
the wife
of a powerful businessman
from high society
was flaunting her
beautiful,
gold-striped fur coat,
bragging about the fact
that she was wearing
the pelt of
the very last tiger
of the Himalayan mountains.
I just didn't want to believe
what she was saying.
The Himalayas are immense,
multi-faceted,
and mysteriously wise –
if there are no tigers left,
then the mountains have died.
You should read the thoughts of the creator
in the eyes of the tiger.

Ballad of Bright Pain

The poet Estaj[1] created the popular folk song 'Ķùsni Ķorlan'.
At the age of seventy-two, sensing approaching death, he
called his loyal friend Nùrlybek. Although he had recently
suffered a fall from a horse, incurring broken legs, Nùrlybek
spent two days rattling along in a cart to come to Estaj's aid.
When Nùrlybek arrived, Estaj lifted his trembling hand with
its worn yet still-glittering ring and said to him: 'Persuade
the old people to let me keep this ring given to me by Ķorlan
as a gift. I parted with her fifty-one years ago, so let his ring
remain with me after my death.' Then he broke into tears:
'O my love, how could you find room for such great love in
such a tiny ring!'

A woman approached me once with her sad story,
words filled with bitterness and anguish:
'What can I do about my own dear daughter,
now, like a candle, almost burnt out?
All my life, I was an invisible sail to her fate,
fanning her hopes and dreams,
so that her first love would find her,
the paragon of beauty.
She grew up modest,
with a bright mind and kind soul,
standing out among her friends
beautiful and pure, as a flower in spring.
But these joined birds of joy and grief,
built a crowded nest in my soul,
which was bound to lead to such trouble,
to love wounded in the bud.
We knew no sadness
until that wound lay on my heart.
Now I am the watchman to pain and grief,
the moon of hopes never rising over our house.
Three years is an endless time to suffer
while happiness seems as if free of time.

[1.] Estaj Berkimbajùly (1868–1946) – singer, composer and poet. His song 'Ķorlan' turned
him into a legend.

An actor who is carefree and happy
can find music and light in her soul,
even if he is married with a child in tow.
It is only me who suffers unbearably.
Year after year I suffer and weep.
She continues to say she is perfectly happy,
yet it is hard to explain how she could
refuse *žigits*[2] with a smile on her lips,
like some mindless roe deer
seeking greenery in scorched meadows ...
I try to tell myself that all is still possible,
that there will be life and happiness in the future,
but my soul has become a snowstorm
of longing and alarm in the breast,
while for her there is no one but him ...
At night she weeps, sad as the moon,
at dawn she puts on a show of happiness.
Her soul is more tender than a primrose ...
How can I save this decaying garden?
Give me advice in the language of the poet.
Give me words that speak from the heart ...'
The mother walked away full of grief,
no surprise, given her misfortune.
Still her words struck me deeply,
and the story of her daughter
walked about in my mind, and I thought:
how a century had passed with so many
elevated by fate in this way. How is it,
that, so busy with our own lives, we don't
notice life passing them by, or
the significance of what has occurred?
Only poets sing about lovers
so the people don't forget their names.
Estaj's poetry went to the heart of me.
Those who truly loved remembered it all.
As for declining Estaj, on hearing
the rustlings of death in the leaves

---

[2] *Žigit* – generally denoting a 25- to 40-year-old male, the term can also be used as an honorific indicating bravery, endurance, fortitude and being true to one's word.

he immediately called his only friend,
and, the story goes, he went on to say:
'Nủrlybek, we have been together so many years.
I am 72 years old, and my end is near.
No one understands me better than you.
I will not give up my life without a fight,
but death is powerful, and I struggle to breathe.
Only you were driven to understand the poet,
so listen to him as he utters his dying words.
Here, on the border of eternal darkness and light,
remember, my friend, that I grasped this truth:
life is nothing without days warmed by love,
otherwise the people's soul is dead.
I grasped this even from "stupid" poets
able to translate wise words.
I knew the river's language.
I held my own with mountains.
For half a century I spoke with them.
For half a century, since our first meeting,
I loved my own Ķorlan, like an endless day.
This meant that I lived.
This meant my life was rich.
Every moment, waking or sleeping,
was filled with a dream of her.
Every hour of every year I was happy.
Every hour of every year I suffered.
But because I was in love
I could forget the world.
My pain was beautiful and bright.
All of you who are young
or young in love,
you should envy my tears …
Even if fate has been hard on me,
how much harder the pain of separation?
Believe me when I say, if we were to part,
I could still survive just thinking about her.
For half a century Ķorlan's ring shone for me.
I could conquer any storm.
For half a century my wife fixed her eyes
to where its light shone on my hand.

I go against the customs of our ancestors,
in asking for Ķorlan's ring to travel with me
on my long journey into the shadows.
Though I am leaving
I remain happy as before,
shining with love at the point of death,
with absolute faith in my single hope
that all paths will lead to my Ķorlan.
That is not a dream that can be achieved in life.
My dream is the sister of eternity,
Ķorlan always with me and me protecting her.'
Thus he closed his eyes.
Thus with one last breath he sighs: 'It's time ...'
When Ķorlan heard about this, she cried:
'From this I see he lived and died a true poet.
He loved and sang even at the brink of death.'
The old woman began to keen,
the shawl on her shoulders shining like the moon.
In her words there was such strength
drawn from the immense power of her love.
Years passed ... and, now giving way to death
having healed for a moment the pain of hell,
she suddenly asked for Estaj's song to be sung,
on the *tenderness that shines in a lover's eyes*,
and immediately we saw this tenderness in hers,
as she whispered, breathlessly:
'My love is boundless, as the sea ... I am hurrying to you ...'
Thus she died ... her soul gave up ...
So do not condemn lovers for being in love.
To love is to be faithful – an incredible feat.
It's much worse to be passed by, by love,
like those who haven't been given a heart to love.
Oh mother, tell me why do we encourage
those who are malicious already drunk with hate,
and who don't forgive human tenderness?
Perhaps life's path will not last forever,
but love's light is only for those who seek truth,
for those who prayed to the light alone.
I beg you, therefore, please –
do not crush lovers.

Do not destroy them
with a tear or passionate word.
A wounded wing seeking happiness,
to protect their fragile souls, is sacred.
Wish them tenderness and passion.
Wish them strength over time in their pain,
where death itself will not separate
the owners of immortal love.

By the Laws of Retribution

To Asanăli Ăšimov

I am explaining to you without ceremony, that I loved you.
I have never felt as strongly for my own brother as I do for
you and God knows, how this came about?
– Letter from Fyodor Dostoevsky to Šoķan Uălihanov[3]

My Fyodor, my friend,
here, as I take my last breath,
it is to you I look towards
with my final thoughts.
Scandals have turned to stone.
White and black are one.
Everything is clear.
Finally my devastated people
carry me into the grave's dark.

My people may be horrified
that in spite of all hopes,
I go to my grave
still believing in God's judgement.
There *are* still those who believe.
When you read these lines,
the turf will already be lifted to bury me …
I owe a lot to today's laws
that seem to rush like an avalanche down a slope.
You were the principal source of my love.
You are the last to whom I send my spirit and words.
It is impossible to smash the turbulent will
of these rivers of the world,
as they travel vast countries
with their wealth and blueness.

[3.] Šoķan Uălihanov (Chokan Valikhanov, 1835–65) – Kazakh scholar, ethnographer and historian, a close friend of Dostoevsky. A descendant of high-ranking Kazakh nobility, Uălihanov was one of the first Kazakhs to be accepted at the Russian Geographical Society. The excerpt from Dostoevsky's letter has been translated by the National Bureau of Translations.

Even the smartest princes
lose themselves in them.
Life's angry pride can be restless
causing the head to spin as it
hurtles towards us –
yet our better selves are like rivers.
Who would dream of treating a great person lightly?
Great river –
who would dare to compete with you?
In your waves all thoughts are born.
We who are just passing through,
can we really understand your depths?
On whom should we pin the blame?
My dear friend. No one can contain you.
Everywhere envy exposes those who try ...
Your thoughts are the cradle of the world.
You are both my shield and goal.
How much I would like the Kazakh people
to love you with the same brotherly love as I.
And now I have stood up with a smile,
                    handfuls of light in my hand.
I would like to flower alongside you,
but my brief past is like a joke ...
and I have carried away many daydreams from you.
The Moon grows scarlet from behind Mount Mataj.[4]
The morning is crystal clear, but the simple star quivers,
as though seeing evil itself.
Šoķan is no more. A torn letter.

But didn't he fight with this chosen age?
Or maybe the age struggled with him.
In the prime of life, strength is all-giving.
At twenty-nine he moves into the afterlife.
A small star quivers in the innocent sky,
and runs from itself into the darkness.
As time passes,
Dostoevsky, the prisoner in Omsk,
goes on to greater fame.

[4.] Mount Mataj – part of the Alatau range of mountains near Almaty. It looks down over
Lake Balķaš (Balkash).

So ... a cemetery for lasting memorials –
Altynemel's cemetery, of eternal night,
is where they buried Šoķan in glory.
One might place some marker here
were it not that the weight of sudden affairs,
that burden which hangs over time,
causes the thought to be carried away
through the years, so you glance briefly
and the thought slips through your fingers ...
Šoķan is worthy of a monument.
His Russian friends agreed about that.
They transported rock from Taškent
and set to with a chisel.
But petty human squabbling
soon brought all sorts of lowlifes
out of the woodwork –
a scoundrel decides to split the rock in two
to cut down on materials and labour.
Not letting on to his customers,
he thought he'd make a killing.
'All these suckers are blind as a bat.'
No sooner had he started chiselling the stone,
than a fragment hit him in the eye,
and he fell down in unbearable pain.
This pain rose to the sky,
while he staggered below on the earth,
biting the dust and chewing the carpet –
leaving future ages to look on his actions,
and judge them as they will.
And in that spring over the hills of Mataj
the flock gathered, and the circle closed in.
All his loyal friends were there
to send news to Petersburg:
the tear-stained grieving face of a friend
felt justice has been done.
There is punishment and the laws of retribution
and friendship is stronger than evil.

Seventh Sense

So you got married.
I'm happy for you.
But it's not only people –
wolves and she-wolves
join their fates,
in order
to avoid loneliness
and provide
lifelong support
to one another.
To marry like everyone does,
and produce a child,
doesn't require
great intelligence.
The question in all of this,
is how will the face that
now looks you in the mirror
be judged tomorrow?

It is not surprising that,
from time immemorial,
people have often confused
their hot and stormy,
passing emotions
with love,
since both can cause
the lightning to flash.

But not everyone
is capable of understanding
that in our human,
all-too-oblivious world,
love – is the highest peak.
The ability to climb up
has been given to only a few happy people.
And possibly unfortunately,
of the ten thousand,
only two

manage to be successful,
on the sharp edge
of this amazing
imprisoning, stormy,
happy holiday,
this eternal holiday
of unceasing delight.

To get physically
but not spiritually close,
is the ultimate sadness.
That's why
there are so many
lonely people in the world –
the wingless tedium
of a single-sided coin.

For them no
one-off flights,
or holidays out of the blue.
Totally deprived
of a happy fate
they smile to your face,
bitterly weeping in secret.

And at any crossroads
of life's path
you are always met
with the inexorable question –
Has your spouse become
a sensitive friend to your soul,
a friend of
your innermost desires,
one who feels
your happiness and torment
with a seventh sense?

If not,
then all your striving
will be like trying to light a fire
on a windy day.
And it means
that you end up
too far away from
the goals fate has assigned you,
too, too far …
That's just how inaccessible,
difficult,
and secret
this multi-faceted,
willfully-choosy
love is.

Call to Courage

(A reply to a *žigit* who feels that he is unhappy)

You wept *žigit*,
recalling the hardship of the road
regretting kindness for which
you were never repaid.
You wept *žigit*,
your sons on your knees,
for a violent youth
that can't be put right.
You wept *žigit*,
about friends, who gave the gift
of betrayal,
considering past mistakes,
cursing transient successes,
your eyes, resentfully scaling
those impossibly high pinnacles.
You wept *žigit* …
only I didn't approve of your weeping.
I know fate
treated you well.
I remember how
you held the road's lashes in contempt.
But who did you become
if you ended up in tears?
What's that on your head:
a hat or a woman's headscarf?
And if it's a hat
cock it jauntily once more.
Wipe away this defeatist melancholy,
like soot from your face.
Your son should not see you cry.
Remember the sons
who look amazed and silent
at the tears in the eyes
and the weak-willed hands of their fathers.
What will they become?
You wept *žigit* …
What has become of your exalted pride?
Where is your generosity

having laid low your trembling enemies?
Courage and cowardice go hand in hand,
just one step between them.
And who told you:
all failure – means unhappiness?
That *tülpar*[5]
never stumbled on a difficult path?
That the white shirt
never became dirty in bad weather?
That goats' teeth
can't destroy the wild plane tree?
Who told you
that all people are good and fine?
That scorched malice
is like an old woman in a harvested field?
That everyone lives by a single truth,
protecting innocent honesty
like a child from lies?
If there are offended people,
it means there are also those who offend.
If there are humble people,
it means those who humiliate are thriving.
Pull yourself together, *žigit*!
To remain on the sidelines is worse.
Insults are just a rusty dagger
thrown into the water.
There is much work on this earth
for the courageous to do.
Forget your tears
and drive longing from your breast.
How can you let trouble
allow your dream to overtake you?
The *žigit*'s dream
cannot gallop behind,
and life's failures
may lead us to happiness.

---

[5] *Tülpar* – in Kazakh mythology and folklore, a winged or swift horse, corresponding to Pegasus. Every major hero of a Kazakh epic poem has a *tülpar*, which grows fast and, through its supernatural powers, helps the hero to succeed in his quest. Nowadays, *tülpar* is used as an honorific term for a horse.

Shared Understanding

Black from grief in this simple room
shrunken and done for with aging sickness,
here Leo Tolstoy is dying.
His wife walks in,
bends down over the bedstead.
'Forgive me, forgive me!
I am so guilty.'
But he remains silent.
He thinks: 'My dear friend, don't weep,
my sadness is no less than yours.
No matter how many tears may fall,
I am at the edge of the grave.
Truly I loved you,
but there was such trouble between us.
I was tormented by your deafness.
You couldn't understand …
I know to be the wife of Tolstoy
is a heavy cross, and all the heavier
for me was the burden of
your incomprehension.
You know you could have understood,
but you didn't want to.
It was a long century for us,
but here is our parting at last.
I forgive you, and ask you to forgive me …'
And he shut his eyes, his tragedy,
the ability to expose a hundred evils,
yet with a wife unable to understand him.
TOLSTOY IS NO MORE.
He has gone to his rest.
How unhappy you were,
the wisest of people.
Where can we find tenderness
that is biased towards us?

Who refreshes us in the intense heat,
shelters us in the fold?
The three measures of life are –
heights,
depth,
spaciousness.
Failing to understand them
leads to the heart of
darkness and deafness.
After all, there are no paths
between one torrential soul and another.
There is no worse curse
than a lack of understanding.
The path from one soul to another is like a duel.
What a steep ascent,
a road in a circle of people.
Incomprehension, what are you,
the misfortune of the innocent?
But to not want to understand
carries a heavy burden of guilt.
O, how many paths I only half-know,
O, how many springs have turned to sludge.
Incomprehension is a traitor and a murderer,
the hangman torturing in the midst of darkness and deafness.
Giordano's fire swirls behind you.
Galileo's trial is also you.
Incomprehension, you lasso the damned Biržan sal.[6]
The starlight eclipsed Úlyḳbek.[7]
Incomprehension has always
been cursed, allowing
no pardon,
no mercy.

---

[6] Biržan sal Ḳožaġululy (1831–94) – traditional Kazakh composer and singer. He belonged to a special category of artists in Kazakh society known as *sal*, who usually functioned as part of a group that included those skilled in wrestling, horse-racing, music or storytelling.

[7] Úlyḳbek (Ulugbek; 1394–1449) – Mirza Muhammed Taraghay bin Shahrukh, a Timurid ruler, astronomer and mathematician. 'Ulugbek' is a moniker, loosely translated as 'Great Ruler'.

You whipped Abaj,[8]
your voice joined those people
who envied Áuezov[9] success,
your jealous eyes not out of your sight
for a moment: he picks up the whisper:
'His novel has no truth,
it fails to reach true heights.'
Áuezov just smiled bitterly:
The people will JUDGE.
The people will GRASP IT.
Yes it really was like that.
What blindness to see
yet not to discover.
If the one who fails to understand
is not to blame,
it is certainly a crime
not to wish to understand.
Incomprehension is
the fog of dank
humdrum days.
It covers the horizon.
It extinguishes the sun
in the daytime.
So –
I am concerned about what happens
when a young poet achieves fame.
He may be misunderstood.
Let's pray for mutual understanding.

[8.] Abaj Ķúnanbajúly (1845–1904) – the most influential of all Kazakh poets, also a composer
and philosopher. He is considered to be a reformer of Kazakh literature on the basis of
enlightened Islam; his works also reflected the European and Russian cultures.

[9.] Múhtar Áuezov (1897–1961) – Kazakh writer, social activist and philologist. The poem is
referring to the extreme popularity of his novel *The Path of Abaj* (1942–52).

Four Mothers

On life's long and difficult path
make sure you don't forget who you are.
If you always recall that your mother gave birth to you,
not forgetting that there are actually Four Mothers fanning
                                        out like wings:
OUR NATIVE HOME – our fate and the essence of our
                                        essence,
OUR NATIVE LANGUAGE: brought to us from our
                                        fathers,
RICHES OF THE SOUL and CUSTOMS – our sacred
                                        rock,
burning for us through the darkness of generations and
                                        years,
OUR NATIVE HISTORY – its degree of bitterness
and sadness, tormenting us and weighing us down ...
No deity is more significant than these Four Mothers.
Without them your head is like tumbleweed.
Anyone unable to love, or take care of his own dear mother,
is unable to understand the greatness of the Four Mothers.
Anyone who forgets about his Four Mothers
will be blown into oblivion by a forgetful wind.
A people who cannot protect the Four Shrines,
will never be fated for happiness.
The Four Mothers are like the fate of our dear ones.
To live means to live only for them.
If you are dying, you are dying for them.

Translated by Belinda Cooke

VLADIMIR GUNDAREV
(19.07.1944 – 25.08.2012)

Vladimir Gundarev was a Russian-born poet, prose writer and translator. He moved to Kazakhstan in 1961 and worked until 1970 for the radio in Tselinograd (now Nur-Sultan), then spent twenty years as literary consultant for the Nur-Sultan inter-regional branch of the Writers' Union of Kazakhstan. Since November 1990, he had been the editor-in-chief of the journal *Niva*, which he also founded.

His thirty-plus poetry collections include *Derevnya moya derevyannaya* (My Wooden Village, 1973), *Zimopis'* (Winter Chronicles, 1976), *Svetlyn'-Reka* (Svetlyn-River, 1980), *Kaplya v more* (A Drop in the Sea, 1982), *Prodolzhenie zhizni* (Continuation of Life, 1987) and *Ya zhivu na planete lyubvi* (I Live on the Planet of Love, 2003). His poetry is characterised by a manifest love and tenderness for his native lands, both Siberian forests and Kazakh steppes. In his *Koreiskie i yaponskie motivy* (Korean and Japanese Motives, 2002–03), the poet tries to construct his own poetic form, taking into account the intricate rhyme system, style and spirit of Korean and Japanese haiku, tanka, sijo, hansi and other forms. Gundarev also authored the non-fiction books *Zhizn' na svetloi zemle* (Life in the Bright Land, 1980), *S zabotoi o zemle* (With Care to the Land, 1985), *Zdes' propisany nashy serdtsa* (Our Hearts Are Inscribed Here, 1994) and *V serdtse i pamyati pokolenii* (In the Memories and Hearts of Generations, 2000). His works have been translated into Kazakh, Ukrainian, German, Korean, Slovak, French, Spanish and Portuguese. He translated many Kazakh poets into Russian.

Gundarev was awarded the Order of Ķùrmet (2005), the Pushkin Medal (Russia, 2012) and the Alaš International Literary Award (2012). He was a member of the Russian Academy of Poetry.

It's Time to Love

It's time to love.
Do you hear me? – It's time.
Poet, put down your pen.
Take your eyes off your work for a moment.
Evening enters like a sorcerer or magician.
Fling open the window.
Let in the evening.
Feel love's living fibre
that you struggle to find in yourself.
It's all around in the life you've been given –
In the fate of
flowers,
nature,
woman,
the earth.
In everything there lives a presentiment of love –
in the tender embrace of the maple branch,
struggling to warm in spring,
in those eyes that look at you coldly
as if the whole world expects to be fired at,
in the inexpressible secret of the young man
fishing for his loved one in the clouds.
Those little glints of beauty
are full of love,
and spicy sharpness,
offering the tenderness of the swan's feather …
It's time to love –
(while there is still time).

The Snowdrop

Silver spurs, clinking and ringing,
icicles break the silence.
Their mouths amazed, blinds pushed back,
windows gaze hard, listening out for the spring.
But up above there is a cheerful white line
and the prattle of noisy rooks,
while the Sun rebelled and bursts out laughing,
as though someone had plucked his rays like strings.
Spring suns itself, turned to the full blaze of the Sun.
Winds stir up April all along the steppe.
Here, the slender snowdrop suffering from the cold,
shamelessly gets tipsy with every chattering drop.
It will take some work from the Sun
before the snowdrop manages to warm himself
in the midday smoke.
But he believes in spring with a pure heart –
and I envy him a little.

Weariness – From Hollow Happiness

Weariness –

from Hollow Happiness.

Weariness –

from Hollow Strength.

Earth's head is tired of

rocking on its own slender axis.

Forget-me-nots are tired of

looking with their baby-blue gaze on
the world.

Cockerels are tired of

being the heralds of the morning.

Dogs are tired of

barking hoarsely from their kennels.

The sunset is tired of

creating a burning fire in the soul.

Water drops are tired of

chiselling into the roughness of
the stone.

The stars are tired of

endlessly blinking at us.

Hands are tired of

speaking with other hands.

My family are tired of

having to welcome me …

All because

you are tired of

loving me.

Black Lily of the Valley

Gentle and fragile,
black lily of the valley,
why can't you get along with me?
Why do you walk past
my all too masculine world?
You have cast such a spell on me,
I'm afraid of getting drawn into a fight,
I feel my spring start to uncoil …
Well then let it.
It's all the same to me,
since you stroke another's hand.
Black lily of the valley.
Black lily of the valley.
The wandering May winds
are privy to all secrets,
yet they cannot understand
our relationship at all.
This wind, this wind is so luminous …
yet my lily of the valley is more precious to me.
Black lily of the valley,
Black lily of the valley
… Why can't you get along with me?

Bach

Beneath this worn out camisole,
his shirt is old,
yet his proud smile is frozen
on his bulging lips.
Though this organist
has neither wealth nor money,
who is greater than
this stooping Bach?
Nothing but lost notes
ring in his empty pockets.
Ah, here he it is –
give it here at once.
Let this note rise to the heights,
so it pierces through,
making you all fall on your knees
before God – who is?
Why Bach of course.
His whole family was poor,
but he always had
music to feed them.
And thus it sounds out,
And what a sound!
A solemn mass.
Drone of a gothic chorale,
beneath a subdued sky ...
O, how frenzied is ailing Johann's
soul as he releases his flock of notes
like birds in flight.
He composes at his instrument
day and night,
even in winter's dark,
him melting like a candle.
... Here as I stand guard at his monument
all is silent ...
The Leipzig night disperses
a slow snowstorm of stars.
And almost perched on the edge
of his writing desk,
a weary and happy Bach
completes his fugue.

I Burst into Your Memory …

I burst into your memory,
burst into your memory.
I am crazy and uninvited,
not kind not loving,
so that later, as usual,
I can sink into obscurity
and carry away with me
the bitter taste of stinging lips …
… On the soft, blue
intoxicating grasses,
I want to lie down and
fall asleep like a child.
I want to wallow
in the tender touch
of amazing dawns,
the source of your
wide-open eyes,
their flowing spring.
And then the earth will
no longer feel cramped.
Crazy now, I am telling you:
give me, give me
a swan song –
I am a clumsy
crane …

Winter Chronicles

The passing chronicles of summer
are again perfected by nature.
And light's transparency has revealed
its width,
depth,
   heights.
      In a single day
         light's bright clarity
            sacredly reveals the soul.
The striving passion of work
once again goes right to the fingertips.
It means that purity and love
have still got hold of me.
It begins like healing.
In the world of the winter chronicles
is my happiness.
Only better to remember in the past,
where the future's clarity becomes visible.
And after the first freshly fallen snow
there is an unsullied whiteness in my breast.
I want the first freshness
to fill dreams and work,
so that the emptiness didn't touch the tenderness,
so that it remained indivisible,
so that the soft hands of the snowstorm
are able to touch the coarsened soul.
My feelings are delighted
by the comfort of the first snow's whiteness.
… The inspiring winter chronicles are everywhere,
responding sweetly in the breast.
This sensation of a white miracle –
I ask you not to pass by my heart.

The Artist

You are a loner,
forgotten in a corner,
in the darkness of a draughty door,
sick of cold.
Artist, take black charcoal
and create white snow for them.
Draw the face of a madonna
that did not know bitter tears,
so this house can heat up
and the soul will be refreshed by the frost.
Moths may fly to the light,
but you'll hardly notice them.
The artist will once more
                    be filled with power,
though still filled with his own weaknesses as well.

The Road Is Like a Ribbon

The road is like a ribbon,
embracing the fields.
The summer was fading
like your jacket.
There is a yellowish glimmer
over the spreading distance.
The forests give off
the bitter smell of almonds.
The Sun is a dim medal
on the sky's shirt.
Time dissolves
in dry blueness.
Shadows of trees
wilt on your sleeve.
The sorrow of withering
is as intense as if I burned
over fire coals.
I am hovering like smoke,
I am hovering …
          hover …

Evening Sunset

My evening sunset ...
burning with a scarlet flame,
before the closing in of eternal night,
what sadness do you predict for me?

Is there anything that I know of it myself?
Called to that region up there beyond the clouds,
the soul strains to the heavens,
collecting earthly sorrow as it goes.

The meadow contours grow faint,
rapidly merging with the twilight.
Everything melts in my memory –
words, events, meetings, faces ...

I regret that I can no longer
put things right from the past,
my breast is so weighed down,
my memory starts to weep and bleed.

Life is such a mix of kindness and evil –
I tried to do my best, yet often
felt I was outside looking in on life,
struggling to make sense of all that past.

Don't change or cross anything out.
There is confusion and turmoil in my soul.
My love lit up my path
but did I pass any light on to anyone?

All of the past was fitted into a single day,
in a single day fate was in place.
And imperceptibly light and shadow
transformed to a dense essence.

But even if I have lived in vain,
and not by God's laws –
evening sunset, do your best,
just keep going – a little longer ...

Tenderness

Tenderness.
Boundlessness.
Snowiness …
The meadows breathe in harmony with me.
But do you know what tenderness is like,
for the likes of me?
Just occasionally I remove my armour –
the trappings fly off and
tenderness lurks in my gloomy fingers,
flaming like the night.
I throw aside my unnecessary staff,
the years of turmoil fall silent and
like a welcoming star
tenderness streams
from my downcast eyes.
Please, protect my heart
from its ludicrous reserve.
Lips redden
like a rowanberry
filled with the juice of tenderness.
Endlessness –
is like the boundlessness
that is reflected in your fate.
I can only hope my clumsy tenderness
will touch you for a moment.

The Whitish Morning …

The whitish morning …
                              merges with the whitish sky.
Morning and sky
            are completely without borders …
Somewhere in the steppe,
                or rather
                      beyond it
                          above the forest,
haphazardly and bitterly,
                great birds started to weep,
their tears merging
              with shining light
                  weaving sun-filled
                      threads of parting.
I walked away into the fields,
                  across the river into the distance,
                    but immediately,
this sobbing flowed and spread throughout August.
How endlessly
                  these birds
                    sobbed –
              like tiny children,
            sensing autumn,
and the burden of migration.
The woods are silent,
dressed in decayed clothes,
         leaves falling …
                golden hues fading …
I feel all of this deep in my core.
I kiss your palms
And your white white hands.
… I am afraid that they are weeping
over this shining midday
not for anything
except our
ridiculous birds of parting.

Five to Twelve

You don't need to chase the future,
dash headlong at each obstacle.
It's already five to twelve,
with an abyss at the first corner.

When called upon it is foolish
to refuse to take part.
In a moment the hand closes up
on the dial of fate.

As has always been the tradition,
and with respect for selflessness,
one must work day to day –
life can't be postponed to later.

The time you waste is worthless.
Idleness and inactivity is a vice.
To achieve a little more than you think
you have to organise your time.

And finally you must acknowledge love,
with a soul that will never age –
given it is five to twelve
and there is still a lot that you can do.

To My Readers

To Zinaida Chumakova, in memory of a delightfully productive meeting in Žezķazġan (Dzhezkazgan) Historical and Archaeological Museum.
– 14 September 2011

Perhaps you are few, but you exist.
Thank you for what has turned out to be an honour,
if you have been able to keep my artless lines in your heart.
For you – my spiritual family,
are more dear to me than anyone.
In February I took the word from the earth and sky,
when the snows were swirling
about the golden birch foliage,
in the dewy morning of mown grass,
when its aromatic aroma
floated thickly into the sunset,
with ripe wheat grain,
with what tender light the steppe was lit,
there at the spring hidden in the thicket,
among forget-me-nots and cornflowers.
Even in the dim humdrum days – such grace –
I strained to guess the future.
I grieved with you in your troubles,
conquered the precipitous pass,
indignant when crooks fleeced you,
happy at the slightest sign of you
rising above yourself smiling
and pleasing others – and not just
those particularly dear to you.
I live with a small part of each of you
in me, inspiring and giving,
so that we share a trembling connection —
for in the most secret lines of love
I took your feelings as a fiery spark
to ignite many years for me.
I took all the best from you,
and learned well from it.

But if I suddenly became arrogant,
forgive me for this affliction,
which may have led me to listen
to other voices for which I have
only myself to blame.
I bared your soul without restraint,
and without that I am
blind, unfeeling and without wings ...
That you were prepared
to recognise me as your own
I thank you, dear readers!

Translated by Belinda Cooke

AKUSHTAP BAKHTYGEREYEVA
(b. 23.08.1944)

Akushtap Bakhtygereyeva is a poet. She studied at the Faculty of Philology of the Kazakh State Women's Pedagogical Institute in Almaty (1961–66), then worked as a journalist for the periodicals *Oral ôṇiri* in Oral and *Oktâbr' tuy* in Taldyḳorġan (Taldykurgan), before being invited into the editorial team of the major literary newspaper *Ḳazaḳ ădebieti* in Almaty (1966–71). Subsequently, she was an editor-in-chief at the film studio Ḳazaḳfil'm (Kazakhfilm) (1971–72), the journal *Žazušy* (1972–75) and the publishing house Žazušy (1975–81). Since 2007 she has been head of the literary association Ḳalamger, and the chairwoman of the West Kazakhstan Branch of the Kazakhstan Writers' Union.

Her first collection of poems was *Ôrimtal* (Willow, 1967), followed by *Naz* (Playfulness, 1969), *Ḳuanyšym, iṇkărim* (My Joy, My Passion, 1971), *Seni ojlajmyn* (Thinking About You, 1973), *Aḳḳanat* (Angel, 1975), *Baḳyt ăni* (Song of Happiness, 1978), *Žajyḳ ḳyzy* (A Žajyḳ's Daughter), *Aḳželeṇ* (1985) and *Sùmbile* (Sirius, 1990), plus other works. She published her volume of selected poems, *Aḳ šaġala* (White Gull), in 2001 and three years later came out *Lebedinaya vernost'* (Loyalty of Swans) translated into Russian. Bakhtygereyeva is also an author of lyrics for numerous popular songs, and translator of many Russian poets into Kazakh.

Bakhtygereyeva is poet laureate of the State Prize of the Republic of Kazakhstan (2018), recipient of the Alaš International Literary Award and of the title Honoured Worker of the Republic of Kazakhstan (2012), and was awarded the Order of Ḳùrmet (2005).

Wild Foal

Father, how you dreamed of a racehorse ...
Hoping for misfortune, and illness
to be washed away with the spring,
you asked for a foal to be put aside
from the best mare in the herd.

You wanted to break him in the *bǎjge*.[1]
You wanted to ride him straightaway –
to greet the steppe at the break of day.
Father, who knew that you would never
ever ride your horse ...

When you left, this horse,
having lost a friend and freedom,
became wild, and unusually vicious.
Only in his stable
he occasionally neighed.

So one morning at first light,
with a single jerk
he broke his lassos,
destroying the wattle fence ...

What instinct drove him from his home?
What far distance did he dream
of travelling to?
The horse flew to unknown spaces,
into the dawn steppe's half-darkness.

Longing for freedom the foal has returned
to his stall, to peacefully drink water
from a bucket – his dreams a mystery.
We also have broken out, before being tamed.
Life reins us all in, in the end.

[1.] *Bǎjge* – traditional type of horse race popular in Kazakhstan; the distance can be from six to one hundred kilometres.

Tell the Žajyķ River

Tell the Žajyķ River,[2] there is a girl,
who is willful and free like him,
writing her poems on his
white sails like a wave's foam.

Tell the Žajyķ – she's like a seagull
on the breast of her own native waters –
having touched you with her wing,
she'll soar into the heavens.

So hard for those without longing
for the shores of their native river …
Tell the Žajyķ this daughter will come running,
come running in spite of petty troubles.

Like the Žajyķ raging in spring,
crazily, her turbulent life
spills out,
far from the shores, as life flings her
into the storm-tossed waves –

now long since washed, and
carried away … Žajyķ's daughter
walks bravely through life,
a ship in her home waters.

'O, my Žajyķ, when I walk with you
my life is a fire, directed and fierce.'
She sings her own song.
She suffers but she sings …

[2.] Žajyķ – also called Ural, a river that originates in the southern Ural Mountains and
discharges into the Caspian Sea. 'Aķ Žajyķ' (lit.'white Žajyķ') is an honorific term.

When There Is a Loved One

If you hear the loud cackles of a goose
circling a lake, you know something's wrong
with the lake – unless your loved one is near, autumn
displaces the spring with its chill and barren gardens.

If music suddenly spills out boundlessly, hearts
speaking easily to another, wormwood
singing trembling and tender –
you know your loved one is close by.

If your loved one walks somewhere nearby,
the sky is particularly pure and bright.
You give an amazed, bewildered glance,
just as the buds are ready to inhale the air.

The Moon in the heights is heavenly,
a whirlwind that lifts the heart high.
It's hard when there's no one to love,
yet to be the loved one is likewise difficult.

Conversation with Mama

I miss your voice, Mama
and I thought I'd go to you.
I wanted to tell you in private
about my joys and sorrows.

Do you have the strength
to have a long heart-to-heart?
Fewer and fewer people understand
the state I am in.

You did not listen
when I asked you
to follow me
and remain near.

You didn't believe me
when I told you
of the cruel, selfish people, who
would give a child to strangers.

Mama, since I left your home,
I can't believe the horrors I've seen.
Singing of powerful love,
I collected white flowers in the garden.

I survived a friend's betrayal.
Raging sadness, the soul's torment
breaks out in this letter – but then
I tear it up, afraid to upset you …

Dreaming about you, I can see your aged face –
I hear you say: 'Take your time
daughter – all in good time.'

And Again About Love

Love, I have come back to you again –
be my theme, repeating once more.
There is no life without love, there is no happiness.
I have nothing more to say.

If you want to endure the hardships of life,
you need a song, you need human contact.
You only have one shot at this one and only life,
life must be loved passionately.

If you truly love, then your eyes gleam differently.
A strong stream begins a new course.
To find happiness and respect on Earth,
first you need to love people.

We must love the white dawn, the radiance of the Sun.
We must be able to love the flower's image.
We must read legends of olden times,
about girls who died, deprived of their chosen loves.

Shouldn't a girl be a wife for a husband, a mother for a child?
We didn't realise there is no joy without girls.
We don't write stories about those who
married by calculation – they leave us no legends.

I have composed poems about love in the past.
Today I return in its defence.
If you are too weak-willed to love a spouse,
I doubt that you can love people …

Steppe Swallows

You touched my heart, just when
I thought I could give poetry a rest.
My steppe swallows,
Why are there so few of you?

A beautiful image of paradise,
with your singing above the hills.
Where are your curved wings,
that compare with a girl's eyebrow?

Where are you today, my winged one?
You, who can't hurt anyone.
Have you moved somewhere quieter,
where your descendants' shelter will be better?

Were you perhaps scared there
might be snakes, disturbing your nest?
Returning from a trip, why is it,
there are less of you to meet me?

Did you feel any danger
with such a tiny little heart?
Why did you renounce the steppe
that you turned into a song in spring?

This little flock that gathered together,
was like a reunion of dear friends.
You seem to retain the kindness
that so many people have lost.

You touched my heart, when I was
about to give poetry a rest.
My steppe swallows
why are there so few of you?

To a Seagull

What brings you to the steppe?
A mystery, given there's no sea here.
Tear-filled grief seems to lie in your eyes –
Could it be you are also in love?

What troubles lie in your breast,
you circling lost, alone,
wings so heavy, across the steppe?
Could it be you are also in love?

What sadness weighs down your eyes?
What wounds have scarred you?
What strength let you circle half the world?
Could it be you are also in love?

White-winged spirit of blue expanse,
will you always be so free?
What winds drive you across the hills?
Could it be you are also in love?

Winter Night

Night distances, filled with
winter silence.
Eyes grow tired
from the intense light.

The flash of dawn is still not close.
Joyfully we head home with you,
loathe to leave from visiting friends
in this time of celebration.

Houses, woods and road,
uniting everything and everyone –
gradually shrouding with
blinding thick snow.

Snow. Snow! Year on year
we do our part and wait for it.
And here it lies, gift of nature,
on our shoulders – like one of our own,

its tracks under the poplar's canopy —
I was ablaze because you were beside me,
my fluffy headscarf all the more
fluffy and warm from the snow.

Was it the beginning of spring –
the day you kissed me for the first time?
Maybe that's why I forgot about the winter,
forgot to shake off the snow when I came home …

… not one word, you didn't let me
realise this, and shook off the snow.
Snowflakes rested on my shoulders
then slipped to the floor in an instant.

As if burned by a sudden flame,
I felt afraid, despaired.
It seemed that my silk dress
was slipping from my shoulders …

Song of the Restless Heart

I just want to be familiar with those
who are open in friendship and all they do.
Whose word is honourable, carrying weight,
where truth is strongly protected.

I only want to meet with those
who don't get greedy when poor,
but have a big soul. Who believe in
happiness, but don't flatter rogues.

I only want to be friends with those
who have a heart that beats strongly.
Who are happy to breathe hope
into the fortunes of others.

Always, I want to spend my time with those
who walk tall through life,
who avoid the gossip of the crowd,
keeping their distance from fools.

Justice

Justice, your place is sacred in my heart.
People rush to where they can see you.
Though you are as high as Everest,
not everyone can live up to you.

You listened attentively to so many
expecting words of truth.
Everyone admired you
as if you were a beautiful girl.

In meetings with fawning flatterers,
you were secretely weeping.
Like so many others I state:
how fine you are – incomparable.

But then we see people
all in with the in-crowd.
Does this mean maybe
your road is not for everyone?

So, Justice, walk the open road –
without you, flowers freeze in the snow storms.
Where were you when a good *žigit*[3]
suddenly met up with some clumsy girl?

Why try to pretend strength is safe from evil?
Why fail to help the good?
Without it there is no peace for anyone, anywhere –
no, not even in the grave.

[3.] *Žigit* – generally denoting a 25- to 40-year-old male, the term can also be used as an honorific indicating bravery, endurance, fortitude and being true to one's word.

Justice – just a few letters. Many use you
just to stupidly point the finger.
Just come and meet us for once,
and we will sit happily around you.

In this world full of battle and victory
did you get worn down and agree to give in?
I hope to meet you, but even if I don't
just make sure you always remain on earth.

To My Father

I grew up like a white-headed flower,
a tender, laughing girl,
but in spite of this you, my father,
insisted in treating me like a boy.

I didn't sleep in the arms of my mother,
always behind you at your heels.
Climbing on the back
of a stallion,
the blue air cut like a stone.

Mama was powerless without you:
I did not eat,
but waited for you.
And then, hugging you by the neck,
I would not get off your lap.

Your look was warm.
You gave me water,
sweeter to me than honey.
When you came back from work
I always met you.

And we would harness the horse together,
me hurriedly grabbing the reins.
You would laugh
saying you would choose
for me the best bride.

But I never removed the
double-barrelled gun from the wall.
When you went hunting
you went without me.

I never played *asyķ*[4] in the evenings.
Your 'boy's' days flowed differently –
till finally one day my hair lay
in long dark braids upon my shoulders …

I don't want to hear you say
that a girl's fate is marked out,
that I have to marry as other girls do –
for I am the 'son' you dreamed of for so long!

[4.] *Asyķ* – knee bone of a sheep, used to play national games, including *asyķ atu* ('hit the bone') in which bones are thrown to knock other bones out of a line. It is particularly popular with boys.

Willow

Great sweeps of snowstorms
touched you on their way,
but spring's arrival
urged you to bloom,
to the trill of nightingales.

All around,
celebrating your birth,
the snowdrifts dance.
Only attachment to your native earth
has saved you from destruction.

Your back has been severely bent
by a fierce gust of wind
but it didn't break.
Speak to me, willow, if only a word …
But you are silent as before.

In place of the wretched cold
a ray of sunshine appears in the sky.
But tell me,
where do you get this strength,
where does your courage come from?

In the Museum

Here are the clay dishes behind the glass.
These walls might wonder, who ate off them?
He walked his path, in love with life like us –
working out the value of good things.

And here is a silver belt,
owned by some high-ranked beauty.
Was life kind to all her dreams?
Who fell recklessly in love with her?

Here are some fragments of people's lives.
We don't know the names of their owners,
all is lost in the cycling of the ages –
carried with them long, long ago into the abyss.

You, sabre, who destroyed
your enemies on the steppe,
tell me, did you ever
dream of a peaceful day?

Like the *seris*[5] of old …
'… once a horseman always
a horseman – in harness …'
Everything that was, is gone.

[5.] *Seris* – traditionally a sophisticated group of artists skilled in singing, composing, poetry, hunting, eagle hunting. They used to wear striking costumes. Nowadays, *seri* is a synonym for a 'refined young man' or a 'lover of women'.

Tell Me, Is It the Same with You?

Tell me, is it the same with you,
is everyone equal before the Lord,
as they tell us in books, or do you also
have clever liars, fools in worn-out chains?

Is there a matchmaker and military man standing there
admiring the heavenly luxury? When people show up
at the paradise gates, do they have to produce
letters of recommendations stamped and sealed?

And can you tell me if you always have spring there,
flower upon flower as it is on the steppe?
Have all been forgiven their faults
or do you need bribes up there for this?

With you, do children abandon their mothers?
There are too many spots on our Sun.
The only people who are satisfied are those who steal –
… By the way, do you have to pay for a drink in paradise?

Paradise before you – hell behind.
Your white horse does not mourn in fear.
Like here, lazy Kazakhs are expecting
heavenly rewards from the angels there.

… When the body is buried deep in the earth,
the spirit dwells in truth at last.
Tell me, do people still denounce each other –
does gossip continue to thrive?

You are far from all human vanity,
you couldn't read but were nevertheless wise.
What can I do about it mama,
if God needed you as much as me?

Translated by Belinda Cooke

TEMIRKHAN MEDETBEK
(b. 6.03.1945)

 **Temirkhan Medetbek** studied at Kazakh State Pedagogical University (now Abaj [Abai] Kazakh National Pedagogical University), before going on to work in the media and creative industries. He was the editor-in-chief at the journals *Aķiķat* and *Žuldyz*. His first poetry collection was *Žanymnyṇ žas ķiraġy* (My Soul's Tender Sprout, 1970). A prolific writer, his subsequent books include *Sapar aldynda* (Prior to the Trip, 1973), *Alys šaķyrymdar* (Distant Lands, 1975), *Mǎrtebe* (Honour, 1977), *Kôgeršinniṇ ķauyrsyndary* (The Pigeon Feather, 1982), *Dauys* (Voice, 1984), *Syrym bar saġan ajtatyn* (I Have a Secret to Share with You, 1989) and *Taġdyrly žyldar žyrlary* (The Songs of Fateful Years, 2002). His notable collection *Kôk tùrikter saryny* (Melodies of Kok Turks, 2002) describes contemporary issues in the form of ancient Turkic psalms of the eighth to tenth centuries. The poems 'Mahambet ruhynyṇ monology' (The Monologue of Mahambet's Spirit), 'Kùltegin' also spelled 'Kul Tigin'), 'Tonykôk' (also spelled as 'Tonyukuk' in English sources) are particularly important in this regard, the last two being a contemporary adaptation of the final rendering of Orkhon inscriptions on steles by Professor Vilhelm Thomsen. Medetbek's poems have been translated into Chinese, Russian, Ukrainian, Tatar, Uzbek and Kyrgyz. He has translated Charles Baudelaire, Mikhail Lermontov, Alexander Pushkin, Pablo Neruda, Yanka Kupala, Émile Verhaeren, and others, along with novels by Heinrich Böll and Vladimir Nabokov, into Kazakh. He has also written critical prose: *Meniṇ Abajym* (My Abaj, 1995) and *Baba dǎstùrdiṇ mùrageri kim: Tuġan ǎdebiet turaly ojlar* (Heritage of the Tradition: Thoughts on our Native Literature, 2001).

Medetbek was awarded the Prize of the Writers' Union of the Kazakh SSR for *Kôgeršinniṇ ķauyrsyndary* (1983), the State Prize of the Republic of Kazakhstan for *Taġdyrly žyldar žyrlary* (2000) and the Order of Ķùrmet (2005).

Boasting Song

Waddle-waddle – I'm not in a rush
the earth is bending under me.
Stomp-stomp – with my giant steps,
rocks are cracking under me.

The heavy riches
of my caravans
transformed the hills
to lowland.
Just watering my mares,
and all the rivers
dried at once.

Enemies were eager so
to become my faithful slaves.
When I spat and blew my nose,
what came out but honey caves.

Lakes of mare's milk in caskets
churned into kymyz[1] streams.
My leather bottles, full to the brim
were cracking loudly at the seams.

My troughs are made of oak,
my wells never dry.
My hat is made of beaver.
My forehead is bright.

One kick of my bird
killed a wolf, now it's dead.
My strong bow's arrow
shook a far-away land.

[1.] Kymyz – beverage made from fermented mare's milk valued in Kazakhstan for its
refreshing qualities; it is a main drink for many occasions.

I kneaded black stones
like bread of clay.
I stole my foe's land
and dragged it away.

When I opened my mouth
my tongue was a sword.
My spit shone like silver
My phlegm was gold.

What a time it was!

Song of a Strongman

A long, long time ago
I was fighting with a rock
The mighty mountain was my foe.
I hit it hard and caused
a hail of stones.
Bang-bang, I hit it harder,
the crag crumbled like a house of sand.
A rocky knot strong as shackles –
was broken by me – that's how I fought.

Drew a sigh –
lightning flashed.
Shook off dust –
earth crashed.

Cast a cry.
Laughter roared,
clouds fell
from the sky.
When I sang
and laughed out loud,
flocks of birds
hit the waves.

Arrogant when confronted with pride,
bowed to people who honoured my side.
For those who dared to go too far,
I readied the fire and caskets with tar.
And those who dared to 'overflow'
I stopped in their tracks and let them go.

When I gripped a stick
it began to smoke.
When I squeezed a stone,
it shed tears and broke.
Lifted a camel, threw it like a pebble.
Who is against me?
I'll drive you into the ground like a stake.

With pride I walked.
With arrogance I stood.

I'm Afraid!

My country is burning
its core is on fire …
Disease overwhelms
my soul.

Our time is bleak.
No spring, it is snowing.
But look, it is not the snow.
It is blood pouring.

Dangerous words
dropped on my heart
like bombs in the Afghan war.
Carpet bombing, I can't hide anymore.
My dreams and my blessings
got stuck in the snow,
frost everywhere, nowhere to go.

Our waters taste strange
as if poisoned slowly.
My country seems deranged
by unholy spirits,
busy sowing discord.

God knows who
roams greedily around.
God knows who
awkwardly avoids you …

My candle, my light
is it dying out?
Like in a nightmare
woods are swaying, trying to move
and abandon my land forever.

Inside me a bonfire
is cutting my life short.
Can't I pour my tears inward?
They are overflowing,
cutting my face,
tearing up my chest.

My orchards
could face a drought.
My mountains
could collapse –
I'm afraid!

Kindness

You are a fresh spring.
Your waters quench the thirst of those
whose throats are dry as a desert sand.

When someone's left
in the dark,
you are a ray of hope
in their heart.
You are a paradise
on this earth,
under this sky.

You are our shelter!
You are our mother!
If you are kind to a widow –
you will pour in her soul
a secret pure as
spring water.
If you help an orphan –
kiss him on the forehead –
you will warm up his soul
with a beam of light.

Your radiance
melts permafrost,
turns ice
into water.
The whole universe
sucks your breast
like a baby,
having a nap
in the arms of its mother.

You are fertile juice
in the root
of a flower.
You are eternity itself.
You are a light
born from
the mercy of Allah!

This light
can't be destroyed
by the bullet.
Can't be pierced.
This light
can't be severed
by the sweep of a sabre.
Light can't be ripped up.

Lamentation of a Kok Turk[2] Warrior's Wife on His Death

The Moon fell
on my right side.
The Sun went out
on my left side.
The star on my forehead
dimmed and died.
My lion fell.
My pillar collapsed.
Who caused your death, my warrior?
You could catch an arrow
on the fly,
snap it in half on your knee.
Where is your skill now?
You took your enemy
like a hare, by the scruff of the neck
and he let out his last breath.
Where is your steel grip now?
You used to take a tiger
by its tail,
lifted it up and flung it away.
Fire burned inside you –
it forced you to
run amok sometimes.
Did this fire engulf you?
You were like a mountain
even when you lay.
When you stood up
you were like an oak.
You were strong as a rocky shore
never overwhelmed by floods.
Who caused your death, my warrior?

[2.] Kok Turk – (lit. 'Celestial Turks') a confederation of Turkic peoples who established the
Turkic Khaganate (552–659AD) and the Second Turkic Khaganate (682–744AD) in the
Altaj Mountains and expanded their territories throughout Central Asia.

Your people are sobbing,
their tears become
a torrential downpour.
When you were tied to a giant poplar,
you just walked away
with the poplar on your back.
Where is your strength now?
You chopped steel like wood,
your hands were tireless.
What caused your death, my warrior?
Your mind
was like a chest
full of pearls and corals.
Your voice was so fierce
it flattened the grass.
Heralds of a *khagan*[3]
couldn't match it.
Black clouds …
rushed into the Altaj Mountains.
Your sycamore house
is shrouded in black.
Who caused your death, my warrior?
My silver womb
was full of your golden might.
When I had cravings,
you gave me a lion's heart.
And I bore you ten children.
I walked in golden slippers
I almost drowned in my happiness.

Tomorrow
I'll tell these ten children of yours
to saddle the horses and fight your enemy.
They will avenge you.
And if they don't,
death will pin them to the spot.
perished by my curse!

[3.] *Khagan* – title of imperial rank in the Turkic and Mongolian languages.

Deluge

What a spring.
What floods of rain!
It's as if all clouds in existence
have gathered here,
in one place.
Someone from above
is pouring giant caskets and buckets
over us.
As if the sky itself
had lost its bottom.
Nothing to stop the downpour.
Necks of heavenly leather skins
full to the brim with water
all untied at once,
causing a cloudburst
as if a mudflow rushed from the summit –
the mountain itself
feels frightened and tricked.
Ridges are circled
by foaming waters.
They look like faltering camels
slaughtered by the torrent.
… A soaked birch
stands in the middle of nowhere,
water dripping all over it.
In this downpour
she looks like a mother
waiting for her child
alone, at the muddy road.

In a Moment of Inspiration

Look at this poet.
Like a blaze on a windy day
he's spewing fire.
All he yells about
is his country:
it makes his heart bleed.
All he thinks about
is his land:
it makes his joints ache.
His eyes are burning coals!
His words are flames!
They burn brightly.
What inspiration.
It is as if
nature itself
serves him, so he can control
rain, clouds and wind.
He alone
carries on his shoulders
the pain and sufferings of all.
He's like a whole nation
fighting for its honour.

Sea in a Storm

A mighty hurricane struck
as if aiming to erase
the Moon and Sun from the sky
and move the Earth itself.
All around
suffocated.
A terrible, fierce sound rose
from the very bottom of the sea
whining and deafening.
Thousands, millions of waves
pushed each other,
drowned each other,
exhaling cold,
leapt towards the sky
and fell rumbling,
then raised their heads again
with the thunder.
Thousands, millions of waves
endlessly sprawled,
endlessly shrunk,
roaring like dragons.
The sea's surface darkened
as if mourning
the end of the world.
Furious tides
played with ships
turning them over like troughs
tossing them into the abyss.
The iron clamps of the hulls
torn in half like threads,
vessels anchored in the bay
turned into giant beasts
trying to break off
their iron chains.
A hurricane pulled the reins,
whipped the ships
sending them like frenzied horses
into a stampede.

Only silent anchors
barely held back
the maddened ships,
roaring like oxen,
bellowing like camels.
Such noise
turned the whole world upside down.
Scarlet arrows of lightning
dived into the blue sea waters
where dragon-waves
swallowed them at once,
smirking at their vain efforts.
These mighty tides
puffed up and swelled,
rising, surging, billowing.
They brushed off the clouds
as easily as felt.
They fought against the cliffs
with such power and angst,
the rocks cracked like nuts …
That's how the fierce sea
showed what it can do.

Beautiful Woman

What a wonder!
One glance at her
and your heart explodes,
bursts into fire.
How much anguish
this woman brings?!
What sorcery her beauty hides?!
Without any hex or spell
she steals your soul …
What was she created from?
Moonlight?
A poet's song?
A white flower's petal?
The purity of deep waters?
Sat next to her,
your mind goes blank.
You're confused
and lost for words.
She raises her eyebrow
and lowers her eyelashes,
you almost faint.
If she chooses you,
you feel like jumping from a peak,
losing your mind,
wandering aimlessly,
forgetting everything
and falling in love.
And then you are burned
by her lips
bright red-hot coals.
Wonder and anguish
is yours!
When her breath warms up your skin
you feel the touch
of a golden rain.
When her laughter
caresses your ears
silver bells

tinkle all around you.
She's graceful as a swan,
supple as a vine,
light as a feather.
Can't take your eyes off her.
When she speaks
her white neck
trembles softly
like a singing nightingale.
What a wonder
and what agony!

Losing Myself

Once
I was silent
instead of telling
the simple truth.
That's how I lost myself.
Since then
I've been saddled
with a misfortune –
cold as ice,
heavy as salt.
I lost myself …
That is why
my inner world
was swept away
by a howling wind.
My mind is cornered
by the army
of troubling thoughts.
They poured poison
into my soul.
An enormous
unknown load
has crashed
my shoulders.
Clouds green as bile
have gathered over
my poor head.

Lies and gossip
are mocking me
gloating,
delighted.
My soul is scorched.
My vision is clouded,
I can't see
what's around me.
No strength to raise
my bowing head
and breathe in full.
O God,
I would prefer
to be dead
than live like that.
But I lament in vain.
One untold truth.
One untold word.
My curse forever.

Translated by Rose Kudabayeva

Thirty-Six Degrees

It is true of – the infant and the wise man,
the shah, trembling on a shaky throne,
the poor man, the coward, the brave man,
the poet whose obstinate line
touches your heart by chance,
the traveller, wandering in the desert,
the climber who conquered the top,
the sailor, sailing to the north-west –
they all have a temperature of thirty-six.
Let the frost in the yard and the blizzard howl.
Let the heat burn all living things.
Let the far north become a sultry Mecca,
a person's temperature will not change.
Water does not boil at thirty-six.
Moisture doesn't disappear from the reservoirs.
Iron will never melt.
You can't even set fire to paper.
But why then does the world mourn a hundred times,
why does it rejoice, seek new experiences,
tolerate disasters, become broken about life,
find the truth, weaken from doubt,
toil, get lost,
pine and seethe at thirty-six degrees?

Photo as Memento

I will not postpone my business till tomorrow.
I will not chance fate.
I will go to the forest today.
I will climb the mountains in the heat.
I will have a photo taken in memory of nature.
Birch-mothers, poplar-brothers,
pine-sisters will surround me in a joyful crowd,
as if I wasn't just on a visit
but had finally returned home.
Birches, poplars and pines
will rustle
happily
wishing me well.
I will stand with them
before the lens
to immortalise myself with a joyful crowd.
It will be as if I had
woken up to
a kinship long forgotten
hugging the bark to touch my cheek
so that a branch hangs onto my shoulder
like someone had taken me
under their wing again.
I will go to the steppe and meet with feathergrasses.
I will catch the attention of the stunned marmot.
I will have my photograph taken with you,
just in case
maybe tomorrow
I won't be able to find you.
The mountain river flooding with trout,
we will take a photo together –
while you are still alive.
After all, it may turn out one day
that we will find here a deposit of expensive stones,
as engineers dress the stream in concrete,
and where will then the trout go to spawn?

Here my own relatives are living in a clearing,
beneath birch, poplar and pine, golden in the sun
and maybe I'll get back late
from some distant journey
and don't manage to see you.
I will not
postpone my business till tomorrow.
I will not joke with fate.
I will go to the forest today.
I will climb the mountains in the heat.
O nature, by way of memento,
I'll have my photo taken with you.

Where Is My Heart?

My heart is gone, is gone from me.
It escaped from my chest cage.
My heart is gone from me, gone from me.
When the ground collapses beneath my feet,
when I am blind from grief and evil,
when I am in despair with endless cursing,
the hands of my friends supported me.
When saved by my friends, I survived,
and my heart is with you.
When the sounds of poetry come to life,
my heart –
is a taut bowstring.
It trembles as in a fierce fever –
ready to fire lines at its target,
ready to rush without looking
into the merciless fight – blood
flowing in an endless bloodbath …
Going into battle
for the truth
my heart
becomes an enemy of peace.
It beats furiously –
then stops beating from tenderness.
It finds truth
and loses it.
Maybe it seems fussy
to someone.
It manages to hold the interest
of the wise for a while,
then casts them aside in disgust.
I do not know,
but, only today,
do not look for my heart in me.
It is there rather
where there is not enough fire.

If it is not torn
between joy and suffering,
if it is not joined
with my friends,
if it does not make an assault
on the enemy,
if one is shamefully
cautious in life,
just banging on one's chest,
tediously repelling all,
then it has surely gone cold.

Translated by Belinda Cooke

SHOMISHBAY SARIYEV
(b. 25.04.1946)

Shomishbay Sariyev (Shalqar Sarin) is a poet. After graduating from high school in the Aral district of the Ķyzylorda region, he found employment at *Lenin tuy*, a Ķazaly district newspaper, and in *Tolķyn*, a newspaper in the Aral district. Subsequently, he studied journalism at Kirov Kazakh State University (now Äl-Farabi Kazakh National University), graduating in 1971. He was editor-in-chief at Ķazaķstan publishing house (1970–74) and head of literary criticism and poetry departments at *Žŭldyz* journal (1974–91). He was launched as a poet in 1961 by *Lenin žoly*, a regional Ķyzylorda newspaper.

Sariyev's debut collection of poems, titled *Baldǎuren* (Boyhood), came out in 1974 and was followed by *Teņizden soķķan žel* (Sea Wind, 1975), *Taġdyr* (Destiny, 1976), *Ôŋ men tùs* (Reality and Dream, 1980), *Taġdyr žyry* (A Verse of Fate, 1984), *Bizdiŋ ġasyr* (Our Age, 1989), *Saġynyšym teņiz* (I am Longing for Sea, 1994), *Ķos ķanat* (A Pair of Wings, 2004), and finally, a two-volume selection of works in 2006 and *Šôl dalanyŋ ùlymyn* (I am a Son of Deserts) in 2008. He is an author of more than 300 song lyrics. Sariyev's poems have been translated into English, Russian, Ukrainian, Kyrgyz, Uzbek, Tajik, Romanian, Czech, Indian and French. He himself translated Robert Rozhdestvensky, Luís Vaz de Camões, Dmitry Gulia, Olga Bergholz, Sergey Vikulov, Andrey Dementyev, Irakli Abashidze and Fazu Aliyeva into Kazakh.

Sariyev published two monographs in his capacity as senior research fellow at the Äuezov Institute of Literature and Art: *20 ġhasyrdyŋ 20-ynšy žyldaryndaġy ķazaķ poeziâsy* (Kazakh Poetry of the 1920s) and *70-80-90-žyldardaġy ķazaķ poeziâsy* (Kazakh Poetry of the 1970s, '80s and '90s).

The poet was awarded the Franz Kafka Prize (2003), the Platinum Tarlan Award (2004) and the Parasat Order (2011), and is an Honoured Worker of Kazakhstan (2006).

There Is a Country

It speaks to me sweetly, just as
life is sweet – like honey.
The vast map of the world
has not yet named it.

There is one beloved country
that strangers rarely cross,
that all explorers have overlooked,
even great Columbus.

Those who know what life is
are so happy there,
they take it all for granted,
they do not feel the time pass.

There's only one such magical place
that the world speaks of.
What lies in store's unknown,
but there each day is happy.

Empowered by that land,
it helps us cope with sadness.
Its greatest law is Loyalty.
It speaks of all that's true.

My companion is my dearest man.
Embarking on this poem,
it's like I'm saddling a horse.
Maintaining the harmony
of that land, I would like
to secure its happiness.

Let's call it our home forever.
Let's draw a line around it.
Let's call it our true homeland
that I'll protect with sword in hand.

It speaks to me so sweetly,
its words as sweet as honey.
You will not find it on a map –
that land whose name is Childhood.

Childhood Friends

You are engraved on my memory, childhood,
I still recall everything, yet how quickly your caravan passes.
Alone and far away from sweet childhood friends,
the road ahead's foggy!

How happy childhood was!
The waves roll on like prancing horses,
like stars that make you forget the time.
My childhood friends, do you still remember me?

Nomadic life has given so much,
its afternoons, hot and fragrant, its beautiful nights.
My yearning heart still cares about you –
those who have left this life, you as yet unborn.

My peers are far away from me.
Their hearts, as white as milk, were pure.
They were like beautiful gardens and all were kin to me.
It was always summer in that world.

We're adrift now on the waves of life, while life
is like a caravan, its destination known to all.
Each of us makes a family and each has seen the world.
We have each our sadness and our joy.

My infancy gave me so much.
It seemed that time would never end.
Its laughter secure in the world around it,
there was no greater happiness.

Waking up as a child is a dream you'll remember
all the days of your life.
Your first friend, your first love –
you'll savour that joy forever …

There was no eye that cried.
Your childhood can never return.
We never sat around that fire.
Rivers cannot flow like a sweet cordial.

The ways of being a child are lost.
So I can only admire that boy
who having sought his friend in vain
finally closed the door.
There is no way now to open it.
We have lost the meaning of that world.

Home

Home is where your heart's at peace.
It's in your heart you know it.
There is nowhere else you'll find such warmth
in all the days allowed you.

From birth, through childhood, and beyond
you'll seek that special place, your nest.
Home starts out as a simple hearth.
Your homeland stretches beyond it.

I placed my faith in it,
leaving my home and country behind.
When a man comes into being,
the steppe beyond his home's unknown.

But when you make your way in the world,
your faith in home sustains you.
It warms your heart and soul.
The highway to life starts from home.

With unfettered dreams,
I pave the way to the world from home.
Safe and sound, I pursue my dreams.
Returning, I know I will be at home.

Glad to know I'm part of a family,
I will find eternal joy.
When I die, I'll say farewell
from my family's seat of honour.

Home sustains me with all I need
through happy days and bitter.
The confines of my home expanded
from fledgling's nest to my fatherland.

A Piece of Bread

It petitions Allah –
Mankind, the servant of God.
Having invented so many things,
it sheds light on mysteries.
Its spaceships, crossing
the boundless void, open up
to Mankind the secrets of the sky.
Yet its most important invention
is a piece of bread.

In all the times
        we have need of bread.
And to you, future generations,
        this is the wisdom we bring –
we give you bread.

Weapons, war, bloodshed –
        such things are a sin.
So we should be grateful for peace,
        and grateful for bread.
To indulge in excess,
        when one is too wealthy –
is no more than vanity.
The essence of life
        is a piece of bread.

Each day Mankind is drawn
towards new discoveries.
Where will its steps lead it?
Though merely passing through,
it wants to exploit the Earth.
Bread –
        is the Stuff of life,
Bread –
        is the Song of life.

Bread sustains humanity
and you will be able to dream
great dreams, when
you have listened to its song.

Robots, lasers, the conquest of space –
so many things are possible,
inspired by the taste and smell of bread.
Hunger and thirst were vanquished
when Mankind invented bread
and then, when it tasted it,
the world was bathed in radiance.
That was the legacy
bequeathed generations.

Song

In spite of great misfortune
my land has always sung, with its humped, wide deserts,
its summits yoked like beasts of burden,
the hearts of my people have always sung.

In spite of great misfortune
my land has always sung, with its gurgling springs,
its green grass, it has always sung,
the hearts of my people have always sung.

In spite of great misfortune
my land has always sung, with its vast, silent deserts,
its transparent lakes, my land has always sung,
the hearts of my people have always sung!

In spite of great misfortune
my land has always sung, with its countless, endless byways,
its dense, boundless forests, my land has always sung,
the hearts of my people have always sung!

In spite of great misfortune
my land has always sung, with its people
weeping along with 'Elim aj'.[1]
Oh, my land of countless dreams!

This world is alive because of the melody
of never-ending heartbeats.
Would my people possess this country,
if their hearts had never sung?

---

[1] The song, 'Elim aj' ('My people'), was likely created in the early eighteenth century during the period of The Great Disaster (Aḳtaban Šübyryndy). This began with the attack of the Dzungar army in 1723–25 that decimated the population of south and south-eastern Kazakhstan, and was followed by widespread drought and famine.

Fishermen

A son whose father drowned
scoured the waters for him.
He asked his mother, 'Is he really dead?
And why was he so in love with the sea
when he was fated to die there,
like his father before him?'

And so, weeping, he searched
for his father and not for fish
in an ice-free stretch of the wintry sea.[2]
However many carp he netted
he remained inconsolable.

His mood was saddened again,
and his heart full of grief,
when he thought that not for the first time
there was a grave in the sea
with no one buried inside it.

Across that ominous grave
the waves raged in a tumult.
Staring forlornly at the skyline,
the fisherman's son sat
absorbed in anxious thoughts.

He gazed at the mountainous waves
and thought of the joyous childhood years,
though at that moment it seemed
he wasn't facing a stormy sea
but the raging of death itself.

He decided then to leave the sea,
without consulting anyone.
Wasn't he himself as free as the waves
that used to ripple on the surface
when he played beside his mother?

---

[2] The poem refers to the Aral Sea, a lake in Central Asia.

Trying to untangle its mysteries,
he thought all night about the sea.
In the morning he was back
in his boat again, exploring
the vast expanse of sea.

The haughty waves pounding the shore –
waves of sorrow, waves of joy.
The fisherman's calling will be pursued
for as long as the sea survives.
Death itself is helpless against it.

A Long Haul

A storm at sea. A ship. My mother in labour …

'A gift from God, my first son,
you were born at sea aboard a ship –
that's the way your life began …'

So spoke my father, revealing the secret,
till I imagined that moment again:
my diapers washed in salt water,
my umbilical cord washed into the sea.

With questions as numerous
as stars in the sky,
I search for a light: like one who seeks
a beacon at sea. A traveller still,
I am looking for answers.
My hopes are high.

My dreams are like white flames
of clouds. The far-off landfall still eludes me
in the sea lanes of my dreams.
How can I reach that humped horizon?
I seem condemned to cross an ocean
as if aboard a ghost ship.[3]

Though I was raised on a playful coast,
the white-capped waves now are raging.
Their tumult must not make us fear.
Like a ship setting out for a long haul,
my voyage, too, will be protracted.

---

[3] The translation hints at the similarity with the legend of 'The Flying Dutchman'.

The Dream

My dream is like my mother, the earth,
too vast to encompass in my arms.
It's like the boundless steppe.
No wonder I'm concerned!

My dream is like the highest peak,
but who will reach it if not me?
My mother tongue will empower me.

I'll strive towards the snow-capped peaks,
and never falter.
I'll reach beyond the clouds and fog.
My foes will cry, my friends will laugh.

But ask about me from the Future –
and who will say how far
beyond the clouds I've passed?

Future days will come,
days filled with bliss.
My shadow trailing after me,
my eyes and heart towards the light,
I will track the Sun.

Translated by David Cooke

Steppe *Tülpars*

The winged horses[4] of my steppes are running.
The stars seem to have dropped from the sky
to join them. In their charge, they are moulding
the earth – as if they are the reason it is round.

One horse is running with the speed of the wind.
The saddle appears to be stuck on his back.
Rolling along with the stallion's legs, the world,
like every mounted horseman, is spinning.

Those still asleep should be woken up –
for the whole spirit of the steppes consists
in a running horse. Everything should move aside
for the stallion of my dreams to gallop on.

Craving the music of the thudding hooves,
the valley people love riding their horses –
even when the wind blows into a gale
under the stallion's wide chest. See –

the stallion presides, like a dark storm
on the horizon, about to sweep over, winged.
Our life here, as we head for the future,
is in the rushing of the horses of the steppes.

---

[4] 'The winged horses' or *tülpars* – in Kazakh mythology and folklore, *tülpar* is a swift horse, corresponding to Pegasus. Every major hero of a Kazakh epic poem has a *tülpar*, which grows fast and, through its supernatural powers, helps the hero to succeed in his quest. Nowadays, *tülpar* is used as an honorific term for a horse.

The Theorem of Love

My dear, you and I have both heard
that Love is not a theorem.
Like a meteorite in the sky it falls.
The thrill of being in love blurs days.

Not many young people understand
being madly in love,
blindly in love.
How they miss out not knowing
this dreamy flower of Love
that denies you all rest. It resembles
the great gravitational pull of the Earth.
Some are pulled into it, then lose;
others believe in it, trusting the power
of gravity in Love. Yet what happens
to the young man when separated
from Love?

       Then he loses
the greatest of all his blessings,
and all his dreams. If Love loses its gravity,
it loses its weight, as if in space.
Without weight, he can't laugh for joy.
Without weight, he can't be grounded –
and chaos spreads world-wide.
When mistakes have been made,
and done with, even caused by him at times,
will he understand? For the gravity of Love
is a powerful thing, even greater
than the gravitational pull of the Earth.

My brother, let me tell you a secret,
my dearest secret: in the sky of youth
you flow. Accept the true existence
of that power and bow down to it,
my brother, bow down!

Far Horizon

O life, pave my way
and give me the chance
to wander around. A horizon
is encircling me and the round world
is spinning. Like a misty desert
of the valleys, where mountain ranges
are invisible, the horizon
is beyond reach.
It is like the stallion from myth
tired of waving its wings
as it gets closer.
Life, o life – the horizon
is unreachable
like unreachable dreams.
It is not to be reached
even if it seems to lie
under strangers' feet,
on the peak of the highest mountain.
The horizon is not to be reached –
like the stars in the sky.
Even if you press your feet
hard on the ground, marching fast,
and get a little bit closer,
the horizon is not to be reached.
Even if you cut it
like a lightning bolt, or ride
the fastest race horse,
the horizon is out of reach,
no matter where or how you go.
Is it good to believe in the unreachable?
For, by moving his horizons,
a man can reach his goals.
This life should not be spent in vain.
Reach it early, or reach it late …
The place where you stand is a horizon
beyond the reach of anyone else.

Run, My *Tülpar* Time

Run, my *Tülpar* time, to my tomorrows.
Do you tell the mystery of fantasy dreams?
Run to the happiness that happens in fairy tales.
Bring me there. I'm holding onto your mane.
Run, *Tülpar* time, to my tomorrows.
Run, *Tülpar* time, to the future.

When I was a child, my dreams were huge.
Should we look, like children do, at life?
Bring me to those peaks of dreams.
Run, *Tülpar* time, to the future.

Run, *Tülpar* time, to the future.
Whoever takes from life should give back to life,
just like someone like me, who owes a lot
to his country, must give something back.
My poetry is for you to keep, so deliver it!
Run, *Tülpar* time, to the future.

Proposal

Red Book,[5] the list in the Red Book
is getting bigger year by year.

There are fewer swans and eagles,
saigas and speedy moose also.
Many flowers are dwindling.
How can they bud if their seeds
and roots are gone? Will this mean
they will never re-appear –
the pink grasses of the steppes too?
For the lawns and trees of our valleys,
for the flowers, birds and animals
of the steppes, and for all living things
on Earth, I am speaking up,
offering my poet's heart.
Most important in life
is for people to show
their modest, pure and honest traits,
their decent, respectful qualities:
what is called courtesy and kindness.
And their true love for nature.
They are losing their habit
of praying to nature the way they pray
to the Creator. In the name
of the Earth, the mighty Sun and Moon,
I beg you to add them in the Red Book.

Every year that book is getting bigger:
the Red Book, Red Book, the list in the Red Book.

---

[5] Red Book – refers to the International Union for Conservation of Nature's Red List of
Threatened Species.

The Flow

I travel to places with my dreams.
I talk about my Country; the core
of myself is in my country.
Many great orators have passed away.
So, world, give me my turn to write poems!

Many poets have passed away,
admired and prized by others.
Mysterious world, open your eyes.
I'm in a hurry to sail against the flow.

Not from the mountain, I am sailing now
towards the mountain. O world,
burn my blood and my soul crimson red,
red as a flame. If you were a lady, world,
and my darling, I would pay you attention

as your gentleman. I am the flow that goes
against the course. And, world,
if you are out of breath, I am your rest.
Far future is calling from the horizon, waving.

Honour and Pride

However far or near,
in whichever country, my dear,
in men –
the people's honour,
and pride of people –
is in women.

Don't let it cause any harm.
For honour I sacrifice my soul.
And to protect my pride's honour,
I must keep my eyes focused on it.

A mark on honour
cannot be forgiven.
A stain on pride
can never be cleaned.

However far or near,
in whichever country, my dear,
in men –
the people's honour,
and pride of people –
is in women.

Translated by Patricia McCarthy

KULASH AKHMETOVA
(b. 25.04.1946)

Kulash Akhmetova is a poet. She graduated from Žambyl Medical School (1966) before going on to complete a course in journalism at Kirov Kazakh State University (now Äl-Farabi National Kazakh University), graduating in 1973. She worked for Žambyl regional newspapers, heading departments at the newspaper *Ķazaķstan pioneri* (subsequently *Ùlan*) and at Žalyn publishing house.

She is the author of more than twenty collections of poetry, including her debut *Aķ gulim meniņ* (My White Flower, 1975) and *Sen meniņ baķytymsyņ* (You Are My Happiness, 1977), *Žapyraķ žazdyņ žùregi* (Leaves Are the Hearts of the Summer, 1979), *Mejirim* (Kindness, 1981), *Bùlaķtaǵy žazular* (Stars Reflected in a Spring, 1982) and *Žasyl žaǵalau* (The Green Riverbank, 1984), written in her early period. Akmetova's poetry is regarded for its portrayal of the female psychology and often complicated fate. The next stage of her poetry (1987–2015) reflects more on issues of national identity, although still presenting the poet as a lyric. These works include: *Mahabbat* (Love, 1980), *Arǵymaķtar dalasy* (The Land of Stallions, 1987), *Sen žanymda žùrseņ* (If You Are Beside Me, 1987), *Baķytty bolyņdar* (Be Happy, 2014) and *Meniņ sǎuleli sǎtterim* (My Bright Moments, 2015). Akhmetova's poems have been translated into Russian, Ukrainian, German, Belarusian and several Turkic languages. She herself has translated into Kazakh verses by Bengali poet Nazrul Islam, Russian poet Alexander Mezhirov and Lithuanian poet Eduardas Mieželaitis.

Akhmetova has received the Lenin Komsomol Prize for the book *Sen meniņ baķytymsyņ* (1978) and was a poet laureate of the State Prize of the Republic of Kazakhstan for the poetry collection *Ķùt* (Prosperity, 2006). She is the recipient of the Orders of Ķurmet (2006) and Parasat (2017).

Prosperity

Everything is wise in nature,
so live and bless life –
each morning, each night,
returns us to paradise.

Roads lead us to history,
to show us the coming day.
Kites, penguins, rhinos,
even small dragonflies –

live praising her abundance.
Let earthly misfortune,
earthly turmoil, and man's
bad temper pass you by.

So much evil in the world!
No one is innocent among the
passing multitudes – as, age upon
age, we reduce the world to ashes.

Shamelessly, we have trampled
over birds and beasts, but has it made us
any stronger, having driven
innocent birds from their nests?

No, it is us who are defenceless,
as much as these poor animals.
Human and animal now one –
the bullet is heading our way too.

And what about tomorrow?
Nature dictates our food and shelter.
As we search for a new path to the future,
direct us and make us understand.

Restore God's world to its fine
luminous beginnings where
the Creator gathered ungrateful
people for an eternal feast.

But, envious and malicious,
we have defiled God's gift.
Forgive us our stupid epochs,
drunk with war and apocalypse.

We've been stuck in this madness
so long, we have lost count …
yet, it did not destroy our native genius,
it did not cause our people to scatter …

Our voice is the master of comparisons,
a poet with an all-encompassing soul,
it offers its unique take
on this great enlightened world.

And my generous people,
who call their *ķuda*[1]
'*ķuda* for thousand years',
be plentiful and holy,
let our enemy fear us.

Let prosperity come.
Let the beautiful spirit blossom.
Let the bright mind sharpen.
Let us make this change.
I look forward to that time.

[1.] *Ķuda* – 'co-in-laws'. Usually, the parents and relatives of a married couple refer to each other as *ķuda* and maintain a warm and respectful relationship; in Kazakh society one would be honoured to be called *ķuda*, and pleased to treat their *ķuda* with respect in return.

Lace

You walked away,
beyond the grey shroud,
the path broke away from life,
and you will no longer hear, *mama*,
the poems that I write…

So what was left for me?
Nothing except to bow silently
entrusting words to the page …
The lacemaker walks away unnoticed,
the lace lives on.

My poetry lives on, just as
objects last longer than people.
How careful we are with our things,
but we cannot keep people safe.

They reflect the night-time stars,
the Kyrgyz[2] earth's flowering…
but not the hands of a loved one,
struggling to plait the little flower.

You must look where those flowers
bowed their little heads,
yellowing with age,
as they await the steppe winds,
                                        or
parting with their mistress?

[2.] Kyrgyz – the poem refers to specific lace ornaments that are known as 'Kyrgyz lace'.

Discoloured white threads,
stir in me
a memory of mama,
her warm hands and glowing eyes,
but I lack the strength
        to comfort myself with memories,
of one so central to me, yet no longer alive.
The lacemaker walked away …
but the lace lives on.

Street

Street like a burbling river,
car-boats sail along.
Here someone squeezes on the bus.
Here a Zhiguli[3] stopped.

Street like the Arys River …[4]
Some look down, others look up.
Two may separate and straight away,
they're entwined in the arms of others.

Endless twitter, banter, and jostling,
falls in a shower on the human stream.
Here they carry a child's crib,
there they carry a mourning wreath.

Here, someone fell to eternal rest,
there, eyes looked fresh upon the world –
as rapidly flowing waves uncover
days of birth and days of parting.

Not surprising to want to pause briefly …
to absorb everything into yourself …
but the crowd flies along the pavement,
mesmerised with the rhythm of life.

The eavesdropper earth readily picks up,
the joy of the first meeting,
the pain of parting and the endless
passion in human thoughts …

[3.] Zhiguli – popular Soviet car.
[4.] Arys River – river in southern Kazakhstan and a tributary of Syr Dariâ.

Spring Poplars

Savage winds started to blow in the night,
powerfully steering the storm clouds,
impossible for the poplars to wait for dawn,
as the powerful call of spring once more torments them.

Their pale trunks like mothers' faces,
painfully awaiting the birth of a new life.
They grab the air with their fingers of branches,
driving the blood through their tense veins.

All night the spring wind bends the trunks,
and storm clouds race through the treetops,
but the dark breaks up
                    and strong knots
become untied on all the green branches,
and the leaves of the poplars start to rustle.

Spring!
        Everywhere in everything we see its signs:
under the melted snow the earth revives,
in the steppe the cold sands are warmed.

Under the life-giving Sun, poplars
and maples breathe in relief, half asleep,
awakening leaves lean towards me,
green light illuminates the tree tops.

Spring.
Fill yourself up with the babble of leaves,
with the clumsy whistle of baby chicks,
with the grasses bursting into flames with freshness,
and skylarks in the pure heavens.

Prayer

I saw mountains – granite peaks in a diamond crown.
I saw the sky – radiant spheres in the endless cosmos.

I saw a cornfield – glowing rays of a paradise morning.
I saw groves – pouring forth their rich aromatic leaves.

I saw waters – great waters, billowing ocean rollers …
They were an angry, roaring animal suffering some great
wound.

I saw storm clouds – storm clouds angrily closing in,
tilting the heavy sky and smoky distance.

I saw the land – a blue expanse of lively rivers.
I saw the grave pole – forever sad about the people.

I saw sandstorms – they wiped out the steppe settlement.
I saw rockets – like visions, they hovered above me.

I saw the air – filled to the brim with poisonous winds,
flowers and trees, and the birds of the east have died forever.

I saw time, returning with heavenly retribution.
O, it is painful to be a writer. Why was I cursed with this gift?

How troubled the world is – primordial fear has come to life
in it.
The tsunami is rumbling and the earth is shaking from
tremors.

The firmament is indignant, as is the abyss beneath us.
And again – typhoons, and again – tsunami waves.

All powerful Allah. The universe is revealed to you.
Save the foolish, have mercy on your own creatures.
Return to the universe the beauty of the first harmonies.
The green leaf – my steppe – in your rainbow crown.
Save us and have mercy.

Save us and have mercy.
Listen.
Hear us, I pray.
Keep my people – my soul …

People and Towns

When fresh snow falls on the earth,
and the powerful forces of nature are dormant,
out of the frost and snowstorms,
a person's anxiety leads him to build cities.

They are like stone mountains.
The peaks develop new, seemingly
endless heights. Courtyards walk to courtyards,
foothills and valleys meet ...

Gardens walk, interweaving with branches.
Deserts walk, merging with water.
Houses close up scrutinising each other –
insensitive faces, closed-up walls.

They are like stone mountains,
great white heights in the night light –
endless ... making it all the more difficult
to understand our next-door neighbour.

The closer the houses,
the more crowded the rooms,
the less we know one another –
so many lonely people in the world!

Will the day come when we don't notice
the person sat next to us – like an empty space,
unable to share happiness, misfortune or beauty
with anyone else in the world?

Ages will pass. The calendar changes,
and the man who conquers planets
will burn from isolation,
destroyed in the indifferent waters of Lethe.

Doesn't this day place you under threat,
as you build your multi-storey planet Earth?
Yet even wild, dry granite
will desperately cling to our neighbour's walls.

In response to my pain, gardens are silent
and I feel orphanhood more strongly –
but then there is no one in this world
who doesn't live in dread of misfortune.

When the person closest to me
lives without knowing my sadness,
he and I remain forever remote …
like this snow … this dead snow.

This great hall – its many expectant eyes,
all keen to hear the solutions to it all.
What the poet reveals gives hope,
causes the bitter pain to subside.

And the dim words are endless,
like clay walls without windows,
blocking out people – though the steppe
still flowers, the grass still stirs.

Water runs agitated towards us,
the earthly expanse widens freely once more …
Can this love that is dying in us
really abandon the earth for ever?

Walking away, does this age just leave us
with a machine to manage our feelings,
good and evil, soulless and certain,
defining the man of the future?

No, as before, the poet is called by the heavens,
to awaken souls on Earth.
to own verbs not words,
bringing harmony to our chaotic feelings.

I always look for a way in verse,
to protect people from disaster.
I pour forth my stanzas like birds,
turning the embittered once more to love.

So to unite the people of the Earth,
I have both hope and anxiety:
children are playing in the sunny dust
at the threshold of my house.

The town has spread its wings over them,
like a wild kite looking for a catch,
and I wish: if only these children
were not strangers to each other.

If only the children who play in my yard
were not afraid of this bird's ferocious habit.

Mother Tongue

Or when they ask you: 'How many languages do you speak?'

When inspiration comes to me
and each word burns as if on fire,
suddenly I know all words, speaking
in tongues, even to birds – to the snow itself,
as it flashes past me like a blue shadow.

My love, don't argue with me right now –
a flash of inspiration and I subdue the storm.
I understand all feeling –
Petrarch inclining to Laura,
Byron in the rustle of the garden.

My verses rise with the flowers,
in tune with the Russian oak forests:
Rossini's music is created
from the birds in the sky –
I can magic his music into words.

I translate from all the languages of the Earth.
Can comprehend the heart and soul,
I seek to grasp the forest's rustling,
the smoke rising falteringly over bonfires –
all will gain in me the living word.

I will give language to the forest and mountain valleys.
With the strength of words I can smash metal.
Like the night, like the very cores of the high stars,
and I understand the soul of someone close to me,
and the bright mind of a stranger.

I understand the movements of pure rivers,
and the bush in flame.
I possess all languages of the world
with my heart,
but I respond to the world – in Kazakh.

Translated by Belinda Cooke

Kazakhstan, My Homeland!

Kazakhstan, you are my song, my dream,
my golden cradle, my black forest.
How can I lack for anything –
where the steppe lies open before me?
Kazakhstan, my proudest possession!

I am invincible with you behind me,
like a wide-ranging master.
I understand
what the rivers whisper about,
and give ear to the cries of eagles
declaiming the poetry of this land.

Kazakhstan, you are my song,
my radiant steppeland.
Giving me life, you lead me on
along your endless pathways.
Protecting the happiness of my child,
you were the darling of my fathers.
Kazakhstan, my homeland!

You are my poetry's cradle,
intertwined with flowers
when plum and cherry blossom.
Unconstrained, my heart is open.
Why would I ever stray beyond you,
Kazakhstan, my homeland?

In the 'Colosseum'

We're having a Christmas do in the 'Colosseum',
enjoying traditional entertainment,
even though we like to think
we're getting up to date.

The guys on the door were stylish
and seemed so full of themselves.
They whisked away our coats and led us
to the best seats in the house.
How good it made us feel!
The music that everyone loves was playing,
the place lit up like a palace.

There was roasted snake on skewers
and bright red scorpions
that looked as if they'd bite you
with French wines and scotch
to wash them down.
There were fruits from Iran and apples.

Once in, we couldn't get enough
of violins and songs,
the flamenco dances, the castanets.
Chilling out, our drinks beside us,
we leaned back and looked up
to the glitzy lights above us.

The crowd that night was laid-back,
though it didn't quite feel right –
when all at once it hit me
and made me feel ashamed.

I thought of the cash I had in my pocket,
but missed one thing. Like an arrow
it should have pierced me
and left me spoiling for the fight.
Where was the Kazakh language,
its sound and its song?

The evening was beautiful, a triumph.
the ambiance so civilised. And yet,
I felt sorrowful for dark-eyed brothers
speaking strange tongues.

Even the lark tweets in the language of birds.
Like slaves ruled by an emperor
whom they would never see,
the young are enslaved by money.
Please God they'll never despise
the values of their fathers
or let themselves be duped
by newfangled notions,
growing ashamed of their tongue.

Our language has made us who we are.
Enshrining our culture,
it makes us a people, undivided and one.
Our future depends on it.

A Prayer for My Son and Daughter

Please, God, watch over Žazira and Žarķyn.[5]
Be their protector in difficult times,
and let them both be sturdy,
as steadfast and true as mountains.

If they are blessed with any talent
allow them to prosper and use it well.
If they're prepared to pick up the cudgels,
in defence of land and people,
give them self-belief.
And any time they speak their mind
let their words hold sway.

When the caravan of time moves on,
please, God, ensure that both my children
look back on their lives with pride.
Let each be granted a virtuous partner,
a golden family, a stalwart friend.

[5.] Žazira and Žarķyn – the poetess' son and daughter.

My Little Calves, My Children

My little calves, my children,
snuggle up to me now
and take me out of myself.
When I lose faith in grown-ups,
I look at you and I'm at peace.

My little brood, you bring me joy,
you soothe me. You are the best of me.
There's no need now to know
the stuff that adults need to know.
There's time enough for that.
So in the meantime play,
and make the most of things –

the songs of the forest and days
when sun sets in a golden blaze,
and swans glide across the lake.
When you draw your pictures,
bring nature with you into our house.

My little braggarts, tell me
whatever it is you have to say
and what it is you want –
those treats I never mentioned,
that I could only yearn for.

My little foals, have your fun.
You are like a green oasis.
Don't disappear like mirages.
You can let off steam and kick your heels.
You can have the run of the house.
With the beestings of my breast
you imbibed your earliest song.

If I need to prove to the world I'm happy
I can just point to your faces.

You now are my strength and joy,
for you're never tormented by the griefs
that in my youth consumed me.
So I will never raise my voice
in pointless admonition
for life itself will teach you
whatever you need to know.

Sewing a Button

You do not miss my kisses as once you used to
and never rush back home these days …
Such were the thoughts in my mind
while I was sewing your button.

What had I done to upset you?
Preoccupied with daily chores,
was I no longer the girl
that once had turned your head?
Your shirt is clean and white,
just as you yourself are –
though the pure are sometimes cold.

I was turning over so much
inside my head.
It seemed you understood me.
Your warm hands were touching my face
when I bent over to snap the thread.

My face was suddenly red,
as it used to be.
Blushing now,
I didn't want to leave you,
when you touched my face,
I froze and made no stir.

I felt compliant
when, like an orphan's, you touched my face;
and sewing that button
onto your sleeve,
I conveyed my longing, overwhelming.

And you relented,
your eyes dazzling like the Sun –
though I wanted to,
I couldn't say a thing.
To keep our love alive,
I've learned one moment could suffice.

Translated by David Cooke

VALERIY MIKHAILOV
(b. 7.09.1946)

Valeriy Mikhailov is a poet, prose writer, publicist and literary critic. He graduated from the Faculty of Geophysics of the Kazakh Polytechnic Institute and Journalism Department of the Advanced Komsomol School in Moscow, afterwards working in the mass media for more than 40 years. He was editor-in-chief of *Kazahstanskaâ pravda* and of the literary journal *Prostor*.

Mikhailov's poetry collections include *Pryamaya rech'* (Direct Speech, 1983), *Vest'* (News, 1991), *Tysiachiletie drugoe* (The Other Millennium, 2006), *Zolotaya dremota* (Golden Drowsiness, 2005), *Pyltsa* (Pollen) and *Dymyashiisya svitok* (Smoking Prayer Roll, 2015). His best known prose work, *Khronika velikogo zhuta* (*The Great Disaster: Genocide of the Kazakhs*, 1990), on Kazakhstan's 1930s' famine, has been translated into Kazakh, German and English to great acclaim. He has also authored biographies of the Russian poets Mikhail Lermontov, Evgeny Boratynsky and Nikolai Zabolotsky for the series *ZZL – Zhizn' zamechatel'nyh lyudei* (Life of Great People, 2013, 2015, 2018), as well as a book of literary portraits *Serdtse naraspev* (Open Heart, 2018), in which he reflected on Kazakh literary figures such as Abdijamil Nurpeisov, Kadyr Myrza Ali, Akim Tarazi and others. He also co-authored, along with Tair Mansurov, a biography of the First President of the Republic of Kazakhstan, Nursultan Nazarbayev, published in Moscow in the series *ZZL – Biographia prodolzhaetsya* (ZZL – Biography is Continuing). His non-fiction books include *Borovoe* (1979) and *Markakol* (1983). He translated from Kazakh into Russian books by Kazhygali Mukhanbetkali, Bek Togysbayev, Sofy Smatayev and Iran-Ghayip.

Mikhailov is a member of both Kazakhstan and Russian writers' unions, poet laureate of the literary awards named after Mikhail Lermontov (Russia, 2014), winner of the Alaš International Literary Award (2007), and recipient of the Order of Parasat (1996).

Golden Drowsiness

Thin as conscience, I flung
an ancient fishing net into the sea-ocean –
with little hope, I sat myself down
drunk from the salty spray.

The distance breathed the outcast's freedom,
the Sun streamed on the dashing wave,
I meditated with a golden drowsiness …
till there was nothing I desired.

Shoals of fish scuttled through the mesh,
and the deep flashed with secrets,
and the golden fish emerged
and muttered something to me.

Lively patches of light in the blue air
flew towards me as if they were mine,
their words circular and gold …
speaking only of love.

The Lantern Rocked and Creaked …

The lantern rocked and creaked,
alone in the inaudible snowstorm,
the snow flew and flew and flew –
higher and higher and higher.

In the dark, in the lacklustre sky,
a milky light shone.
In the dead of night at the gates
the lantern groaned in the wind.

A world so strange, so strange, so strange,
snow coming up to the roofs,
our own house flew in from heaven –
closer and closer and closer.

Deep in my soul, deep in my soul,
somehow it had got lost.
No windows or doors in it,
only funnels of light.

Along the Country Road
Forsaken by God

Along the country road forsaken by God,
in that steppe, where there is nothing but feather grass,
I stroll mindlessly along,
barefoot, hearing the tender dust.

Feather grasses are brooms clinging to the wind.
For a hundred *versts*[1] not a village in sight.
What do I care for lies circling the world.
How warm is this golden dust!

In this land forsaken by God, perhaps
the greatest kindness would be
to allow you to roam the field for an hour,
barefoot in the dust, like a light-bay horse.

While the clouds keep away, the dust
is gentle, the sun-filled light is warm.
I would happily stroll indifferent to meaning –
futile to look for it where there is none.

[1.] *Verst* – an obsolete Russian measurement of length, each *verst* equivalent to 1.1 km.

To Be Free of Everything

To be free of everything,
to float somewhere like a cloud,
glittery snowy whiteness
over the Earth turning to evening.
And there is nothing that you need …
To try to catch the last glint of the Sun,
to fly rose-winged
to reflect the last light
to someone in the distance,
where the darkness thickens.

Khlebnikov

Steppe flowers sang to him,
frogs turned bronze like buddhas.
He was a thoughtful stork in the grass.
His pupil drank in the far spaciousness,
and the migratory permanence of the wind
streamed freely in the blue.

Numbers flew like a flock of cranes.
The meaning of the times, melted like a shaky wedge.
Happy and light, his view of the world
drank in the bird's perennial wedge of the ages,
the ripe living dew of the falling stars,
and the steamy milk of clouds.

The earth breathed with the clay of creation,
while the grasshoppers' abrupt singing
rang out like gold heat.
The melodious haze stood like a pillar,
and a harmonious cloud of insects
pierced the blue – feverish and transparent.

The language of stones was a deep rumbling.
Currents of fire snaked beneath the earth.
The Ural's sleepy ridges, the passionate Caucasus,
were grumbling and shifting,
while magma oozed like leprosy
through the ancient, fragmenting layers.

The naive and savage people,
trampled nature's flowers like elephants.
Horses wheezed from furious races.
There was the flowering of black suns,
while girls flew in a marriage dance,
like butterflies, drawn to a comforting fire.

He listened to the voices of his own people,
to the word's deep resonance,
to words weathered over time.
Spring roots babbled
their rosy inflexions came to life,
and melted on whispering lips.

The human sea rose to the heavens,
their grief wandering like a hungry animal –
Rus' swam in crazy blood ...
He believed it was the torment of rebirth,
the sacred redemption of all the earth –
and he sowed the pure vision of love.

Earth flew like a sailing boat in the cosmos.
The world was the word. This word sang
and waves struggled to get on air.
Only the song was not subject to evil or decay,
and by her singing command
Velimir located his place in the heart –
the impoverished chairman of the earthly globe,
and the tremulous observer of waves in Khvalynsk,[2]
the ardent priest of meadow flowers,
favourite of the clouds and birds,
the disinterested wanderer of heavenly will,
never having been shackled by the earth.

[2.] Khvalynsk – river port town in the Saratov region, Russia, located on the Volga.

The Log

Dense gloomy log, alone in a dry bonfire.
You won't burn, but there on the golden fire,
you arrogantly hiss and smoke
as if it is at someone else's festival.

The flame crackles and eddies around you,
generous with its sparks, flying full of life.
Yet, you, a callous stone close in on yourself,
unwilling to look at the playful child.

Now the joyful bonfire burns out.
The wasted darkness grips it.
In the grey ash the twigs subside,
without strength, without hope, without mind.

Only you, forgotten log,
suddenly rip out the flame from the inside
and, belatedly, selflessly continue
your bluish fire till morning.

We all depart into the sky gradually …
What is our flame? Only such longing,
and straw and a powerful log –
it burns you with a tender blue flame.

Only the endless sky is imperishable,
reclining over the world with its starry sparks.
One day it will flare out like the log,
causing everything to transform once more.

Blue Fences, Grey Houses

Blue fences, grey houses.
Although the locks are weak, it's still a prison.
Black sheep, like a red-brown camel in smoke.
Along the steppe people are scattered by a heavy sky.
In the dull heat haze the ages are melting.
Here, since birth they have dragged on like a life sentence.
You know, there is such a desert all around ...
Where can one find one's fate?
The grey poles are like a cordon.

Stately and tall, the clay brick of the town
of the dead flowered in the neighbourhood.
Dusty *mazars*[3] are dumb and blind,
their crescent moons drinking the empty sky.
The tearing wind shakes the weed grass ...
Is it a dream or a waking reality?
A train will pass through – and all that is there
is a funeral moon, a telegraph pole.

[3] *Mazars* – mausoleums, or 'dwellings of the dead', for rulers, saints, distinguished figures
and scholars of the past.

Why Were We Born into the World?

Why were we born into the world?
No one knows apart from God.
In a country that no longer exists,
not now or in the future.

And in this world night
is it still not clear to us
that we are the last rays
of a star that has gone out?

We continue to fly in all directions.
Other luminaries shine on us.
The star, long since cooled,
is burning down.

Winter Rainbow

And it shall come to pass, when I bring a cloud over the earth,
then my rainbow will appear in the clouds, and I will remember
my covenant, which is between me and you ...
– Genesis 9, 14–15

Once, just the once, I saw a winter rainbow ...
The snowstorm raged furiously in cascades of whirling snow.
The frost fiercely detested all the world, right to the heavens,
when suddenly, brightly lit, it climbed over the dead steppe.

It was on an early morning at a stop near Majķùdyķ,[4]
where hunger once tortured the exiled more powerfully than
hell,
where ever since the earth has seemed to groan,
estranged and hollow
where the black hands of the dead, crying for mercy, stick out
of the snow.

'I will present you with my rainbow ...' – the wind blows icy
                                    cold,
'... that it was a sign of the covenant ...' – (Who will
                                    understand this?)
'... between me and the earth ...' – and no one noticed
this winter rainbow as the people hurried to work.

The cramped, long-awaited bus crawled along: one or two got
                                    off, one squeezed on ...
The snowstorm whirled more intensely and burned with frost
                                    to the ground.
This rainbow was in the sky a while as a brief interlude in
                                    compliment to the season –
till it disappeared – perhaps due to a cloud of snow from the
                                    snowstorm.

[4.] Majķùdyķ – *auyl* in the Ķaraġandy region that suffered greatly in the famine of the 1930s.

I only think of one thing when I remember the winter
                                    rainbow,
in that steppe where my flesh and blood were lost.
If hell on earth is the path to heavenly paradise,
did God send this colourful vision of light for those dying in
                                    winter?

The War Against Us Hasn't Ended

The war against us hasn't ended.
This war will last forever.
Russia, only you remained,
like a star in the heaven before God.
From one edge of fate to the other,
the precious path lies.
So burn without dying out …
from hell to bright paradise
not for long, not for much, just a little …

Wine

Homer as we know was blind.
At parties he would mix his wine with water,
which earned him much respect from the Muses
admiring his strength of character.

Socrates was the wisest in the world –
he knew that he knew nothing.
He took his time and never got drunk,
apart from hemlock which he downed in one.

Omar Khayyam[5] was an inveterate drunk,
(only in poetry of course – not in real life).
So Allah was happy to give him his due:
a crown – and drink-filled happy days.

Then the green-eyed monster hard liquor appears.
Rimbaud and Verlaine drank absinthe like crazy,
but Baudelaire, well, he did one even better –
drinking himself early into his grave.

Europe rocked our boat, and now
even Russia has taken to the drink.
Yesenin choked vodka like an enemy.
Blok was carried away on a river of wine.

As for our age – don't even start.
They drink to the death, like it's their last battle.
No one seems bothered about the Final Judgement,
but it's not beyond the mountain …
not beyond the mountain …

[5.] Omar Khayyam (1048–1131) – Persian mathematician, astronomer and poet.

The Derkul River

There the sandbanks of fine mist thickened with poplars.[6]
There the heron snatched small fish to feed its young.
There wedding songs rang out like toads in the evening.
For a full hour water rippled against the shores.

There a sterlet cut away a silver path with its sabre,
and sensed, with all its senses, gambolling in the depths,
how free, how smooth and intoxicatingly sweet it is,
to glide along the wave with your own light, like a flying moon.

[6.] Derkul River – river bordering Ukraine and Russia.

Two Waltzes

1.
The whole of my life
I won't forget you –
the way you flooded me
with light.

Eyes fixed on you
like a child's,
I was a blind calf,
trailing after you.

Lighter than an air balloon,
flying off into the clouds,
a tiny flashlight,
grieving inside.

And like a miracle,
the earth shone for me –
and it flew, everywhere
glowing with your light.

2.
The whole of your life
you won't forget me –
and then later you will
still remember me.

Me, eyes fixed on you
like a child's,
a blind calf,
trailing after you.

How, lighter than an air balloon,
I flew off into the clouds,
a tiny flashlight,
grieving inside.

And like a miracle,
to the end of my life,
you shone everywhere,
for me, for me.

Night Rain

1.

As I listened to the rain, falling in sheets,
my soul was freed of its shackles,
like leaves in the darkness from burning dust.
Fresh thoughts floated somewhere,
rising and spreading freely, to meet the stream
that flowed rhythmically down from the sky,
so my soul, soared freely upwards,
breathing the night's pure moisture.

2.

Rain fell all night – and the meeting was put on hold.
An unknown strength carried my soul
into damp spaciousness, in its hollow darkness,
where there is neither space for will or mind,
but only the sound of many wide waters
and the song of the lonely water drops,
where the word dissolves away into the distance,
like an echo in the sky of leaves and earth.

Translated by Belinda Cooke

NADEZHDA CHERNOVA
(b. 15.01.1947)

Nadezhda Chernova is a poet, novelist, translator and critic. After graduating from Kirov Kazakh State University (now Ăl-Farabi Kazakh National University) she worked for various mass media and creative organisations in Kôkšetau and Semej, before being appointed as an editor at the poetry department for the Žalyn publishing house and later to the same position for the journal *Prostor*.

Chernova is the author of more than twenty books of poetry and prose, including *Vozrast avgusta* (The Age of August, 1978), *Tsvetushiy saksaul* (Saxaul Blossoming, 1979), *Pomnyu* (I Remember, 1982), *Kochevnitsa-zhizn'* (Nomad-Life, 1986) and *Brodyachie syuzhety* (Wandering Stories, 1988). *Nebesniy dom* (Heavenly House, 2006), *Veter zhelanii* (Wind of Desires, 2011) and *Letyashie v tumane* (Fliers in the Fog, 2019) are regarded the poet's most notable collections of lyrics.The prime subject of her poems is Kazakhstan, for she is drawn to the history and traditions of the Kazakhs. For instance, 'Ķorķyt' (Korkut; about a legendary musician and philosopher), 'Găkku' (Swan-Song), 'Drevnii rod' (Ancient Race), 'Altyn dala' (Golden Steppe), 'Dala' (Steppe), 'Ķobyz', 'Kipchakskaya osen' (Kipchak Autumn), 'Ladon' stepi' (Steppe's Palm), 'Skazitel' (Storyteller), introduce to the audiences her experience of Kazakh culture. Being a Russian writer with an excellent knowledge of Kazakh, she delivers the unique music and tone of Kazakh language in her notable 'Dva yazyka' (Two Languages). Poems and prose by Chernova have been published in a number of journals in Kazakhstan and former USSR countries, as well as those of Israel, South Korea and France. She has translated works by Kazakh, Turkmen, Ukrainian, Bulgarian and French poets into Russian.

Nadezhda Chernova has been awarded the Order of Ķùrmet (2006) and the Alaš International Literary Award (2008).

The Chase

Drunk with heat, the grapevine
clung to clay walls and fences.
Apples shone, the sand reddened.
You were after control of my mind.

The market as striped as a melon,
through plum-skins, midnight glinted.
You were chucking coins in the ditch,
each ripple slipped off and was gone.

You caught up. In the ebbing light,
you gathered young drops in your hands.
Alive in the fields and channels,
in your palms, their brightness died.

And beyond a distant wall,
just then, my fleeing mind
saw a girl, far off and behind you,
peer out from under her shawl.

The Old Fisherman

All day, all night, he's up there on the roof,
whether or not a storm is on the rise.
The hot air breathes. The sand is on the move.
The salt gnaws at his insomniac eyes.

Below, the mountain village lives and dies,
bears fruit again. It bathes in sand. The saltwort
drowns the rounded kilns. What paradise
it is to own a house of mud, it is thought.

He sits immobile on that flat roof, though,
his eyes fixed on a blue blur in the distance,
the living sea
        that left an age ago,
out there beyond the wall of midday mist.

He knows his tackle hasn't rotted, so
he's waiting, and his low-hulled boat is still sound.
Time is on a different watch. Governments blow
from other shores, the old life is burned to the ground.
All this bustling around!
Like ash flung from an urn,
it will all fly off and settle on the seabed.
The sea is timeless, it's got to return.
He keeps his eyes set on it, straight ahead.

The Full-Moon Dreams

The night's awash with silver light, the stars
ring clear here while they circle, chained together.
Across the booming steppe, the speaking grass,
the jangling summer wanders on its tether.

They dream, the wolf-cubs warm beneath birch roots,
the opening lures them to the sky. The tears
of milk are here: their mother's scent is acute.
And then,
            out of their eyes the moon appears.

She dreams, the white-downed, nostril-bothering fox
among the golden fields of oats. That quail
that called her evening song across
the steppe let out a cry to no avail.

He dreams, the weary crow. So many eyes,
open, green, in the fallen sky! But though
he's finished pecking eyeballs, and off he flies,
there's nowhere now at night for him to go.

A herd of motley cows dreams up a pendulum:
blue meadows' waves, the waves in a stream,
the faithful path the moon takes round the heavens,
the waves of moments and of timeless dreams.

The herdboy's shabby sheepskin coat: his bedclothes.
He's leaned his shoulder on a shaft of light.
He dreams a glaring eye, and as he dozes
under the cosmos, crosses the valley in flight.

He dreams of the time before he was born,
before dawn calls, cow-horns and grassland herds,
when face and name
had not yet taken form,
and there was only flight and shining worlds.

The Fliers in the Fog

These cousins in fate have strong rapport,
these two white horses that rush through the mist.
Neither will fall for the noose any more.
Try shouting, they'll raise their legs and resist.

Their consonantal trot is inspired,
the pair of them breaks the air as they go.
Who'll fall first on the wild grass when tired?
Who'll singe their lips on the year's first snow?

In autumn dawns, whose call is that loud
when keeping the sky in sight is a slog?
A pair of stars among restless clouds,
these two white horses that fly through the fog.

These two white horses that fly through the mist,
relentlessly following on at our heels,
across the land where crops don't exist.
And an eerie joy is what my spirit feels …

Both in the Future and Present

Both in the future and present,
just like in the past as before,
life passes, nothing more
than a flight of fowl
en route from 'was' to 'wasn't'.
In a blink we go from love
to the swift arrival of grief,
a moment as feathered and brief
as the call of an owl
that sounds, one night, from above.

My Only Begotten

A strange kind of wish we have here,
to grasp at a moment's picture
of a tomtit, a cloud, or a deer,
then flick through our pages even quicker.

My only begotten, are you
a calfskin scroll, worn through,
or writing scratched on clay
that's starting to crumble away?

But maybe at least a page,
a verse or a word will be saved
among the ash and dry dust.
From the skies, fire falls in waves,
mute, and talking in tongues.

Not knowing its worth,
the Creator sets fire
to His earth
so often you can't keep up.
He turns our pages in the wind.
He doesn't stop.
He doesn't tire.

What Happens Is Going to Happen

What happens is going to happen,
there's nothing I'm bitter about.
I've had such heaps of happiness,
my mind can't sort them all out.

Did you ever see bitterness bend
all the way down to the ground?
Oh all my bitter tears
are gone, they're ocean-bound –

and there, they'll descend and settle
in the light and quiet on that floor
to grow a pearl the size
of a grain of sand, in a jaw.

In the World Reversed

In the world reversed, where nothing is firm and assured,
where newspapers tire of printing their crime reports,
dictators swarm, and malice gnaws at understanding,
the Aral Sea shrivels, diseases crawl onto land,
where the world seems ruined, vanity unchecked,
where words and air are poisoned, there's need and neglect,
where it's all collapsing, the threads that were once our guides
have rotted and severed, crumbled and vaporised.

In this phantom place, this spectral, deceptive world
where beautiful people breathe in as intoxicants swirl,
night rippers seek and slash their prey, messiahs
from left and right keep saving their skin with lies.

As the sunset burns itself out, as history halts,
hold on to me tighter, forgive me my faults,
hold on to me tighter, now we are out of defences
apart from our love.
          Hold on to me now, as tenderness
breaks our heart. We're not dead yet, our lives
are still ours. Though darkness descends, we will see first
                        light.

Moses

Ancient Moses wasn't great with words.
He walked along those mountain cliffs,
issued his prophecy, and then transferred
the pain in his soul to Aaron's lips.

But a bush caught fire as he emptied his lungs,
bright seas would part at his oral skills.
Perhaps that's the poet, just silver-tongued
translator of somebody's loftier will.

Conversation with Love

No birds but springtime bells are sounding their notes.
I've left where once I arrived, devoid of all hope.
In that building without a way out, the condemned
have a ward, where I saw how the light in their eyes had
                                        dimmed,
where air attacks the larynx, rooms reek of carbolic,
green aprons gleam, where you hear the pathologist
on his rounds, and the mournful lie with their face to the
                                        wall,
and because they believed the chrysanthemum's white
                                        spheres,
the spring at the window, and me, there was no time for tears,
and I smiled and promised a life to them all.

I've left where once I arrived, devoid of all hope …
As if love had thrown me from a saddle as I rode.
I lassoed it; trapped, it went out of its mind,
I chased it away – and then I ran on behind.
'Get real, say no, he's not yours!', shame whispers.
'Go on, be brutal and take him!', love insists.
'You're divided by blood', shame says, 'hands off!'
'It isn't forever, just think of the moment', says love.
'Don't shout! Let go of the dream. It's misplaced.'
'You're frightened of love? You looked death in the face!'

And only fate kept quiet in all this. And still does.
Damn it, what was it that made it introduce us?

Translated by Alistair Noon

Songs of the Žajran Steppe

(According to Kazakh folklore)

Over the Mountains
(*kùj*[1])

Like a darting lizard, the flame
glances up from the fire – tell me
dombyra,[2] who is it just walked in
under the cover of our yurt?

The flame flickers a moment
in the fine ash. Having plucked
the strings, he doesn't leave –
they have their own language.

How the *dombyra* rings and plays –
it drives away
my herd.
      The horseman gallops,
tall and young.

Having caught a star in the well,
he urges his horse onwards.
How my string laughs
at the tracks.

Three moons have passed.
Three days have withered.
I broke my lash in anger
on my horse's back.

[1.] *Kùj* – musical genre (composition) based on a story arc, created for and performed on a number of traditional instruments.

[2.] *Dombyra* – the most popular traditional musical instrument among the Kazakhs. It is made from wood and stringed with animal intestines. It comes in various shapes, with 2–4 strings and 8–24 frets, but the most typical is an oval shape *dombyra*, with 2 strings and 12 frets.

In my hurry I flung away
my red-trimmed hat.
The early frogs sang
in the distant reeds.

Cranes playfully circled
over the fields.
Having freed his herds,
the horseman took his *dombyra*.

The song which warmed hearts
and turned cheeks to ice –
how melancholy my string is,
how it calls him.

Two Legends of Kelintôbe[3]

1.
Dark night over the clay castle.
Grave stones everywhere.
No one can help the town any more –
all the men have been killed in battle.

As long foretold, the wise man said,
Earth's ruin approaches –
sin's retribution must fall
on rich and poor alike.

People gathered in mourning dress
at this last encampment.

The enemy approached, churning up the dust –
their black horses neighing loudly –
their teeth shone in the early morning light,
their dragon helmets glittering in the early morning glare.

The crowds jostled each other, then froze.
Born from the billowing clouds,
born from the flames of the Sun,'
the beautiful woman mounted the walls.

She stood, naked, before the greedy horde
while they gave her their darkest looks,
blind with malice and blood,
yet chained by her beauty.

The mists swirled away like a mirage,
dissolving completely in the morning smoke.
She then vanished into their winged *kibitka*,[4]
reserved for the most desirable women.

[3.] Kelintôbe – (lit. a 'hill of a daughter-in-law') refers to the *auyl* (see footnote 8) in the
Žaŋaķorġan district of the Ķyzylorda region. It is believed that Queen Tùmar (or Tomiris)
of the Massagetae-Skythian people defeated the invading armies of Cyrus the Great in
530 BC, killing him in battle in these parts.
[4.] *Kibitka* – carriage with a covered top.

The castle she'd saved, sparked into flames,
it lit up its dome, built new walls.
... the castle she'd saved collapsed like sand –
and only legends survived ...

2.
On the clay castle night circled,
like a woman in a mourning shawl.
No one can help the town anymore:
men and boys have all fallen.

A wise sage spoke up, grey-haired as the age:
'Haven't we a single warrior left?' Clutching
their daughters, widows started to weep,
nothing left to them now but their shame.

The ornate wooden doors began to quiver
as a voice sounded out in the mosques.
Light and fine, like morning light,
in a swirling crimson dress –

she walked in – and sternly rebutted
the women's sobbing and cursing:
'No one has ever been able to conquer us –
we did not bow to storms and misfortune.

In battles and military campaigns
we followed the *batyrs*'[5] tracks.
Swallowing our tears, our faces visible,
we unfastened the serpent's ring.'

She stirred them up, brandishing her whip,
so they gathered together like a flock of birds –
young girls with their fathers' swords,
widows with their husbands' sabres.

[5.] *Batyr* – originally a term for 'hero' or 'valiant warrior', roughly equivalent to the European knight; nowadays the term signifies military or masculine prowess.

The enemies flew down, countless as the dust,
dry as the dust,
down on the town – thousands
were slaughtered on the bloody feather grass,
choking and wheezing in their death throes.

I saw the last, gloomy detachment,
digging the graves of the dead,
scythes glittering at this castle of wars,
under this red, vindictive sun.

Peering from their helmets, pierced by swords,
they meet the heavenly patches of light ...
... The truth of this legend
only the voiceless sand can tell ...

Buryltaj[6]

(Ancient ballad)

I save a brown foal.
Not one star or marker.
No crossing for the deep ravine –
only winds on to the steppe's expanse.

I gallop on a lively racehorse
to the place where my love lies –
empty save for the winds of the fields,
a whirlwind of ash on the sand.

Nothing but the coldness of a long-lost story …
Who, my love, secretly carried you away?
Midnight moon, my heart,
The moon in my breast has choked with tears …

[6.] Buryltaj – a song by composer and poet Biržan Sal Ķožaġùlùly (1834–97). The song is dedicated to a girl that the author is searching for for while riding Buryltaj, his beloved horse, but cannot find. The poem reformulates the lyrics of the song.

Storm Clouds over Baânauyl

(Ancient ballad)

Storm clouds over Baânauyl.[7]
The midday sun never shines over the earth.
The red fox that flashed like a flame through the pines
tries to get the kite – but cannot do it.

The yurt is pegged and tied for the people's summer camp.
Our *auyl*[8] is silenced and the fire reduced to ashes.
Never will I see my loved one again.
The yurt's white bird departs – a nomad on the earth.

Translated by Belinda Cooke

[7.] Baânauyl – area of natural beauty and home to a number of endemic species in the Pavlodar region (north-eastern Kazakhstan); it became a national park in 1988.

[8.] *Auyl* – social-economical formation considered to constitute the heartland of the nation and a basis for an ethnic and cultural union of the nomadic community. Consisting of 50–70 yurts in the eighteenth century, it developed into its current permanent state of 'rural settlement' (of a minimum of 100 dwellers) when Kazakhs adopted a settled mode of life in the nineteenth and twentieth centuries. *Auyl* can also be used as a synonym for 'native land' and 'homeland', concepts revered by the Kazakhs.

IRAN-GHAYIP
(b. 7.06.1947)

Iran-Ghayip (Iranbek Orazbayev) is a poet and playwright. He graduated from the Faculty of Mining of the Kazakh Polytechnic Institute (1970) before going on to study at the advanced courses of the Maxim Gorky Institute of Literature, graduating in 1980. Over the years, he worked as an editor at the Žazušy publishing house, head of the poetry department at the *Ķazaķ ádebieti* newspaper, head of the literary department of the Mùsirepov Kazakh State Academic Theatre for Children and Youth and editor-in-chief at the Editorial and Repertoire Council of the Ministry of Culture and Information of the Republic of Kazakhstan. Currently he is an editor at Žazušy.

Iran-Ghayip's poetry includes *Žùrek žyrlajdy* (My Heart is Singing, 1974), *Žeti ķazyna* (Seven Treasures, 1977), *Tùnniņ kôzi* (The Night's Eye, 1979), *Dùniežaryķ* (1987), *Ômir-ôlen* (Life-Song, 1982), *Mùnar, Mùnar, Mùnarym ...* (dedicated to the poet's son; 1992), *Iran Bejne* (Reflections of Me, 1995) and *Ķorķyttyņ kôri* (Ķorķyt's Grave, 2001; about the legendary musician and philosopher). He has also written about thirty dramatic poems, including *Kieli kùnà* (Sacred Guilt, 2006), *Batķan kemeniņ bejbaķtary* (The Wretches of the Sunken Ship, 1990) and *Ķorķyttyņ kôri*, translated into several languages. He has translated works by Dante Alighieri, Adam Mickiewicz, Ovanes Shiraz, Taras Shevchenko, Vladimir Mayakovski, Mamed Ismail, Bella Akhmadullina, Mikhail Yukhma, Ida Verber and others into Kazakh, and published a thirteen-volume edition of selected works in 2006.

Iran-Ghayip was awarded the State Prize of the Republic of Kazakhstan (2002), the independent award Platinum Tarlan (2003) and the Order of Parasat (2006).

I Have Everything ...

I have everything.
Everything about me is human.
Anything you look for you will find in me:
poison in my blood, poured by sadness,
honey in my soul, collected by joy!

My heart,
my liver,
a pair of lungs, still intact.
God save you from the blackened lungs –
they will burn you from inside.
If everything about me is human,
should I feel guilty about my silver tongue?

I have thirst
and a river inside me,
not to mention tree ...
No way I'm hopeless
like the scorched earth.
I can smile
when I'm crying inside –
don't be surprised by that.
Sometimes I'm a fool,
sometimes a prophet!

There's summer inside me,
and autumn
and winter
and spring –
good to own all those.
But the one thing I don't own –
is an animal's instinct to follow others blindly.

I have everything.
Everything about me is human.
Anything you look for you will find in me.

My Song

My song –
still the same old one –
even when tied up with chains –
given the chance,
it attacks ignorance at once,
slapping a dumb person on the head.

My song –
is the voice of eternity,
it knows what suffering is,
will never give up and fight
even on Judgement Day.
It won't burn in fire
or be drowned in deep waters.

My song
chooses the right path,
it hates all sorts of deception.
Sometimes the choking fumes
from the fires of our times overwhelm it, forcing it
to vomit bitter bile.

But my song stands firm,
the voice of life itself.
It can put up with everything –
suffering from poverty
and misery,
disappointed
and brittle –
it's still alive.

My song –
may look like an elephant on the street.
This mortal world howls and barks at it
like snappy cowardly little dogs do,
a grey daily life with all its mediocrity
tries to oblige rich patrons.

My song
is beautiful as the blue skies
strong
as the earth,
as full of life as the
breathing heart of the whole universe.

My song –
is the voice of the weary Sun
rushing headlong into the night's embrace –
the spiritual mystery of the creator
voiced in the Qur'an, Torah, Gospel and Psalms.

Duel

Pushkin …
Duel …
d'Anthès …
Blood[1] …
A lesson in life for me –
to be always on guard.
What's going on here – a duel?
Any sign of blood?
Always at my back, a coward
in white on a white-grey horse.

He prefers not to argue with me,
he knows what he will get.
I'm not Pushkin,
I'm a gun –
a self-loader.
With a trigger – pulled by itself.

---

[1] Russian poet, playwright and novelist Alexander Pushkin (1799–1837) died from wounds
sustained during a pistol duel with Frenchman Georges d'Anthès.

Tender as a Flower ...

Life is Truth,
Death is a Lie,
don't be sorry to die.
Just enjoy the Sun's light
while you can –
likewise, the earth's warmth.
Have the strength of a tombstone
while it is not above you.

A tombstone,
a human being
a flower –
all are the same, only in three
different forms, different states.
Don't favour one over the other –
take all three at once!

This fleeting moment hides the truth –
a flower bows before a human,
but a human bows to a tombstone.
A lie revels in a death
seeing the world deprived of such abundance.

Can't you see that
even a flower is human
as is a stone –
neither able to exist without the other.
Life is Truth
Death is a Lie,
is there anyone who doesn't run
from this Lie?

There is another secret unknown to us:
a flower is drawn to a human
and a human is drawn to a stone.
Keeping track of time
as they merge into each other.
Their unity grows stronger.

Those who are in the know
could make the night shine like day.
So whether happy or sad
be honest with yourself.
And don't grieve for the fact
that one day
your body,
now tender as a flower,
will turn into a stone
and find its resting place.

Two Breaths

As far as I know there are two kinds of breathing:
the first makes you a part of mankind;
the last tortures your soul
and extinguishes the light of truth.
One breath is far, another near,
between them – a whole glorious life.
Since man was first called a man,
two sighs – Archangel Gabriel and Azrael.
Two breaths.
One – before,
another – after.
I wouldn't be me without my first breath.
My last will be as quick as the grains of sand
in an overturned hourglass.

Two breaths:
two worlds – life and death …
One I can conquer,
another one will conquer me.
I sobbed as a winner, I sobbed as a loser,
gasping for air between two fires.
Enough sobbing.
I won't cry.
Both breaths are mine,
I'm paying the highest price for them.
Both worlds are equal to me,
ice cold
I'm ascending the throne of eternity!

Life is hell, but I'm not sure that death is paradise,
Sometimes you can't tell them apart.
And who would guess
that I'm sad –
not able to sacrifice my hell for a heaven.

I'd Love to Die ...

'I'm not stifled by life on Earth.
My mind is up there with the sky!'
However, in a world of poetry
I am not as powerful as Abaj.[2]

Words are a tricky staff to carry, believe me.
So don't be hard on me.
I'm only a human, how could I
please everyone, be good to them all?

Read my poems, try to understand them –
I was born a poet so you could.
I'd love to be immortal, but what about my soul?
I'd love to die, but don't have the right to do so.

[2.] Abaj Ķùnanbajùly (Abai Kunanbayev; 1845–1904) – the most influential of all Kazakh
poets, also a composer and philosopher. He is considered to be a reformer of Kazakh
literature on the basis of enlightened Islam; his works also reflected the European and
Russian cultures.

Joining Your Ancestors …

In you I found my strength.
For you I can sacrifice myself.
Live long, my love,
let me fade like the green grass under the Sun.

Don't sigh, don't grieve –
let the Moon and Sun bewitch us.
As long as you walk on this earth,
there's no end for love and no end for me.

Don't be weak, my love.
We are as strong as a tree knot –
our love swings us in its cradle,
bringing us close to each other.

We will avoid loneliness,
sometimes carefree, sometimes sad.
We'll join our ancestors when our time comes –
together, always, till we turn to dust.

Burning in a Fire ...

You are softness itself
I'm completely the opposite,
But shall we find a bodily harmony
And start the sweetest life
Together?

We had our share of bliss
Our souls sang like nightingales,
We drowned in a sea of sweet feelings
Following our earthly desires.

... But in each other's arms,
We found the purest of all fires.
Our bodies intertwined.
Our passion making us a whole.

Love You, Dear ...

When my jaw
drops
for the last time,
and all my poetic inspiration
is silenced by the grave:
I will still
be in love with you,
my dear,
as a dead man
is in love
with his resting place.

Getting cold
from the icy embrace
of the black
earth:
I will still
be in love with you,
my dear,
as Allah
is in love
with his creation!

Illogical Logic

Why create us Human in this way?
... With all our consciousness!
Totally illogical!
Only the Creator Himself
should possess
such a free-ranging mind.
Or maybe
He was so bored
of His loneliness,
that in a moment of desolation –
He just did it.
Eh ...
Who can be equal to
Him?
No!
No!
No!
It's all a lie!
Everything is half-baked
and shoddy!
It can't be!
Couldn't be!
It's impossible!
All right!
... What can you do.
Let's not complain –
He created you!
So live your life,
accept your fate.
Be born!
Cry!
Laugh!
Sob!
Drink!
Eat!
Take a crap!
Die –
play the ape ...

Become
a stray dog!
If you hadn't been born,
didn't cry –
or laugh –
or sob,
didn't drink –
or eat –
or take a crap,
didn't die –
you would turn into Him!
… and that's absolutely impossible!
He is the only One!
Admit it.
Show your humility –
bow down like a slave –
feel that
He is the Truth!
Beg and
worship –
with your body and soul.
Don't doubt for a moment –
… Otherwise,
pride and arrogance
will ruin you
in the end,
poor thing …

Oh, Well …

I frolicked
and laughed:
learned that everything is pointless.
I cried
and grieved:
realised that even more things are futile.
I ate,
relieved myself.
My tail tucked firmly between my legs.

He Is, Allah

He is not
in the sky –
He is not ...
on the earth –
He is not!
in the cradle –
He is not
in a grave –
He is not!
Don't look for Him –
in vain:
He is not
at the door –
He is not
at the *tôr*.[3]

... In Tora,
Psalms,
the Gospel
and
the Qur'an –
He is not!
... In my
soul –
and heart –
He Is, Allah!

---

[3] *Tôr* – place of honour located opposite the entrance at the back of a yurt or a room, reserved for guests or for the oldest man in the family.

Greetings

Greetings to you,
my native land!
The country where
I was born
and raised.
And will be buried –
covered by dust,
I will go into the ground –
in my 'Ķorķyt-grave'![4]

Patron
of me unfortunate,
is the Dead – *aruaķ*.[5]
Greetings to you!
What a pity that
my 'birds –
nightingales',
singing grouse –
all are in a 'Trap'!

Greetings,
'bronze-
sculptures':
moving
changing
shapes!
Greetings to you,
my relatives ...
Are you still
alive?

[4.] Ķorķyt – an eighth/ninth-century philosopher, poet and musician. According to legend, he sought immortality as his life drew to a close. In lonely torment, he hollowed out a precursor to the *ķobyz*, a classical Kazakh stringed instrument associated with shamanic healing. Playing its music, he staved off death until he fell asleep and was bitten by a venomous snake. Thus the saying: 'Wherever you go, there is Ķorķyt's grave' (i.e. you can't avoid death in the end).

[5.] *Aruaķ* – ancestral spirit. It is believed that *aruaķs* protect the living descendants, thus they are treated with deep reverence. Kazakhs visit their ancestral graves to ask for guidance; they make vows in the name of *aruaķs* and call their ancestors' names in a battle cry.

Are your lives
going OK?
What kind of mood –
are you in?!
Where is
insidious Death –
Azrael,
who will
take my soul?

My paradise –
is hell,
My Nirvana –
torment:
let your life
carry on and your bazaar
not to be closed
because
'Your poet –
will die!'

The poet –
doesn't die …
People:
multiply –
and be
reborn!
If a poet
dies:
the Sun –
goes out,
the Sky itself
expires …

Cry from the Heart

Hey,
black trees,
grown –
in my yard …
and
all trees –
growing on the earth!
Which of you
will become:
a cradle …
Which of you –
a coffin?!
Well,
which of you
will become gallows?

Tell me!
Why are you
all silent –
your heads drooped?
Are there
any executioners
and traitors
among you?
… If you shackle
a poet's song,
if you put his heart
in a coffin
and hang him
on the gallows:
I'm right here in front of you!

Who Owns Today?

Who owns Today?
'The God of Bribes' – 'Money!'
Corrupted – from the very beginning,
'Secret tricks' – bind them together!
Scoundrels conspiring with each other,
those who have abandoned honour and conscience!

Who owns Today?
Vile people! Rogues!
falling over themselves.
'Scammers' – stopping at nothing!
Crawling before their superiors,
earmarked 'Slaves'!

Who owns Today?
Gluttons from 'Dens and Pits'!
Hungry louses – *'Oâk-buâk'*,[6]
Their ideas are dirt ... 'Unclean!'
They crushed pure nature and shame,
servants of Devil they are ...

Who owns Today?
Arrogant-Stubborn-Stuck-up people!
Strangers, Aliens – 'Folks'–
Those-who-come-and-go ...

Oh, things are bad, very bad:
It's good time for 'Mockers',
a bad time for Kazakhs ...

Translated by Rose Kudabayeva

[6.] *Oâk-buâk* – shortened versions of *ol žak and bul žak* – 'there' and 'here', which are
expressions considered as part of an uncultured person's language.

SERIK AKSUNKAR
(b. 29.03.1950)

Serik Aksunkar is a poet, essayist and journalist. He graduated from Ķaraġandy Pedagogical Institute and went on to study at Kirov Kazakh State University (now Äl-Farabi Kazakh National University). Subsequently he was employed at the Ķaraġandy local newspapers (1977–87), later becoming the executive secretary of the Ķaraġandy regional branch of the Writers' Union of the Kazakh SSR (1987).

Aksunkar's debut collection of verses was *Kôktem tynysy* (The Breath of Spring, 1975), followed by *Ķyzylaraj* (Swallow) in 1980. These two books attracted attention from the literary community for their proud civic pathos. His next publication, *20-šy ġasyrdyṇ žiyrma säti* (20 Moments of the 20th Century, 1984), a reflection on the present and future of the world, was later revisited by the author and republished in 2012. Aksunkar's bibliography also includes *Ķyzylaraj* (A Red Dawn, 1990), *Ġasyr kardiogrammasy* (Cardiogram of the Age, 1992), *Adam Ata – Haua Ana* (Adam and Eve, 2000), *Ômir degen kùndi ajnalu* (Life Is Revolving Around the Sun, 2005), *Tôbemnen žauhar žauyp tùr* (The Diamonds Falling from Heaven, 2005), *Ķypšaķ ķissasy* (Stories of Kipchaks, 2008), *Ķaraorman* (Dark Forest, 2012), *Mocart pen Sal'eri* (Mozart and Salieri, 2015) and *Kôkejimde – Kùlteginniṇ žazuy* (Kùltegin Inscriptions Are My Preoccupation, 2015). He also published a two-volume edition of his selected verses in 2014. His poems have been translated into Spanish, Azerbaijani, Russian, Ukrainian, Turkish, Kyrgyz and Mongolian. He himself has translated poems by Marina Tsvetaeva, Nazym Hikmet, Evgeny Evtushenko, as well as by Asian and African poets, into Kazakh.

Aksunkar is an Honoured Worker of the Republic of Kazakhstan and a poet laureate of the Alaš International Literary Award.

Midday Dream

The world is full of delusions.
Generations are at war, sons
with fathers. Trying to talk
to Abaj[1] in the audience –
such a blustering fool.

The son is looking worked-up,
pumped full of revenge.
How can he possibly love Abaj
while hating Šăkărim?[2]

Many Kazakhs went mad,
full of unspoken thoughts.
How can they love Alaš
while inwardly hating Maġžan?[3]

The professor is in a rage.
He has a grudge against us.
Mayakovsky is his theme –
Mùķaġali[4] is drinking in the street.

When I was eighteen, I saw this
in my mind and soul – a nightmare.
O my saint, what does it all mean?
Explain it all to me, please.
Mùķaġali is drinking in the street.

---

[1] Abaj Ķùnanbajùly (Abai Kunanbayev; 1845–1904) – the most influential of all Kazakh poets, also a composer and philosopher. He is considered to be a reformer of Kazakh literature on the basis of enlightened Islam; his works also reflected the European and Russian cultures.

[2] Šăkărim Ķùdajberdiùly (Shakarim Kudaiberdiuly; 1858–1931) – well-known Kazakh poet, philosopher and historian, Abaj Ķùnanbajùly's nephew.

[3] Alaš Orda – political movement and later a party opposed to the Soviets during the Civil War (1917–22). Their supporters among the Kazakh intelligentsia were initially tolerated, but ultimately executed in the 1930s, during the Stalinist purges. Maġžan Žùmabaev (1893–1938) was one of the most influential Kazakh poets and a member of the Alaš Orda Party. Accused of being a Pan-Turkist and Japanese spy, he was persecuted and ultimately shot in March 1938.

[4] Mùķaġali Maķataev (Mukagali Makatayev, 1931–76) – outstanding poet who enjoyed a devoted following among ordinary Kazakhs. He translated foreign literature into Kazakh, including Walt Whitman and Dante's *The Divine Comedy*.

Childhood Is Like Honey

Childhood is like honey.
It is a vine with fresh buds.
I was thirteen and one day
a sixteen-year-old girl asked me,
'Have you ever kissed a girl?'

'No', I replied, my eyes crossing
with her bright eyes, my heart
beating fast, my blood burning,
my brain boiling. 'Come on',
she urged. 'If you don't tell anyone,
let's kiss each other every day
like that.'

A front yard: late autumn,
the moon shining.
Lips touched lips. We were attached
to each other and to the earth
in a magical geometry,
rotating at 180 degrees,
the temperature soaring.

As a neighbour,
I witnessed a lot.
We often kissed
after that, and I looked out for her
from the window, day
after day, waiting impatiently
for the girl who kissed me.

This lasted about a year.
My heart beating fast, my blood burning,
my brain boiling, we used to kiss.
Once, walking home,
I saw her kissing a young man

in the same place,
the same yard …
Her loved one was not me
but someone else.
That day I hated every girl.
But how they bewitched me thereafter?

We Are All from a Distant *Auyl*

We are all from a distant *auyl*[5] –
sick of songs from our youth.
Stomping about in dusty *auyls*,
we were the drizzling rain.

A hovel is a song,
a mountain is a song
and a rock is a song
telling of Arķa and Balķaš.[6]

The name 'poets' that you pin
on us is an idle word,
for we are famous the world over
as drunkards.

We are created from storms.
We are the rain which, once started,
never stops. Even an *auyl*
is called after us: 'Drunkard'.

We go here and there: Rome,
Crimea … If we get money in our pockets,
we travel further and further.
In the Soviet era we multiplied
but were then destroyed like moss.

Spring was our soul's bliss.
Many legends surround us,
and the holy man, Yesenin.
We are honoured to be linked
to seven grandfathers.

[5.] *Auyl* – social-economical formation considered to constitute the heartland of the nation
and a basis for an ethnic and cultural union of the nomadic community. Consisting of
50–70 yurts in the eighteenth century, it developed into its current permanent state of
'rural settlement' (of a minimum of 100 dwellers) when Kazakhs adopted a settled mode
of life in the nineteenth and twentieth centuries. *Auyl* can also be used as a synonym for
'native land' and 'homeland', concepts revered by the Kazakhs.

[6.] *Arķa* – refers to Saryarķa, or the Kazakh Uplands (also known as the Kazakh
Hummocks), a large plain extending throughout the central and eastern regions of
Kazakhstan. Lake Balķaš (Balkhash) is a – major lake in Central Asia, located in south-
eastern Kazakhstan.

Yet poets have bad names now ...
You will see –
is the end of the world near?
We are like an Indian tribe.
We are out of stock.

Monologue of a Wolf

I hate dogs.
I fight them.
I brawl with them.
I am a wild creature
of the wide steppe –
such magical wildness
I possess as I ride land
and air. I have
an abundance of power.
I can break a man's sharp knife
with a single fang.
I am proud of it!
All the *ülys*[7] were distracted
by their frequent bloody fights
with dogs whose smell
still reeks on the steppe.
It is said we have the same genes
as dogs. Is this true,
my wolf-ancestors?[8]
Such stories fill
the heart with revenge,
make us curse fiercely.
If we are related to dogs,
what about our wolf origins?
Are we to be overcome by the *tôbet*?[9]
Why are you silent, my wolf-ancestors?
Whose descendants came to life too weak and unworthy?
Why are you silent?
This is a silent night.
I'm lying here, among enemies.
The rim of the sky is disturbed
by voices of barking dogs.

---

[7] *Ülys* – refers to 'state', 'country', 'nation' or 'people'.

[8] Wolf-ancestors – according to Turkic mythology, a she-wolf nurtured a boy, a single
survivor of a great battle. The boy became a warrior and claimed back his country: all the
Turkic nations descend from his ten sons.

[9] *Tôbet* – also known as the Kazakhstan mountain dog; a livestock guard dog of ancient
lineage in Kazakhstan. In the context of the poem, *tôbet* is used as a derogatory term for
a dog (as opposed to a wolf, the totemic creature of the Turkic people).

Spell Song of Gold

'I'll buy everything,' said gold,
'I'll take everything,' said steel.
– Pushkin[10]

Stepping over the shame,
I seduced
mind,
honour,
a grief,
a man, then bought him.
Who is man?
Who am I? As a man, you need to understand
what power is – for
I will sell you again if I get pushed.

You haven't yet seen me in a rage,
I'm not afraid of a *pushka*[11] –
nor even of Pushkin.
Don't be angry, biting your lip.
I ruined your country,
ruined your land ...

I'm not afraid of the snake's burrow,
of hydrogen,
atoms,
of neutron bombs
which will have my name on them
if they are used playfully.
I invented them all.

---

[10] *Literature and Money*, ed. by Anthony George Purdy. Rodopi, Amsterdam-Atlanta, GA, 1993: p. 28.
[11] *Pushka* – Russian for gun or cannon; a huge sixteenth-century artillery piece.

The kings are my darlings,
my most-loved children,
even if they are mischievous.

If you harm executioners,
you'll meet my rage:
they're my bastards from my maidens!
the soldiers are my slaves in the saddle.
I am the God of War on Earth.
They will die for me.

As a poet, you will get a mourning song
but bodies of soldiers cover my face
and there's no proper price for dead slaves.
All my wives are beauties,
so the rumour goes.

When I am shaped into a ring,
I lead them to bed. You can see
from my face I am not afraid of anything,
not even of a hero.
On earth I speak boldly.

I say exactly what I want to say:
'Black earth!' and 'O, my castle.
When I have time, I will have fun!'
Is Giaconda the epitome of beauty to you?
I'll give you her price when I have calculated it.
After all, I am Gold.

Noble

I believe an unlucky son of a sad khan[12]
accidentally deposed from the throne
was the same as you.
You worry like Žajyķ, and are as alone as Edil.[13]

If a man grieves for his people, let him grieve
      like you.
Taking people like children into his arms,
impatient with the troubles of the rich.
Your kin was noble.

When, Khan Kene[14] stepped down from the throne,
your grandfather also –
Žaâu Mùsa[15] dismounted from his horse.
Abandoning everything,
he devoted himself to God. God's code
was in our genes, but it was pecked out by the foxes
of a godless country.

Every time Kôk Bôri[16] howled,
how didn't your bitter mourning reach Alaš?[17]
It will reach Alaš in the end.
… Because Allah hears everything.

[12.] Khan – title of a ruler in Central Asia, equivalent to a king.

[13.] Žajyķ (Ural) and Edil (Volga) – rivers crossing territories in West Kazakhstan.

[14.] Khan Kene – refers to Kenesary Khan, or Kenesary Ķasymùly (Kassymuly, 1802–47), considered to be the last khan of the Kazakhs. He headed a Kazakh national rebellion against Tsarist Russia (1837–47).

[15.] Žaâu Mùsa Bajžanùly (1835–1929) – prominent Kazakh poet, singer and composer.

[16.] Kôk Bôri – (lit. 'celestial wolf') metaphorical name for a wolf, a totemic creature for the Turkic people; here it refers to the legend mentioned in footnote 8.

[17.] Alaš – common name for the Kazakh people.

O Motley Snake that Came Out from Within

O motley snake that came out from within,
you are seriously ill – what is the medicine
that would cure you? The Motherland
which created me gave birth to you too,
so what can I do?

How deep were your thoughts
when, cracking open two of your eyes,
you stung your own mother
while lying on her breast?

I will not be able
to flourish, you will see. The enemy is near,
my body is becoming cold – you, nasty snake,
have gone through my chest!

You won't leave
my house and my side is unstitched;
you sleep with me,
poison flowing from your mouth.

I wanted to leave the crowd and sing my song,
but I am stung by a snake that came out from within.
Now I am dying from its poison.

I was vulnerable because of my patience.
And now we are taking a break together
in a grave – no holiday in a foreign country
for me. When I die, you will slink
from my side and lie down, stinging me,

yes … lie down stinging me. Take my dream, then,
and I'll pretend to take a nap.
If you don't stick your forked tongue into me,
I will resurrect myself again.

Happy God

Happy God, whose hemline waved on earth
and in heaven, met a man weeping.
'Come,' he said, 'divide the share of earth
which is enough for both the king and slaves.

A warrior attacked the fortress,
the children found slops,
hunters filled the dense forest,
pasture was used up by the cattlemen.'

God helped the deprived people;
no hope was turned down,
even mean ones on the golden steppes.
Sly men captured the air.

'Where are you going? The sky is mine,
don't forget. Come back here.
You will have to pay for breathing air.
Those who disobey me will die
of suffocation.'

The poet wandered off
and thought – To hell, what else
is God going to take? All that remains
is a black coffin; even the sand and water
belong to that bastard god of greed.

'Where were you off to? What kind of person
are you without a will and greed?'
God persisted. He looked coldly at the poet.

The poet said, 'Please
forgive me. As I can see,
there's enough suitors after all this wealth.
Occupied with thoughts of the world,
I forgot about humankind.' God smiled,

deep in thought. 'Fly away', he said.
'When fire gets into your wings,
I will open that sky for you.
There is no consolation left
for a poet on this earth.'

May Allah grant his blessings
and give the support of the spirits,
whether this is dream or reality. Ever since,
I have been walking among the clouds.

Poem of the Nomadic Scythians

I am
the poem of the ancient Scythians.
Even though I walk about in exile,
covered in blood, there hasn't been a moment
when I have kept silent – even when I rode
Pegasus, my steed, my tribe behind me.

I look around at the mortal world,
my soul accepts it yet grieves over it.
When exalted from being mounted
on a tall horse, and singing,
my tongue became tied, for most of my people
were on their feet.

How confused I was, then,
and I kept to myself a thought
that came from Allah.
In front of every ruler
I spoke fearlessly like a dragon.

I jerked the world's hem as I pulled it.
I moved along the horizon
and entered the blackest cloud of the black sky
that was pouring black rain.

I ran from the steppe into the sky.
And a white cloud kissed my wings.
I inhaled the perfume of Hafez;[18]
I managed to push Pushkin into a husk of millet
and I was angry with *kaffir*.[19]

---

[18] Khwaja Shams-ud-Din Muhammad Hafez-e Shirazi (1315–90) – Persian poet, known by his pen name 'Hafez' or 'Hafiz'.

[19] *Kaffir* – non-believer or infidel in Islam; in Kazakh colloquial speech also a synonym for dishonest, ignominious or cruel.

When I descended from the white cloud
and sat down, crossing, then stretching my legs,
he offered me vodka.
Once I had drunk it, I vomited.

Then I broke through the black clouds
and went down to my father's house.
The steppe was wild with light.
I headed for Kôk Tăņir[20] and flew up
into the sky.
But my Alaš was left behind.

[20.] Kôk Tăņir – (lit. 'celestial Tengri') primordial deity in the religion of the early Turkic peoples; god of the sky, the only creator of the universe, often paired with the 'earth-mother', Ûmaj (Umay).

My Destiny

My destiny, luck,
was woven by an ancient Runic inscription.
Kùltegin[21]
sat on the knees of Elteris[22]
Abaj
sat on the knees of Ķùnanbaj.[23]
Ălihan
sat on the knees of Nùrmùhamed.[24]
Mùhtar Maġauin
sat on the knees of Maġauiâ.[25]
Burning from the fire inside me,
and suffering from a court named conscience –
how Caesar sat in the Senate –
I sat on the knees of old men …
Those knees are my gold throne
but they vanished like a mirage.
They came from Karlag[26] saddened,
and without bowing, not obeying Stalin,
the God of earth.
My destiny, luck,
was woven by an ancient Runic inscription.

[21.] Kùltegin (Kul Tigin; r. 685–731) – outstanding military commander of the Second Turkic Khanate, formed in the seventh and eighth centuries after the liberation wars against China. He became famous as a brave soldier and participant of many Turkic military campaigns.

[22.] Elteris (Ilterish) Khagan (r. 682–694) – founder of the Second Turkic Khaganate; the father of Kùltegin.

[23.] Ķùnanbaj Ôskenbajùly (Kunanbay Oskenbaiuly; 1804–86) – prominent Kazakh politician and leader aġasùltan (leader) of the Middle Žuz, and bi (judge), the father of Abaj Ķùnanbajùly.

[24.] Ălihan Nùrmùhamedùly Bôkejhanov (Alikhan Bokeikhanov; 1866–1937) – Kazakh statesman, politician, publicist, teacher, writer and environmental scientist who served as the Prime Minister of the Alaš Autonomy from 1917 to 1920. He was leader and founder of the Alaš Orda national liberation movement. Nùrmùhamed Bôkejhanov is his father.

[25.] Mùhtar Maġauin (Mukhtar Magauin; b. 1940) – prominent Kazakh writer and publicist. Maġauiâ is his grandfather.

[26.] Karlag (Karagandy Corrective Labour Camp) – one of the largest Gulag labour camps of the USSR. It existed between 1931 and 1959 and was located in the Ķaraġandy (Karaganday) region of Kazakhstan.

Kùltegin
sat on the knees of Elteris
Abaj
sat on the knees of Ķùnanbaj.
Ălihan
sat on the knees of Nùrmùhamed.
Mùhtar Maġauin
sat on the knees of Maġauiâ.
Burning from the fire inside me,
and suffering from a court named conscience –
how Caesar sat in the Senate,
I –
without obeying or bowing to anyone –
sat on the knees of Aksunkar …

Life Is Revolving Around the Sun

Vibrations
Crashes
Hearing and listening –
today my
soft Earth
is revolving around the Sun
while the Sun panics
at the Front approaching.
Carriages
Tribunes
Prisons
revolve with the Earth.

There is a daily walk
in a caravan.
The body is watered by the Spirit,
as is the country by the Earth.
I also go around the Lady Sun,

round and around the Sun,
in sad thought,
with a lake of tears.
Life is
revolving around the Sun.
Turning into ashes
means death.

I cover my *asyḳs*[27] with gold,
freed for a moment from sad thoughts
to welcome a new age
with my mother-Alaš
who revolves around the Sun.
Noble ones are turned into flowers,
ignoble ones into ashes ...

[27.] *Asyḳ* – knee bone of a sheep, used to play national games, including *asyḳ atu* ('hit the bone') in which bones are thrown to knock other bones out of a line. It is particularly popular with boys.

A Letter to My Mother

Tăte,[28] in the midst of renewed grief
and longing, I disturbed your *aruaḳ*.[29]
I want to go on foot tonight
from Ḳarḳaraly to Žirensaḳal.[30]

I wandered about these green fields
often, full of yearning
until I reached you.
Strawberries stained my legs,
up to my belt I turned red …

On the way is a graveyard of ancestors.
Your son is coming – still crying.
Even if you leave this mortal world,
a trace will be left of a paternal home.

[28.] *Tăte* – depending on the region, a form of address to an older woman or man, meaning 'aunt', 'sister' or 'uncle'; it may also signify 'mother' (as in this poem) or 'father'.

[29.] *Aruaḳ* – ancestral spirit. It is believed that *aruaḳs* protect the living descendants, thus they are treated with deep reverence. Kazakhs visit their ancestral graves to ask for guidance; they make vows in the name of *aruaḳs* and call their ancestors' names in a battle cry.

[30.] Ḳarḳaraly – also known as Karkaralinsk, is the oldest town in the Ḳaraġandy region, an area of outstanding natural beauty. Aksunkar worked there in 1978–87. Žirensaḳal is the highest mountain peak (1,403 m) in Ḳarḳaraly National Park.

Hiroshima. 999 Paper Cranes

Nine hundred and ninety-nine paper cranes
made by a Japanese child, victim of Hiroshima.

At the instant of death, when the light
of his eyes was blowing out, he said,
probably in his delirium:
'This is my dream, not reality.'
He was imagining his one thousand cranes,
and a single unfinished crane
that proclaimed: 'This is not death.'

The satanic claws of the atom
represent the twentieth century.
I will raise a monument for Him in bronze,
nine hundred and ninety-nine paper cranes.

The Last Heir of the Yana Tribe

'You look like a rusted sharp sword.
Where are your eyes like lightning that spewed fire,
where your weighty words, last heir of Yana?'[31]

'Soul-less
Won't you look at me?
In my heart: the sorrow of descendants
dying ... over and over. Will you gloat
over this, child of civilisation?'

'Apologies ...
Descendants will analyse
the animated evil intentions.
Why do you think
mankind will gloat over me, and blacken me?'

'Will I say to the Devil
who shed my blood,
and left a black mark in my heart:
"Mankind cherished me in the palm of its hand"?'

'We become bait for rash notions –
we all do; you didn't understand me.
In a life short as a whip handle
you left, interested in nothing.'

'Who dragged the Earth into filth?
Cracking his lips:
your Yellow Gold – your Yellow Devil
that I will divorce forever.
Open your eyes!
Observe the graves!
Black clouds have captured the valley.
I'm not going to change my bow.
to your commotion named Neutron!

---

[31] Yana – tribe originating in South Arabia or Yemen, and which finally settled in Syria before the Islamic conquest.

I couldn't hug the sky like you did.
Let me love my Wide Steppe
and Blue Space
for I am going to stay in that space.
A spirit will support my body.
I was born in the steppe
and I want to die there.
Yet the place I worship
is vanishing from my eyes.
My birth in the steppe is my grief.
Maybe I will die in the city.'

'Don't be angry.'
'If I attack like an angry dog, forgive me, my child.
The history-fate tore my land to pieces like a dog.
I am the sole survivor of the tribe.
When the century ended, you came to me,
though sunlight and flowers are alien to me now.
God forbid you will repeat my destiny …
God forbid. Mankind!'

'I understand:
our descendants will get to the truth.
Is it true that because of this slaughter, my friend –
not one person, but a whole tribe
will disappear like this?'

'I know what you're getting at.
God: in forgetting their conscience,
they kill and ask who did the killings.
(How strange is mankind.)'

Translated by Patricia McCarthy

NESIPBEK AITULY
(b. 22.09.1950)

Nesipbek Aituly is a poet. He studied journalism at Kirov Kazakh State University (now Ăl-Farabi Kazakh National University) in Almaty, graduating in 1974. He went on to become head of poetry at the *Baldyrġan* journal (1974–84), an editor at Žalyn publishing house (1984–94), literary consultant at the Writers' Union of Kazakhstan (1995–96), and finally head of department at the *Žŭldyz* journal and *Ķazaķ Ădebieti* newspaper (1997–2001). Since 2001 he has worked for the Presidential Centre of Culture at the Eurasian National University in Astana. He is also the editor-in-chief at the *Altyn Tamyr* magazine.

His debut verses were published in 1972 in country-wide periodicals, his first collection appearing in 1974. His other collections include *Ăke turaly syr* (The Secret about My Father, 1974), *Žŭrektegi žaŋġyryķtar* (Echoes in My Heart, 1979), *Tŭnde ŭšķan tyrnalar* (The Cranes Flying at the Nighttime, 1980–84), *Ruhymnyŋ padišasy* (The Owner of My Soul, 2000), *Mŭķaġali-Želtoķsan* (2001) and *Băjterek* (2003). He is well known for the long poems *Bas sùjekter* (Skulls), *Žasynnyŋ synyġy* (A Fragment of the Lighting), *Najzaġaj* (Lightning), which were highly regarded and won national poetry contests multiple times (in 1976, 1977, 1978 and 1979). He is also the author of epic poems dedicated to well-known Kazakh historical figures and events. His Kazakh translations include selections from the works of Junus Emre, Bo Ziuyu, J.J. Rhodari, Mikhail Isakovski, Agniya Barto and Sergei Mikhalkov, as well as the Russian medieval classic, *The Song of Igor's Campaign*, and Ali-Shir Navaii's *Alexander's Wall*.

Aituly is poet laureate of the State Prize of the Republic of Kazakhstan (2012), an Honoured Worker of the Republic of Kazakhstan (2011) and a recipient of the Order of Parasat (2004).

A Rock Will Never Weep

The true poet refuses to leave a word unspoken.
What could a frozen heart or a worn-out mind conceal?
You are a falcon soaring high in the sky,
I am a rock unable to move.

A rock without feeling will shed no tears.
Mysterious birds equal to you
will not be born again.
Unless you rouse me with your lightning,
my deaf soul wouldn't flinch.

The Illusion of Wealth

Instead of living in a royal palace, feeling under siege,
it is better to own a simple abode where you're left in peace.
Even with parents as rich as Croesus, nothing's to stop you
losing your stash if wheeling and dealing lets you down.

The illusion of wealth, like a tiger, is always
prowling around, on the look-out for a sucker.
Don't polish your scythe in winter, saying you'll mow in summer.
If your steps are toxic, no grass will grow on your path.

You can't reach the edge of the world by running,
for life is short. Take the time to look into your brother's eyes.
However thrifty he may be, the glutton devours his store,
keeping nothing in reserve for that rainy day.

It doesn't matter who you are, a narrow grave
is all you'll claim from these wide-ranging lands.
A giant's body, toppled, will only hit the rock once.
What do you gain from all your lucre
when, in the end, it might as well be dust.
It won't redeem your soul when you face the grave.

You'll never make it across the water
unless God decides to patch up your sails.
At the end of your days, however skilfully
you handle a rod, you won't even catch a shrimp
in that boundless ocean.

There's nothing at all
in the world's tight womb
that won't in the end be destroyed.
Only the man who repents is proof against all evil.
Boiling water over and over doesn't turn it into oil.
Turn down the heat beneath your steaming kettle.

Living a Wonderful Life

Do you share my dreams, my darling,
when day and night I lie awake
like running water? Life then is resplendent,
a riot of colours, as all night long

I savour honey dripping
from the nightingale's tongue.
My eyes always see you in blossom
foaming on the apple tree.

Forever seeking the beauty I lack,
I ask the skies to grant you a magic carpet,
while I, dreaming of paths that lead
to the Milky Way, gaze down
towards the bottom of a deep abyss ...

Passing through the veils of mists
time and time again, I am a light
guarding the sky's lower reaches.
I am the servant of God.
With grace I allow the spirits to pass,
immersing you in bliss.

Oh, how sublime my life is!
Shaking out the stars as morning comes,
I rise in haste to reach you.

My head filled with weighty thoughts
I am sad as Kendebaj on his horse Kerķùla,[1]
when their colts with gold tails vanished.
Each morning, I return again exhausted –

but why would I tell all this to you?
However gently I leaned over, I would only
waken you and not disturb my great country
with my exquisite dreams.

---

[1] Kendebaj – warrior in Kazakh folk tales. Kerķùla is his spotted horse.

The Onagers' Playground

There are no onagers here, though it is still
called the 'Onagers' Playground'. The boundless
lands are calm. There is silence all around.
If you step forwards, invasively,
the snake attacks you from the bushes.

Where are you, onagers, the ones we know from legends?
You have left no trace apart from your name.
Will I also be reduced to a memory
that disappears like an August mirage?

There are no people either –
merely the ruins of winter camps.
The wind blows through rickety frames.

Our poor fathers who tracked the onagers
wandered across the hills as if
they too were among their number.
These hills have seen so much suffering.
It does not matter if you laugh or cry.

My poor people have always
shared in the fate of the onagers.
Weighed down by burdens in their own land,
inured to extremes on steppes and mountains,
they traipsed across them like drifting clouds,
and never laid claim on others' lands
even though they were dispossessed.

Where have you wandered, true onagers?
I am repulsed by the donkeys we have around these days.
Our poor land cries like a motherless creature.
Who can say where its onagers are?

Come, the empty mountain is silent,
It shudders then sleeps, paying attention to no one.
It's like a giant bird laying eggs for posterity,
but the eggs it lays are rotten.

I look at the Onagers' Mountain with a broken heart,
as if I'd received a hundred lashes.
That lost way of life in its death throes
is like a stallion struggling,
as if it were tethered in a woven-hair strap.

The Onagers' Mountain, you are not to blame.
Whenever you come to my mind
I can only grieve, recalling my own losses.

Take Pity on Sorrow Too

The last thing I ask of you, my soul,
is to take it easy and slow down.
If your sorrow falls asleep, exhausted,
leave him alone to take his rest.

God will grant him what he needs,
however moody he gets.
Perhaps he's pining for what he lacks.
Have pity on him once in a while

and leave him alone with his desires.
Let him have this drowsy night
to soothe those tortured feelings
buried so deeply in the heart.

Don't let him feel disappointed,
but recognise his worth.
Don't shake him awake too suddenly.
Lull him as you would a child.

Who else, but you, can help cure sorrow,
the sorrow that still pursues me,
corroding you, my soul?

You are the one who accepts
whatever I've been saying,
the one whom I can trust.
My anxious soul, take it easy.
Don't put such pressure on me.

For Our Sake

There's only one land for us and one flag only.
Why were we born as men, if not to defend it?
Our umbilical cords were cut in narrow rooms.
Our swaddling clothes were washed in bloody tears.

A man has to be a rock for his people.
God forbid that we are ever slaves again.
When your father dies, you yourself will be the father.
You cannot let the homeland perish.

If your father or mother should die, you'll weep,
you'll swoon, then stand again if your child dies.
But if your homeland dies, you'll never rise again.
You'll follow it to your death.

Once our Country died, but then revived.
Our Flag fell and was raised up again.
If I proclaim my country's name,
the spirit of perished heroes will rise.

Our Land and the Sun above it are one.
Pray for the wholeness of both.
Young man, the true worth of this country
is known best by those who once had no country.

We are ready again to lay down our lives,
prepared to face whatever may come.
Two hearts cannot beat in a single chest.
There's one Land and a single flag for the Kazakh!

So Many Troubles

There isn't a soul alive who hasn't had some bad luck,
but I've had more troubles than the hairs on my head.
There are so many people suffering in this world
and so little luck to go around. So how is God
to be expected to let them all have a share?

A poor man never gets a coat even if they fall from the sky.
God seems to favour the rich, even when their purses are full.
When a cow loses its calf because its udder would not yield,
it still won't relax for the poor man to milk it.

What becomes of a soldier, if the commander's a fool?
He'll lie down and die in a desolate canyon.
When I think of my past and reflect on today,
I see I'm surrounded by burial grounds.

The skilful stallions have all been maimed.
The giants moving the mountains have all died out.
Hard times will follow when the nation's troubled –
like a mangy dog losing its hair.

In ancient days the Kazakhs grew fat on water.
With no food or clothes they never gave up on life –
just as a camel in the depths of winter
gnaws its knees in despair, when it's tethered
to a spike and goes around in circles.

Like slaves we lost our mind in fantasies.
When we lost our self-respect, no one seemed embarrassed.
Stuck in the swamps up to our waist,
we brought advisers in from distant lands.

Even when we're boiling with rage,
the hardships of life will take their course.
Even when there's water in the depths of the abyss,
the bucket can't escape its chain.

If a burden is not removed by the will of God,
how can the poor man bear it?
An ass only works as hard as it needs to.
The wretch has never served the people well.

What would a fool know, who gives up his people's dreams?
He is like a chicken scavenging on every dump.
For an owl the top of rock will seem the highest peak.
For a mole his burrow is filled with light.

It is vain to boast. When we lie on bare ground
the rocks will cripple our backs.
If I fail to see you in the heaving crowd,
are you there at all, freedom fighter?

If you are, I'm sorry I never recognised you.
One of your nails is worth far more than any gold ingot.
Who will seek out the descendants of nobles?
I long to hear the sounds of falcon's wings,
what use is the squawking of cranes,
however many they may be?

Please, God, be our support in all our tribulations.
Wherever we go, wheeling and dealing tears us apart.
A shameless thief has taken us by the throat:
he spends our blood instead of money.

He sells the Qur'an. He trades the name of Allah.
The worst nightmares all come true.
There's even a price on running water!
Just wait, my brothers, and we will see
how justice will prevail
when the day of reckoning comes to pass.

Hard Times

When the snowcock[2] bird shrieks, the other creatures
forsake the mountains. When disaster strikes,
however far underground, it shakes the surface.
When times are hard, badgers lick the lamb's rump,
the lizards will cling to the cows' teats.

The bear yields to the wolf, and only attacks him from behind.
Abashed by the eyes of the locust, the snake retreats.
A well-fed kitten sniggers behind the dog's back.
The eagle hunts for mice in the owls' domain.

There's misrule and chaos on every front.
A filthy ass is braying at the sight of a mangy mare.
The tiger runs away at the sight of a dead lion's skin.
A camel is horrified when it sees a dead bull's head.

A spotted snake emerges from a length of twine
that someone tied around their waist.
Then when it creeps around the yurt
your body's convulsed with fear.
The nastier people get, the more abused
the decent folk will be.

Your dead father
will never return, however much you cry.
How tough we need to be
to see and endure such things.
There's no one to set up a stone
when a poor man dies.

---

[2] It is widely believed that snowcock have a special cry for when they feel unsafe.

If a slave collapses,
he's left to rot in dumping grounds –
the slave who owns nothing except his soul.
He was born and died, and then was lost to sight.
There are too many of those in power,
who claim to be descended
from men who ruled in the past.
Their descendants now have muddy boots
and the seats of their pants are worn.

Even if your name is on the ballot,
what throne, you think, will be awaiting you?
Resent the clouds, if they prevent
the Sun from shining bright.
If you are a true-born Kazakh,
go on, keep up with others:
when your brother passes by, set your dog on him.

A Dog's Life

I met a stray dog in the street.
He was too forlorn for words.
His appearance broke my heart,
as if a storm had just blown in.

He was so scrawny you could count his ribs.
His life was like a bowl with a hole in the bottom.
His eyes sank into his head
like two spoons of mercury.

He stared at my hands imploringly,
no longer caring for those
who'd chased him away.
Like a thief who searches for hidden wealth,
he rummaged around in every tip.

When I brought him home,
he began to howl, however. His tears,
like seeds, were ready to burst.
He wouldn't calm down,
even though I'd fed him.

He didn't like the rope chafing his neck,
so I had to let him go,
for he's determined by himself
which path henceforth he'd follow.

I Saw a Colt in My Dreams

I saw a colt in my dreams today,
I saw it playing and running free.
My fellow creature, where did you come from?
For a long time you have been at the bottom of my heart.

A pretty spotted colt with a flowing mane,
see it appearing from out of nowhere.
I thought back to days full of delight
when I myself played like a colt.

Not letting the dust settle on him,
the little animal goes tearing along.
It doesn't even notice
that flimsy strap about its neck.

Meanwhile I'm far away
in the city, seeking fame as a poet.
You don't know as yet, dear colt,
that straps will rub your chest,
your soft back subdued to the saddle.

Skittish colt, with the mane of an onager
and a falcon's face, are you in love also
with all the things around you?
You are my rock, my stallion.
You are always the first in the crowd.

Your mountains and plains are waiting for you.
I will never be finished listing their names.
My dear steed with wings of the wind,
you have no idea
of the traps that will entangle you.

For a long time you have been
at the bottom of my heart.
Today you trouble my soul.
I still think of your innocent eyes,
that I could gaze into a thousand times.

I saw the steppes in your eyes.
I saw the flowers.
I saw the sky and the Sun brightly shining.
It was a mystery to me
to think that a rider might whip you cruelly.

Green fields and grass are far from me now.
I think back to the days of childhood,
when I was free of all sins. Dear colt,
come across and say hello,
please visit me once in a while.

Translated by David Cooke

Black Notebook

Before me lies a shabby notebook
with cracked black binding.
Work your way through it,
slowly and carefully,
to discover a world
that is pure and rings out.
My soul flies there,
a dove with an injured wing,
to the steppe's open spaces,
to the dusty tracks, the winding
mountain passes,
unheard-of happiness,
the bitter taste of trouble,
the call of ancestors,
of bright flowers, meetings
and partings with parents.
Notice those lowered hands
refusing the kindness
they would wish to give.
There I left the tracks
of my feelings, of days
that cannot be forgotten,
moments of thirst
without a sip of water,
the waves of a clear blue life.
This notebook sings
of a dream,
of a son's sadness in a father's house,
of the beauty of a girl I loved,
promised to another ...
Of the days when that lost love
froze my heart, and even more,
the days that burned it.
Yet, still, I was thoughtless
and young nightingales
always sang in my soul ...
Now, slowly take a closer look:
in these lines is a world

that is pure and rings out,
where perhaps my soul weeps,
like a motherless foal.
Here are past and future ties –
mysteries, secrets, echoing spaces,
all drawing together in verse.
My dawn and sunset
gradually approaching …
The pain of failures,
unfinished business,
summits not reached,
my own deficiencies –
my happiness …
I sang about it,
I sang about it all
without a thought,
at the moment of falling short.
Here is my black notebook,
with all the rough copies.
When I laugh or grieve,
my poems are the springs
to quench my thirst.
Look into my world of words
torn from the heart.
The wind will burn your face,
and lead you into the hill's shadows,
that's when you will remember them
at that fertile place,
in spring time,
during the bad weather
in the midst of silence.
Then, the world of my soul
will expand all around
amidst the ridges and hills,
till you take your place in the whole.
And in time you and I
will be one as friends,
sharing in a single belief …
In this notebook I was
generous with my lines of verse –
willingly I squandered my heart.

Night Flight of Cranes

I heard the whooping of a flock of cranes in the sky,
as it completed its night flight.
Neither stars nor the Moon – just cranes, flying away,
suffering as they fly over the wide breadth of the fields ...

What longing in that whooping sound, such hysteria,
such closeness. My heart trembled like a wounded bird in my chest:
Maybe people shot you heartlessly in the wing?
Is the trouble now past? Or is it still to come?

Grasses sleep quietly, eyelashes closed.
Calling out to one another, you fly away from us.
Who drove you into the darkness, defenceless birds,
Who aimed their bloody claws at you?

Your anxiety has become an unexpected mystery,
as if for you, happiness will never be realised.
Is it just change that has cursed cranes with the task
of carrying to people their darkest news?

Beloved Steppe

To hunt you would need
to be in your own homeland,
where the steppe grasses stream
in an endless flow,
at the foot of the mountains.
It is a long time since
I have flown headlong
in pursuit of the golden eagle,
my right arm poised …
Without me you grieve,
like an arrow for its bowstring.
Tiger-like mountains,
compacted snow in your mighty ridges …
When the soul suffers,
who now will provide us
with these wide open spaces?
Who will give us a hand
leading us along beauty's trail,
to bring even greater joy
to the sweet miracle of hunting?
Steppe, no time to waste
in drawing your son into
your warm embrace …
… Sometimes I have such a deep longing,
and then it is a mystery –
what causes this eagle
to suddenly burst out in my soul?

Dusk

Once more twilight descends on us,
the expanse of the flowering steppe embracing us.
A sad shadow nestled up to the flowers,
the straight trail slipped into the grass.
Only the sky's fringes light up,
a last hint of sunset, like a bright scarlet ray.
Night, extinguishing these bursts, comes,
like a loved and weary traveller,
fog-ridden and dark.
The mist crawls like snakes into the expanse:
seeing neither grass nor bush –
even the high mountains have disappeared.
I walk directionless on the grass,
momentarily, in a haze.
I am only stirred by the thin song
of the cicadas for some reason.
I love the sounds of those cicadas,
their song goes on.
Now as I recall my young life,
did the Sun ever go down before the dawn?
I am in the freedom of the steppes
and mountains and rocks,
where tirelessly with my eyes
I sought that desired loss,
whose sweet name I so often whispered …
As I cover my eyes
I see flashes of dawn.
Here the fresh dew glitters,
to the song of the high-pitched cicadas …
The young wind whispers to me:
'It is as if the world has been reborn.'
Its loud heart beats in its chest,
like a winged skyrocket.
In this my native, familiar world,
where the old merges with the new,
you can see how great and small combine,
and how love meets hate.

It is hard to deal with life's difficulties
as you travel the wide expanse of the Earth.
But in your native land you can see
both great and small.
I see in the hints of a twilight dawn
that the darkness will disappear ...
It is not forever.
I am not in the past,
I am in the future –
laced with the life of today.

Translated by Belinda Cooke

BAKHYTZHAN KANAPYANOV
(b. 4.10.1951)

Bakhytzhan Kanapyanov is a poet, translator, screenwriter and film director. He graduated from the Kazakh Polytechnic Institute in 1974, before working for a year as an engineer-researcher at the Institute of Metallurgy and Enrichment of the Academy of Sciences. In 1975, his poetry was published in the journal *Prostor* and he subsequently worked as an editor at the Ķazaķfil'm (Kazakhfilm) studio. After two years at Ķazaķfil'm he took a degree in scriptwriting and film directing in Moscow, graduating in 1977. He has written the screenplays for more than twenty films. From here he embarked on a literature course at the Maxim Gorky Literary Institute, becoming senior editor at Žalyn publishing house as well as literary consultant at the Writers' Union of Kazakhstan (1984–91).

During his prolific career as a poet, Kanapyanov has not avoided controversy. He was disfavoured by the party apparatus for his poem 'Pozabytiy mnoiu s detstva yazyk' (The Language I Forgot), published in the journal *Prostor* in 1986, for daring to find fault with the USSR's policies. As translator he has helped popularise Turkic poetry for Russian speakers. As a social activist he famously visited the site of the Chernobyl nuclear power plant in the first days after the accident, subsequently writing 'Aist nad Pripyatyu' (Stork over Pripyat, 1987), which won the Lenin Komsomol Prize. Since that time, he has been actively involved in the creation of the anti-nuclear movement Nevada–Semipalatinsk (Kaz. Nevada–Semej). He is currently an academic of the Crimean Literary Academy, and chief editor of the literary anthologies *Literaturnaya Aziya* and *Literaturniy Almaty*. His contributions to the arts and social activism gained him the Independent Tarlan Award (2003), the Order of Parasat (2011) and the title Honoured Worker of Kazakhstan (2011), as well as a number of other national and international awards.

313

Listen, Listen In

You plunge your fingers
into the music box,
hear the bright cries
of black and white keys.

Their music lights up
what happened
on a whim:
I remember that street,
where we met by the pine.

Lose the frown: I'd better
listen, listen in,
listen in all I can
when we meet. The street lamps
squint behind the window
so no one will ever
wait in the wrong place.

I'll lead your slim fingers
away from the box.
When the music stops,
the road goes quiet.
All along it the street lamps
are lighting us up,
or is that music
sounding within us?

Lose the frown: we'd better
listen, listen in,
listen in all we can,
there at that pine.
Behind the window, our music
strolls down the street:
you can hear the bright cries
of black and white keys.

Inside the Ravine

The river flows over its bed,
whirls round what Heaven gave –
the blue air the mountain sheds
is a clean, cascading wave.

Within the ravine
the bark lets loose
the resin it holds,
and a ray of Sun
            will gleam:
they want April to come.
And over the sleeping spruce
in all of its blues
the mountain air goes cold.

In this World Where You Seldom Find

In this world where you seldom find
much sense, a shudder proclaims
your shape at the window frame.
Its only friend in the moonshine
is the taste of the young wine.

Nature has given us gifts
whose worth is beyond our grasp.
Its presents arrive as we shift
into Autumn. Fashion is fast.
Freedom and love are what last.

The Forest's Heavy Silence

The forest's heavy silence
is holding the snowflakes in balance.

A bird flaps in the branches,
but doesn't disturb the darkness.

Today's date – anyone know?
This morning's drowned in snow,

the fume-filled city too. Before us
the forest lies like a thesaurus.

Doing some grafting, I'm poised
with a branch, not far from that noise.

The snow that floats in the sky
begins to pour into my eyes.

On my shoulders, I steady this time
of hush, in these woods that are mine.

My Lover's Breathing Will Shake

My lover's breathing will shake
ever so slightly the air,
as if she were in the care
of a ghost in a butterfly's shape.

I will not try to find
the reason she keeps so calm.
The moonlit bed. My arm
extends to draw down the blinds.

Medeu

The mountain road would loop
along the hillsides,
the summits filled with the whooping
and honking of car-rides.

Tyres would swish, you'd observe
bright flag-masts, again
and again the skids round the curves
would drive you insane.

Repeating their turns, the skaters
would nimbly glide
and slice the ice with their blades
up on that mountainside.

The spiral of movement would sound
and tickle the nerves.
A seismic zenith was found
in the depths of the earth.

On scales and swings, we've swayed,
time after time,
points and scores our grade
at the finishing line.

Like mountain springs, everything
is set to unwind,
but still an invisible spindle
links heart and mind.

Where dung fuel stinks for eternity
by the misty banks
of a stream, the shepherd girl's free
among her lambs.

We Don't Know Where We're Going

We don't know where we're going,
we've come from who knows where.
We've nailed our final loan
and live in an age of despair.

Perhaps there's a path we must
walk down to the final sea,
where all prediction is dust,
and the stars are a swarm of bees.

They saw how my words would fall
by divining each stitch in a seam.
Like a gypsy clothed in a shawl,
my muse suddenly gleamed.

Hiding like files on a disk,
on the other side it appears,
that image the poet picks
before the daylight is clear.

Within the Leaves

What bird was that,
the bird whose wings
I just heard breeze
through the tree?

Maybe the leaves
high in the treetop,
those leaves are hiding
its body.

But the bird doesn't want
to nest up there,
to make its nest
in the treetop.

Held in the leaves,
it flaps and flaps
inside the leaves
incessantly.

The Tulips

Springy,
perhaps
    from dampness,
but with petals
    like litmus paper
that redden
in the air's
precipitation
from the tenderness
of numb fingers.

At the resort
it is the off-season.
Mountains.
Tulips.
The south.

I Remember the Moment I Froze

I remember the moment I froze
when a snake in the midday heat,
as if for eternity, rose
like a question, ahead of my feet.

There wasn't a way to turn back
or even leap to one side.
This was the end of the track,
and I stood there, petrified.

Just a metre away, as mute
as the wind, the snake rethought its route.
And its scorching stare, glass-stiff,
disappeared from the granite cliffs.

Translated by Alistair Noon

Mountain Road in the Mist

Mountain road in the mist,
visibility has become drowsy,
it nevertheless holds your gaze,
draws you in with a mythical attraction.

Somewhere on some slope
the chain of time has reversed.
Everything has changed radically,
though I don't know why.

The chronicle of past life
cuts off its run at the bridge.
My twin changed his lenses,
worked out his role from the sheet.

He grasped my mistakes.
He grasped my dreams.
No carefree smile,
just an arrogant grin.

Because of the mist
my double is hardly visible in the night.
The invisible wound aches,
won't move to the side.

My twin sits somewhere
in a car that is still running,
like an angel from the next world,
there to take me by surprise.

We will be friends, however.
We will succeed in crossing the pass.
Though I didn't recognise him at first,
when we came to the road sign.

We miss each other at the turning.
We'll flash our headlights before meeting.
Without a word we'll embrace each other,
silently, we will understand each other.

I will open the door at the ravine.
I will smoke at an uncertain hour.
Damp paper, like mist,
conceals an important decree.

But I have other driving licences,
my double took away mine.
With the wind my diary will carve out
these snowy days beyond the mist.

Along the Mountain River on Horseback

Along the mountain river on horseback,
from the lake all the way up the slope.
Sitting in the saddle, my life has been
arranged according to the season.

Along the mountain river on horseback,
to the bay's uniform step,
from without, I restored in myself
the Turkic roots of my language.

I understood flying dragonflies
and the flap of the Chinese hoopoe.
Tibetan stone grew on my chest,
beyond the river near the ford.

Turks, Tibetans, Chagatay,
brought forth writing on stone,[1]
weaving them with mountain epics
for future generation.

The eagle traced with its wing
the immortal poem of Tăņir,[2]
the horse kept driving me further
from the Saki[3] to the departed Hungarians.[4]

The grass came and went once more,
here before the yurt beyond the ravine.
The trail of the prehistoric Turk
does not break off.

---

[1] A reference to petroglyphs found in Kazakh lands, inscribed with all the mentioned dialects/languages.

[2] Tengri (Tăņir) primordial deity in the religion of the early Turkic peoples; god of the sky, the only creator of the universe, often paired with the 'earth-mother', Ümaj.

[3] Saki – also Scythians, a group of nomadic and semi-nomadic tribes who around 1000 BC lived in the Eurasian steppes.

[4] In the fourth and fifth centuries AD, the Hungarians moved from the west Kazakhstan territories to Europe.

Signs

On this stone, where there is morning dew,
I learned the runic signs:
here is a vertical line, the victoria[5] from the end
of the fourth century – when the Saki disappeared.

Parchment replaced animal hide,
then comes the era of rice paper,
but stone is eternal, preserved by these signs,
made by pioneer magicians.

Here is the sign of a signal flag – the path will be successful.
Here the sign of the bend – the right road.
I grasped the essence of the rune.
In it I saw God's command.

Here is a sign – like an inverted 'И'[6]
it removes the feeling of a closed circle.
You preserve it with your energy.
Under this sign you become free of disease.

Here is the sign of an angle – I see the landscape in it.
In hillside gardens frost does not melt.
I remember my childhood: my mother knitting a wool scarf,
with an incomprehensible pattern –

the magical stone *galdstraf*[7] that could travel to the stars.
Here you can predict fate from the Ritual Night
I seek the protection of the runes.
This is a means of curing myself.

[5.] Victoria – runic inscription comparable to the Latin 'V'.
[6.] И – refers to a Cyrillic letter with the sound 'ee'.
[7.] *Galdstraf* – magical pattern combining several runes in one image.

Tamġa Ystyḵkôl

Tamġa of Ystyḵkôl.[8]
Here you will get a suntan,
as it takes you along this mountain path
to the sacred stone,
where you sit and
dream of something good,
sensing the arrival
of your dusty footsteps.

Tamġa of Ystyḵkôl,
is tied to your antiquity,
with a ritualistic scarf,
and to *arša*[9] that lives near the stone.
There, also, there is the pass
that wakes a wanderlust in me,
and beckons Ḵašḵar[10]
out of invisible karma.

In the settlement of Opal
lie the ashes of Ḵašḵari.[11]
He opened to the world
the wealth of those
Turkic dialects,
showing how they lay at the root of all dictionaries,
thus carving out a name for himself.

I'll work out myself where poems come from,
and who has provided the key
from this transcendental sphere.

[8.] Tamġa Ystyḵkôl – resort settlement on the southern banks of Ystyḵkôl (Issyk Kul), rich
in petroglyphs.

[9.] *Arša* – plant, a species of juniper.

[10.] Ḵašḵar (Kashgar) – a city in Western China. For more than two thousand years, Ḵašḵar
was a strategically important trading post on the Silk Road.

[11.] Ḵašḵari (Mahmud ibn Hussayn ibn Muhammed al-Kashgari; 1005–1102) – Kara-
Khanid scholar and lexicographer of the Turkic languages from Ḵašḵar. He composed
the first comprehensive dictionary of Turkic languages.

Here, sitting by the stone,
tears wash away sins
and I will leave like a monk
with my poetic faith.

Tamġa of Ystyķkôl
rises like a lake-chalice.
This cracked amphora of moisture,
complements your image.
And the bird *samŭryķ*[12]
will build its nest beside the stone,
having touched the sacred paper
with its prophetic feather quill.

Translated by Belinda Cooke

[12.] *Samŭryķ* – in Kazakh folklore, a gigantic, powerful, typically benevolent mythical bird
which acts as a mediator between the three worlds: celestial (gods), earthly (man) and
underworld (the dead).

LYUBOV SHASHKOVA
(b. 28.11.1951)

Lyubov Shashkova has lived in Kazakhstan since 1971. She studied journalism at Kirov Kazakh State University (now Äl-Farabi Kazakh National University), following which she worked for various literary and creative organisations, including Temirtau local papers, Ķazaķ Radiosy (Qazaq Radiosy) radio station, Žazušy publishing house, the Writers' Union of Kazakhstan and *Kazakhstanskaya Pravda* newspaper. She has worked as deputy editor-in-chief on the *Prostor* journal since 2003.

Her ten poetry collections include *Pora podsolnuhov* (It Is Time for Sunflowers, 1984), *Dialogi s nadezhdoi* (Dialogues with Hope, 1991), *Iz treh knig* (From Three Books, 2000) and *Lug zolotoi* (Golden Meadow, 2006). The major motif of Shashkova's verses is the beauty of Kazakh and Belarusian landscapes. She also published the non-fiction story collection *Rasskazhi mne o sebe...* (Tell Me about Yourself, 2014). Lyubov Shashkova's *Hraniteli ognia* (Keepers of the Fire, 2006) creates portraits of major figures of contemporary Kazakh literature and culture, including Äbdižämil Nùrpejisov, Erkeġali Rahmadiev, Akim Tarazi, Olzhas Suleimenov, Ajman Musahodžaeva, Žaniâ Aubakirova and Žâmilâ Baspaķova. The book *Dva vol'nykh kryla* (Two Liberated Wings, 2011) consists of her Russian translations of works by Kazakh intellectuals of the early twentieth century, such as Ahmet Bajtùrsynov and Magžan Žùmabaev (Magzhan Zhumabayev). Her works have been published in Kazakhstan, Russia, Belarus and Korea, and included in Chinese, Ukrainian and Russian literary anthologies.

She has been awarded the Order of Ķùrmet, medals Eren Eņbegi Ùšin and 20 Years of Independence (2011), and international awards, as well as the title Honoured Worker of the Republic of Kazakhstan.

Song

Erejmentau, appear before me.
– Imanžùsip[1]

This great steppe.
Erejmentau melting in the haze.
Like a bullet fired into the steppe –
weary the golden eagle returns.

Hurled like an arrow,
the exhausted horse returns.
The tired Sun
rests beyond the far slopes.

The steppe is great
its borders – Erejmentau!
The steppe is great
for hunting, battle, and glory.

Only her song
flies in the blink of an eye,
soars above the ground
rises high into the sky.

Only one song
embraces the whole world –
all the great steppe
in the heart of the poet!

---

[1] Imanžùsip Ķùtpanùly (Imanzhusip Kutpanuly, 1863–1929) – composer, poet and singer.
The quote is from his song, 'Imanžùsiptiṇ ăni', (Longing for freedom), written during his
imprisonment. Erejmentau is an area in the Aķmola region.

In Vishnyovka

For Brother Ilya

The way the morning starts is simple –
we go to Vishnyovka[2] for milk.
Father sits on the bike.
I settle behind him on mine.
Having attached the milk churn to his rack,
he slowly pedals,
through the village, the forest, on the highway.
I know all his paths,
all his habits by heart ...
and I am desperate to tear away into the vastness.
I want so much to overtake my father,
and I quickly turn my pedals.
But we have an unwritten law
that he goes ahead on the track.
Before me lies the beauty of the neighbourhood,
cars flying along the road,
and for half an hour all I can see ahead
is my father's bent back.
But now at last – the Vishnyovka turning.
And some damn devil pushes me,
and I cheekily cross my father's path
out into the road, me rushing,
without looking where I'm going –
Don't worry there's no disaster ...
just a nervous cry of: 'Hey, look out!'
But there was actually no one there,
just me alone wheeling my bike.

I look closely. And from the abyss
the hidden back becomes visible.

[2.] Vishnyovka – agro-town (until 2009 classified as a village) in the Minsk region of Belarus.

Golden Meadow

Golden meadow in the morning at sunrise,
bird and bee-filled intoxicating grassiness.
But where does it go, this golden meadow,
where does it lead my heart and sight?

Golden meadow in the evening at sunset,
Sun's rays among pines, cast in copper.
Neither heart nor sight is ever enough
to carry away this golden meadow.

Golden meadow, with its honey aroma.
O, to lose oneself, to remain in this green country.
It still soars above its dandelions,
only it is no longer there for me.

O, golden meadow …

How Much Patience Is Needed to Judgement Day?

How much patience is needed to Judgement Day? –
God help me to love those who love me.
How much hope is needed – to wind this thread,
before blood, before prayer – to love and to love?
How much faith is enough – to forgive and forgive
those whose evil pride tries to break this thread?
How much love is needed – to tie the knots,
to fasten them with hope, with hope once more?

There Is a Pause Between Breathing out and Breathing in

For Bakhyt Kairbekov

There is a pause between breathing out and breathing in.
Having taken a breath in the forties,
with what kind of intoxication does the epoch
carry off the holy faces of my peers?

How distinct, how close are their voices.
How young do their eyes ever remain.
How eternal their strict souls …?

They are still all here. Still visible.
A minute, a minute of silence
in order not to finish telling –
but to listen …

Washing the Horse

Go on, wash the horse,
white-maned with its white apples. Let it walk into the Nùra.[3]
Like a boat lowered in the water, and into the air and into the sky,
it carries suntanned lads,
neighing loudly
to their slender-legged girlfriends.

Go on, listen close
on all shores
all shallows.
This victorious,
booming cry –
even the river will reply
with the hundredfold echo,
the distant song
of the winged steppe herds!

[3.] Nùra – 978 km-long river in north-east and central Kazakhstan.

Steppe

For Akim Tarazi

What a deep horizon there is
in winter below Ķaraġandy.
It is measured by heaven's *versts*,[4] so far –
that your gaze won't reach there;

that even birds are too weak to fly there,
that a rider is too weak to gallop.
To be left in the steppe
in winter – means death.

Here my soul lived,
in the vastness carried by the wind,
attracted to the far mirages,
embraced by the steppe …

Beyond inconspicuous Nùra,
lost beyond the snow fall,
at a completely different time,
here the same horizons drifted.

The train rushes at random
along its steel road from the station.
Far, far from that age long ago,
I know it is not coming for me.

It wasn't us who marked our paths
measured by the heaven's *versts*.
I look at the steppe in the empty gloom.
I recognise it and I weep.

[4.] *Verst* – an obsolete Russian measurement of length, each *verst* equivalent to 1.1 km.

A Sigh

Mama, your sigh – an added weight on my shoulders …
– Fariza Ongarsynova[5]

There, where spring sand
trickles through the cracks,
aryk[6] dried up.
The unhurried creak of the cradle
is audible.
Or is it a mother's sigh?

There, where the sky
plunged into the eyes
of the Berezina,[7]
the sighs of a prayer
are audible
both day and night.

Ah, they are a mother's sighs,
an added weight on the shoulders –
all the time so heavy.
But why is it that life is no lighter
without them
but somehow more painful?

… Where is it that
your aeroplane forces
its way through the clouds?
The mother's sigh
follows it
like a flying cloud.

[5.] From the poem 'Anammen ăŋgime' ('Conversations with Mother') by Fariza
Ongarsynova (see also pp. 75–93), translated by the National Bureau of Translations.
[6.] *Aryk* – small aqueduct used to irrigate land and provide a settlement with its water needs.
[7.] Berezina – river in Belarus, a tributary of the Dnieper River.

Apple Harvest

For Valery Mikhailov

Apples, apples – put them by for winter.
August comes. And with it the apple *Spas*.[8]

In childhood apples would lie in the child's skirt.
Such happiness for so many to lie on your native land.

Apples fall into the Berezina.
I cannot catch this wave of stolen cache …

Ah, the river flows away,
hardly visible from the distance …

Since that time I have tasted apples to the full.
I know the secret of their rich tartness.

The secret of the river reveals itself in time.
It is the essence of my life.

The secret of Mount Tabor's[9] light
remains till then, a mystery to me –

Perhaps, that's why there is so much grief
for those who wander in darkness on our native land.

Will we be touched by the Transfiguration?[10]
Apples, apples … apple *Spas*!

[8.] *Spas* – one of the three summer holidays devoted to Christ the Saviour ('saviour' in Russian means *Spasitel*).
[9.] Mount Tabor – in Christian tradition, the site of the Transfiguration of Jesus.
[10.] Transfiguration – a holiday in the Russian Orthodox Church that celebrates the Transfiguration of Christ.

Geranium

And guardian angels talk to children
– Mikhail Lermontov[11]

… That never to be forgotten gift of childhood
wakes you in the early morning –
the Sun with a smell of geraniums.
Scarlet ball through the curtains.

Whose were the most delicate fingers –
that joined each tiny petal to another
to gather together this living flame
into this fiery flower?

So that a heavenly angel
on invisible roads
could just pop in
with its soft song,

so that in peace, and in harmony,
and under his sacred gaze
a new day could begin
filled to the brim by the Sun.

So that, like a full ball of geranium,
the day could be lit from inside
by the endlessly generous midday
and the tenderness of the late sunset.

So that family tradition could be
laid out in the book of life:
childhood. Scarlet ball of geraniums.
Angel. Grandmother. And I.

[11.] From the poem 'Svidanie' ('The Tryst'); translated by the National Bureau of
Translations.

There, Where There Is a Little Log Cabin

1.
In the foothills grass grows up to your waist,
honey poured into the air.
Angel on the left. Angel on the right –
Georgie and Nikita.

A child's palms
hold my open hands.
The world is known to be good –
wherever Georgie and Nikita are.

And the roads have no end.
Good God, help us,
here are Nikita and Georgie –
protect them and direct them.

2.
There, where there is a little log cabin,
where the mountains circle over everything,
where the stream burbles close by,
morning comes in on the porch.

A small ray of light, as a hare hops
from the door to the ceiling.
Then to Nikesha and Gosha:
Come outside – it's a lovely day!

Come on, you've had enough sleep!
Don't lie in everyone – it's summer.
Take your place on the planet,
start to make it better.

Valley

1.
To wake to a roll call of cockerels
and the sinking shadows of invisible little birds,
and the far lowing of cattle,
adds to the neighbourhood's plentifulness.

The morning is as if thoroughly washed out,
burning, overflowing, playing.
A light breeze runs its fingers over
the leaves of the *ķaraġaš*.[12]

It is the most peaceful place in the world,
lying between the Tùrgen Hills –
Oh what was that! Suddenly something in the night
seems to be shaking the earth's foundations.

What is it that is quivering there in that mass of rocks,
reeling with horror before us as if to attack?
No – calm down. It is a whale-fish
lightly turning in the lower depths …

The day will rise and the best of world's
life-giving light will be lit.
The nearby cockerels singing will compete
with your endless cries at night-time terrors.

2.
The valley rests in the palms of mountains –
a flowering place like God's paradise.
When it trembles it is a trembling giant.
O what is this earthly trembling?

In the Lord's palms the earth lies warm.
Only madness and filth send us into the abyss.
Your will is master and sovereign over all.
Do not hold your hands out to anger …

---

12. *Ķaraġaš* – lit. 'black tree', a common name for an elm tree.

Tau Tùrgen

For Andrei Kozlov

The mist circles the mountains,[13]
day plunges prowling into the drizzle
but you start to peek through its gaps:
and see it is not autumn's late malice.

Moisture and spring rains driven,
speeding up the arrival of future greenery
with its cloud of foliage. It is already
turning light through the darkness.

There, shaking off the rain,
the branches of the apricot tree start to tremble.
It is the trembling of birth.
It is the world at its beginning.

Pushing through the curtain of mist,
flashing with heavenly eyes,
the first needle tip of the very first ray
pierces through the gaps in the mountains.

Here, the edge of the heavens is touched,
capturing thrones on the hills.
And then, and then – the light catches,
and the hills and valleys light up.

[13.] Tau Tùrgen – recreational site near Almaty.

Time of Berberis

1.
The slopes above the burbling river,
become consumed with a red flame.
The world, that yesterday was still green,
now enters the time of the berberis.

At the time of late heat,
things have been stored up for winter.
So that life could flow on
with a tart autumn flavour.

2.
In the confusion of wild branches
there is a world of prickles and violets –
the burning flame of the wild rose,
the ripe hawthorn is like a pendant.

I force my way through the prickles:
Am I enjoying this?
Is this work or pleasure?
Hey! Who's that whistling on the branch?

You there, my friend, don't be sad.
The first frost will strike.
Crazy leaves will fly off,
and then the fruit will be easy to reach.

You are right, fortune teller bird,
for me in this moment before winter,
this revelation of late berries
is more precious than in summer.

3.
Along the red Tùrgen slopes
a childish hubbub winds below,
boils merging with the river,
and flows under the eternal sky.

To continually extend this tie
of light carefree sounds,
so that, playing and laughing,
life flows to our grandchildren.

Translated by Belinda Cooke

TYNYSHTYQBEK ABDIKAKIMULY
(b. 20.07.1953)

Tynyshtyqbek Abdikakimuly began his working life as a specialist in various practical fields (electrician, miller, turner, driver, projectionist) between 1973 and 1989, and subsequently went on to study Kazakh language and literature at the Semej Pedagogical Institute (1989–95). He has worked for various creative arts organisations over the years, including the Literary Museum of Abaj, Semej regional branch of the Writers' Union of Kazakhstan and the newspaper *Alaš ùni.*

Abdikakimuly wrote his debut poems when he was fourteen, but published them in nationwide newspapers in his thirties. Much later, he published several collections of verses, including *Akšam hattary* (Evening Letters, 1993), *Yrauan* (Dawn, 2000), *Alkoŋyr dùnie* (Mysterious World, 2014), *Besinši mausym žùpary* (The Aroma of the Fifth Season, 2017), and two volumes of *Kas sak aŋkymasy* (The Knowledge-Revelation from God about the Pure Scythians), printed in 2001 and 2003. Literary scholars consider him to be a representative of emphatically intellectual poetry, on account of his erudite, ornate style and daring linguistic experiments. In his works, Abdikakimuly endeavours to analyse ancient cosmic principles, but through the unique prism of a Kazakh worldview. His poems have been translated into Spanish, Chinese and Kyrgyz.

He has won numerous awards, including the State Prize of the Republic of Kazakhstan in Literature (2018) for the poetry collection *Alkoŋyr dùnie*, the literary prize named after Tôlegen Ajbergenov (1989) and the Grand Prix of national poetic competitions (1990, 2007). He was awarded the Eren Eŋbegi Ùšin medal in 2011 and the State Scholarship in Literature, first in 2003 and then 2011.

Frosty Feeling

With my eyes opened,
my legs stretched,
I arrived into this world!
Is it consciousness of people?

Was my heart feeling presence
of some strange mountain spurs?
What kind of terrain? ... Unknown.
I only know for sure it was winter.

January, with its frozen ashen ears,
doesn't listen to anyone.
I shouted,
and a rainbow burst out
of my mouth ...

Did crows become fat
pecking on the steppe's brain?
I want to disturb the tranquillity
of the silent steppe.

Our life is so brief – and I failed
to find one truly honest soul.
All my life I groaned with anguish,
now I'm dead ... and in tears.

Red fringes of thoughts
are nibbled by the moth-sorrow.
Winter is dancing around me
its bones crunching.

The cold-blooded stars will appear.
I'm too lazy to feel anything.
The Moon smells my face
Wolves – my death ...

Word

In mysterious moments
when your head begins to sink into the abyss of sleep,
you may be amazed, you may be angry,
you may feel stressed or even ashamed,
hearing the words that shout inside your brain.
Words – radiant people without any form or shape –
only you can hear and understand them.
This is their only difference from the real world.

In a brief moment when you feel free
from your slavish existence
let's take a deep look into the images of words, my friends.
Some words are like the breeze of a thousand heavenly
dreams.
Some words are impossible to utter, they will instead cry.
Some words are like a rope thrown over your neck.
Some words are fairer than a beauty.
Some words can revive the dead!
Some words can ruin your life altogether.
Some words are a thousand times more
meaningful than the Bible and the Qur'an.

Our brains are rife with so many evil words too –
yellowish smelly things –
they rattle inside us, alien like a *kaffir*.[1]
If we are able to control them,
they will make us happy
with their thousands and thousands of caterpillars.

Spring is upon us.
When the light-rain pours on us stormy feelings,
the brightest brains that travel in a form of clouds
will produce thunder and lightning!
That will be the day when people
will realise their divine purpose.

[1.] *Kaffir* – non-believer or infidel in Islam; in Kazakh colloquial speech also a synonym for 'dishonest', 'ignominious' or 'cruel'.

So let's think about it.
We can't control our minds and our feelings.
Yet you call this existence a real life?
Tomorrow,
when we expect to meet our end
coming from outer space
speaking in human language,
when we have finished our last meal,
only the sacred Word can lift us up to God!

Sometimes

Sometimes,
when the frost is as angry as forty devils
I can leave the home
without trousers … and in a wet shirt.
Sometimes,
I can speak with the humans like an angel.
Am I innocent?
Not at all, I have no shortage of sins.

Sometimes,
I go into the city greeting
everyone on my way, full of songs.
Sometimes, I bring bright laughter
to a room full of darkness.
Am I carefree?
Not at all … Sometimes I lose my senses
not able to wipe away the tears.

Sometimes,
I bow politely when I see a strikingly beautiful girl.
Sometimes, I happily splash about in a pool playing with a
foolish child.
Have I nothing else to do?
Not at all … Sometimes I even want to plant an apricot tree
but only in my

mind …

Sometimes,
when my brain is full of night tremors,
I just want to catch the worm of sorrow with my hands.
I want, briefly, to die and fall into the grave,
and ask how's life of Aŋķyr and Mùŋkir, the angels of an
afterlife.
Am I mad?
Not at all … I managed to steal even from the devil because
of my cunning.

Sometimes,
a sobbing soul inside me
is at peace even with locusts.
Sometimes, I happily agree even with the slander of the
damned one ...
Be that as it may, at least I don't run back and forth like the
others,
between meals and toilets.

Muse

She's a miraculously beautiful Girl …
But,
I will never hug and kiss her tenderly,
even if I would die for want of it.
I'm only concerned that someone
can jinx her or gossip about her.
Next to her – even the Flower of Happiness
is just an ordinary flower …

When she's around –
I'm always comfortable – be it a grave
or the most honourable place,
I will grow grass from my sighs,
move the time itself back and forth,
in the form of an angel.
For you who don't believe these words,
I wish you could be in love like me.

When she's around – I'm God in my own way:
I know how to solve any unsolvable riddle,
I forgive an unforgivable sin …
Just to talk about her was a relief
for my suffering heart, life was good.
I won't let my eyes look at her beautiful body,
I won't smell the pure fragrance of the flower pinned on her
                                                chest,
otherwise I will end up in one bed
with a shameless devil.

She's a miraculously beautiful Girl!
Next to her Spring's light is just an ordinary light.
And me – I'm just a Thought
and a Bird of Happiness made a nest on my head.

The Same Illumination

The same illumination, which remained a mystery
                                    even for the Qur'an.
I never cease to be surprised by its secrets.
Even a snake that manages to pass right through It,
becomes a full-bodied creature.
Musk turns into a flower with sadness.

If It really wanted,
It would be faster than the light,
which travels a thousand times quicker.
Or It would read poems to the Earth.
Or It would sit down and listen to the Sun.
Even an animal would be more like a man,
following It everywhere.

Does It own both love and knowledge
speaking in the language of Blue Sky?
When the bullet of conspiracy hits one side of It,
it flies out from the other side in a form of a singing
                                    nightingale!

What's the point of talking or not talking about It.
It is such a marvellous illumination
which has the right to eternal life:
The Poet's Mind!

End of August

End of August.
The soul is in love with everything around.
Milk's surface in the wooden bowl shudders.
Yellowish leaf falls on the table,
no one to pray at its funeral.

My excitement died down at once.
Shall I wait for one in turban[2] for this dead leaf?
I whispered something about autumn and greenery.
My prayer was always a poem.

Light green song ... did it dispel any sadness?
Gloomy October ahead ...
I called for a wind to cast a spell. It didn't come.
Poor leaf ...

I buried it, covered it by soil.
Laments would be plenty ...
I felt as if sadness
was consuming me.
The wake passed.
My wooden bowl is empty.
Sincere blessing ...
I smell like winter ...

[2.] 'One in turban' – mullah who is invited to read a funeral prayer.

I Confess

I confess,
I'm a very stubborn person.
Muscles of steel – that's me.
If anyone tries to block me on my path to goodness,
I will just punch them right in the face.

If those who became rich dishonestly
try to command me,
I will happily kick their asses mercilessly,
leaving them with blue bruises
for life!

I am fair in my own way.
Oh, if only people understood it!
If some husbands beat their wives,
I will beat them with pleasure
in front of their spouses!

The main thing for me is to keep my body
and mind in shape!
Thinkers and people of religion,
who cause ordinary folk to suffer
should certainly receive the lash,
despite their arrogance and the khan's[3] power,
so the good are not enslaved by the bad.
And, as for those
who betrayed their Father's language –
these – I will shoot on the spot!

My sorrow is cruel but very honest.
It is a pity that this crazy saint – the law – exists.
Otherwise, I would make all scoundrels scream with fear.
I won't be afraid of what sin I commit,
because a thousand people don't find the strength to raise as
the banner
the words that I have cherished:
'My country!'

[3.] Khan – title of a ruler in Central Asia, equivalent to a king.

If My Paper Should Die

If my paper should die, its bones yellowed with age, let it be.
If my pen should die it will bleed to death.
That's the unknown for you.
Rich and enlightened, listen to my poems
written on the brow
and full of the fragrant musk of sorrow.

The Sun's energy – its thirty-two rays
are in my thirty-two teeth.
So I can even watch over the darkness,
and I can see the animal in human form.
There is an angel on the tip of my tongue.
There is an infinity inside me.

I love life tomorrow and today.
My heart carries a load heavy as the sky.
I would even fall in love with the *albasty*[4]
if her dream is bright enough.
There's even a hidden glow in the mischievous base of my
thirty-two vertebrae.

All sixty-two veins of mine form a divine root.
My sadness is a special one, different from sorrows of
the mortal.
I am like a tiny bud inside a fragrant thought,
able to perceive God as well –
I'm that poor fellow called a Poet.

[4.] *Albasty* – in Kazakh mythology, a demonic female creature that can harm a mother-to-be
and a lone traveller.

Hope

I usually sit in the room for songs,
where I'm almost absorbed by a sadness-swamp.
God sits in the room for guests,
reading my fate and smiling.

We are together in one house.
There's only one wall dividing it into two parts.
When I open the door, there's no one on the other side.
That frightens me.

But I know for sure one covenant.
I'm not a child.
God will open His arms for me,
once I can walk through walls.

Well, I'm not a poet yet.
And my song isn't a poem as such.
Every day
in the morning
I check the wall poking it with my forefinger …

My Room Is Full of Books

My room is full of books.
I know most of them well.
Some of them are about science.
I smell some of them every day,
as if they smelt of my homeland's juniper.
Some of them reek of the dead oceans.
So much water turned into paper at once.
Some books are labourers, shedding sweat.
Some shed tears from their pages.
And those that are 'sent from the sky'
don't know that the Sun has its own miraculous mind –
they are dark fairy tales.

Yes, there are eloquent ones among them,
all equal in their own way.
Some books are dead already, waiting to be sent to a grave.
Others are like treacherous rivers driving you crazy on their waves.
There are books that take you to history's shores like a real crossing.

There are many books.
Some are like wine,
others taste like *šūbat*.[5]
Some leave me altogether following my guests.
There are wise books among them showing the way …
If I should try to measure their combined energy,
would it be a billion horse power?

There is finally one book that is written
only by my angels –
I dream about this book often …

[5.] *Šūbat* – beverage made from fermented camel's milk, popular in Central Asia.

Fifth Season of the Year

With views as warped as a shelduck egg,
theocracy talks nonsense all the way.
Technocracy exalts itself as well.
With the pricked-up ears of the radars
and other devious gadgets,
We sit between them amazed,
looking alternately left and right.

Oh, Son of the steppe,
who recreated the breeze
from the miasma of the world's waste,
don't be like us.
Blossom.
Be inspired.
Then, before you leave for the Blue Sky,
please slowly explain for the benefit of people
the meaning of a false existence.

Whatever you say, say it
with a breeze's gentleness –
if you show your anger,
this generation with its mind and brains
armed with lasers, computers
and raving electronic senses,
will aim and shoot
straight into your bulging eyes!

If, before the giant gods
of different countries you say:
'Listen!
The Sun's bright needle will play melodies
of the four seasons on a vinyl disk of the
rotating Earth ...'
I shall have my conclusions.

Fire is a right-hander and water is a left-hander.
But what about wind and dust?
Leave it ...
A great mind's concept blessed with fragrant thoughts –
we call it *Paradise*.*
If two of us – like-minded people – should say this,
everyone apart from deaf people,
will humiliate us.
The laws of hell?
What about our heads?
What about technology?
Don't shudder.
May is wrapped up in a yellow cloud of buds:
talking non-stop about the meaning of life.
Animal world,
insects and all wildlife,
birds and fishes,
everything –
– came from the Grass Stem.
Oh, computer friend,
let Ķydyr[6] bring luck to you as well!
Let the chlorophyll bring you happiness!

Inside my brain, a chemical thought process takes place too.
My chromatid turned the stench into a pleasant breeze.
That's the merit of a Paradise in my head.
My dearest Son of the steppe, support me too.
Support me and then rush to the Blue Sky!
There you'll find a true Paradise-brain!
Sitting in the star valley of a limitless universe,
talking about the whole world, flowers falling from his mouth,
smelling forever with an aroma of a photosynthesis-musk.

[6.] Ķydyr – legendary saint who brings luck, happiness and prosperity; he also grants
people's wishes and helps those in distress. In Kazakh mythology, Ķydyr can appear in
many guises, hence the saying 'One of the forty is Ķydyr' (that is, every person should be
treated with respect).

Technocracy exalts itself as well.
Theocracy talks nonsense all the way.
Blind Faith,
food and drink...
They don't care about anything else.

There's Paradise-luck in our heads!
The sun is a Paradise!
The pure sun!
Kôk Tăņir[7] together with the heavenly consciousness
makes everything around fragrant.
Spring is Paradise!
Summer is Paradise!
Autumn is Paradise too!
For eternity.
Winter itself sighs Paradise on your window.

*One's luck (heavenly consciousness).

[7.] Kôk Tăņir – (lit. 'celestial Tengri') primordial deity in the religion of the early Turkic
peoples; god of the sky, the only creator of the universe, often paired with the 'earth-
mother', Ůmaj (Umay).

Actor

The Galaxy – a brocade curtain,
closed to all.
Clouded Clio's voice …
Did you solve its mystery?
Is it heavenly or hellish?
Don't pass by not paying attention.
That space is full of mirages.
It sways and bewitches …
A fragrant aroma of songs wakes up its senses and casts a shadow
full of *aruaks*.[8]
An orchestra's fingers are barely shaking.
How many days will stream down from the face of your fate?

Be quiet!
Can you hear in a whisper of this mortal world,
how someone is walking pompously
with a mask on his face,
making quick and silent predictions,
enflaming the inner questions of the audience?
Maybe he's looking for honesty everywhere –
from earth to sky?
But you can feel a whiff of a demonic cold
every time he moves.

Theatre hall – space,
your skull – a spoon hungry for truth …
This being walks confidently
in his constantly changing mask:
a savage,
a demon,
a fairy,
a dog with a black spot …
These images light up one after another.
Only death is not among them.

[8.] *Aruak* – ancestral spirit. It is believed that *aruaks* protect the living descendants, thus they are treated with deep reverence. Kazakhs visit their ancestral graves to ask for guidance; they make vows in the name of *aruaks* and call their ancestors' names in a battle cry.

Melpomene, Terpsichore ... All Muses are his favourites.
He wears endless nuances of feelings – laughter, tears.
If accompanied by a patron with huge horns,
he's ready to play God with passion!

For you and me –
the green steppe,
red sunrise,
autumnal fog,
bluish snow.
There's nothing artificial in all this.
An owner of the mask brings suffering
to an ever-changing society,
everyone but babies is a member of this drama.

Even a king had to play the role of a slave.
Beauty is seduced and sold by a pimp.
Grief was flying from the church's bell as well:
the wretch was beaten because
he 'didn't become an archimandrite'.[9]

If you realise that it is impossible to live like that,
take off all your living masks and throw them away.
Continue to throw them away as if you're enraged by the revenge
till you get to your saddest face ...
And after that carve this law of stone
with your own front teeth:
'Saints should never cross the threshold of the theatre.'

I also considered myself a genius and lectured everyone.
Meanwhile, a creator-playwright's pen was busy ...
Only the hostile master of masks watches us all closely.
At the very end, he covers the stage with a shroud.
Interval.

Galaxy – a brocade curtain,
fluttering in space ...

---

[9] Archimandrite – in the Eastern Orthodox and Eastern Catholic churches, 'archimandrite' originally referred to a senior abbot whom a bishop appointed to a supervisory role.

Sometimes, You Know …

Sometimes, you know, my eyes and soul
want to solve the secrets of credible innovations,
somehow hiding all my fears and doubts.
But,
behind all books – comparable
to laudatory inscriptions on stones,
people shout, hungry for truth.

Sometimes I want to drink the wine
of reason to the last drop …
I want even to go to prison,
in search of justice.
But,
some devil holds me back,
repeating: 'Stop-stop!'
I feel sick that I should have behaved like that then.

Sometimes I want to go somewhere,
just wander off,
to distance myself forever from fools.
But, wherever I go,
As soon as a wooden block sees my head,
It starts to look for an axe.

Sometimes I really want to be a devout believer of some religion –
to prostrate on a prayer mat or to cross myself.
But damn this sort of slavery
when you are torn all the time
between the mortal world and the Creator!

Sometimes cruel night,
its face burned by smallpox,
leaning in with its bright moony ear,
overhears endless questions
rattling in my mind.
Aŋḳyr and Mùŋkir – angels of afterlife –
are questioning me ...
How many times I sobbed terribly
before this merciless court of consciousness.
But,
in the morning,
with something tasty boiling in its pan,
life with all its temptations awaits ...

The Night-Sky Charms

The night-sky charms with its
never-ending rainbows.

I'm moved:
as if I'm back to my childhood!
This night – a balmy one, and everything in it – from the
beauty that spills from my heart to all living things around –
all are my people ...!

Night-sky.
Living sky.
Continued into a non-existing World.
One breath is equal to ten centuries.
I think it indulges Itself
in bright-green limitless thoughts
like a mystery song
in the dream of the sleepy black earth,
all because it's a second miracle after God.

I want to live my life
like this beautiful Night.
I want to hug alders growing in its abyss.
I want to be naked like its Moon,
to bark as its idle dog I want too.

God-*Kumalakšy*[10] (who is above everything)
tells fortune using stars –
their lives and deaths becoming one.
Unceasingly reborn, unceasingly blooming,
Oh, black sky,
your greyhound breeze
sniffs my body from time to time.

[10.] *Kumalakšy* – fortune teller who uses 41 beans or stones or sheep dung (*kumalak* means sheep dung in the Turkic languages) sorted in piles, to predict the future.

This Night – a Night to arouse all the senses.
This Night – the fears and joys of all thinking beings.
… I poured in one gulp into my consciousness
all the bats and moths
that can manage
to reach the tailed stars.

Translated by Rose Kudabayeva

YESENQUL JAQYPBEK
(10.02.1954 – 14.11.2013)

Yesenqul Jaqypbek was a poet and composer. He graduated from Kirov Kazakh State University (now Äl-Farabi Kazakh National University) in 1990 and worked for various cultural and mass-media organisations in Žambyl district over the years, including the newspaper *Atameken*, where he was editor-in-chief.

His recognition as an improvisatory poet came when he won several *ajtys* (traditional poetry contests) and became the first poet laureate of the republican television competition of *ajtys* in 1984. His verses were first published in a collection of young poets of Kazakhstan entitled *Ķarlyġaš* (Swallow, 1984). His individual volumes are *Aġymnan žarylamyn* (I'll Tell You Everything, 1986), *Biz ekeumiz* (You and Me, 1990), *Žeriṇe tabyn* (Bow Down to Your Land, 1994), *Žanķissa* (The Tale of My Soul, 1996), *Esil dùnie-aj* (O, Life, 1996), *Bizdiṇ eldiṇ žigitteri* (Žigits of Our Land, 1999), *Būl žaz da ôter* (This Summer Will End, 2001) and selected poems in two volumes (2014). He initially tried to revive forgotten Kazakh folklore traditions in poetry, and some of his later works are considered to be fine examples of philosophical-meditative reflections of life and death in Kazakh poetry. Jaqypbek is also acclaimed as an author of popular *terme,* a genre of lyrical morality poems in Kazakh folk art that weds verse and melodic compositions. Among them are 'Ķara kùz' (Dark Atumn), 'Ôziṇdi aṇsap' (Longing for You), 'Ôner adamy' (The Artist), 'Žùldyzdar bärin bolžajdy' (Stars Foretell Everything) and 'Tùmandy tùn' (Foggy Night).

Jaqypbek has been awarded the medals Eren Eṇbegi Ùšin (2010), 10 Years of Independence (2001) and 20 Years of Independence (2011) and the State Scholarship in Literature (2011).

I Have No Secrets

I have no secrets.
Whenever I have any, I never keep them.
My temper is like a pure, wide ocean.
I treat my loyal friends with frankness,
opening my heart wide as a gate.

I have no secrets.
I have told them all.
My friends know every secret I ever had.
People only have secrets when they dread
losing their position, betraying the truth.

I have no secrets.
If I had one, you'd know it.
You might even laugh at it,
but there are rogues keen to use my secrets
as weapons against me.

I have no secrets.
I told every secret I ever had.
I do not have a hidden tempter.
… But, my dear girl, I did have a secret,
one that I kept from you and could not utter.

O, Life

I never winced when I was called 'bad',
and goodness knows why I was hurt when called 'good'.
But O, my heart, why did you become sick?
Did someone touch harshly your gentle soul-string?
When we face the Ka'aba and pray, we are loved by God
yet it is so hard to please a man.
Life, O Life, why are you such a puzzle?

We don't notice what is white and what is black –
the world of people has such variety.
Words, though, do differ, coming from multiple sources
and my poor heart aches when words curse.
What do I fear from those in power?
Why do I feel everything so personally?
A fight for thrones or for luck seems to me
to be the fight of white and black, proving
that the Augean stables still have not been mucked out.

O Life, dear Life, is there any cure for this?
I was proud when someone said to me, 'You are bad.'
I trembled like a summer leaf in a breeze.
Yet when I heard someone say, 'You are good',
take note, my heart could not stop shaking.

To My People

My people treated me kindly.
They still express their love for me
and for a long time I have taken refuge
in their strength. Although my life now
is near its end, I keep struggling
to live it as best as I can.
When I took refuge in my people's strength,
they pitied me, sympathised with me,
loved and understood me.
Arrogant ones edited my verses,
high mountains cast their shadows,
but still my heart is full of gratitude.
Many pitied me while sympathising
and would not leave me alone.
I was a tree whose flimsy branches were bent by birds.
People's kindness made me a sturdy tree.
When my throat gets dry from thirst,
people wet my tongue with drops of water.
Even if some are ignorant,
many, on the other hand, are good.
Nobody has surpassed me in this life
yet I have never beaten anyone in a race.
I think deeply about my people, and believe
true wealth means having a native land.
What would I do if I was treated as something
that could be thrown away?
All the treasure I possess consists of
good intentions and an honest soul.
I am the poorest person in the world,
but my dinner is like that on a lord's table.
Whenever in life I experienced hardships,
I witnessed my people's kindness.
When I recall the past, I feel like weeping.
Life will go on, time will pass
but kindness is a gold that never grows old …
May kindness never wear out.

A Foggy Day

When the mist unfolds its sails,
foggy clouds float over the land.
Even though fog blocks my mind,
I love you more than ever.

Fog, fog, foggy …
The fogs of doubt lie dim in my heart.
Have you also been missing in the fog,
losing your way in the thick mist?

Fog, fog … A foggy day weeps.
The dimmed earth and sky are sad.
When I long and yearn for you, my soul,
I love these foggy days more than ever.

A Poet Is Walking

Having lost his audience,
a poet is walking along the street.
Why not offer him a drink
and invite him in for a glass of water?
The poet walking along the street
used to say what was black and white.
What a poet! When he was clever
with words, many women fell in love
with him. When he showed the guilt
of a ruler, everyone supported him.
When he was pushed aside by his rivals,
his real friends stood by to help
and pulled him out of the dark water.
He had many envious glances
as his reputation grew, although those
envying him were few in number,
growing like thorns among plants.
Everyone enjoyed listening to him
when he read his verses exuberantly.
But he is famous no longer,
never heard of. He is not welcome
at feasts. Alas! See him now:
a beggar walking along the street.
He hasn't washed himself for ages.

Missing You

Spring and summer pass by and I miss you.
What shall we do with these years of longing,
eternally yearning for each other?
Like the Moon and the Sun we are.

My charm, although I loved you so much,
I couldn't express that love in words.
How happy must the land be and the people
that drink you in with their eyes every day.

My dear heart, you are the amulet around my neck.
You must be lonely, though you will be loved
by everyone you meet – that's for sure.
Our souls are linked in heaven, never forget.

Verses, Verses

Verses, verses,
my lifetime solace –
like me you are mortal, born on earth.
I tell myself there is a land of wonder
that will console my soul with your help.

My verses heal me,
they are my voice.
I am dazzled by your beauty
although you grow old, too,
just like a young girl becomes old.
Now it is as if I am flying
on a steed with eternal dreams dancing
in my head. A beggar singing verses
in the market street might be happier
than me if he has his youth and life.

When people judge you
by your appearance,
they never see the tears of pain
inside. My hunger is only for words, so –
instead of food, I buy paper pure as my heart.

Verses, verses,
my favourite solace,
my immortal spirit in life.
A tiger hidden in my chest
disapproves of a dog's life.

An Honest Man

He expects kindness from shameful people,
and goodness from the bright dawn.
He doesn't attribute evil intentions to anyone
since he has no bad in himself at all.

His face is set in a broad smile –
it is obvious he is a positive person.
If you stand in front of him with a gun,
he will think you are playing a game.

Every day is a challenge for him
he is so wrapped up in everyone's concerns.
If you shake your head at some things,
he winces with pain as if some harm is involved.

His honesty is the banner of his pride
and, like every good man, he would never show
failure. If you fear finding human filth,
no word can express what his soul would feel.

To the Poetess Who Asked for Advice

Being a poet is not a good thing, my dear.
It means lagging behind your mates
when your mates are happy,
living a life of joy, without any woe.
You'll be waiting for your time to come,
lamenting to the distant Moon.
You won't have real friends on this Earth
since being a poet is a link with space.
Although you beseech and peer at the skies,
no help will come from there.
When your friends have gone their own ways,
like seasonal birds late in spring,
you'll feel you are missing your chances.
Being a poet is not a pleasure; it is a pain –
like being an illusory bird. When late
to adapt to changes in society, you'll fail
and won't receive any thanks.
Your soul might well flourish and bloom –
but have you ever seen a poet with a throne?
Your family will reject you, call you selfish.
This will be your future, your fate.
In a greedy society, we won't flourish.
Some hope still leads us on to bright dawned mountaintops.
From slope to slope, we pace with pride
and stride among the tulips.

Don't Ache, My Heart

As if my name was blacklisted,
my chest ached non-stop.
Don't enquire about me,
please don't.

My life is passing me by
while I obey flat-headed governors.
I respect everyone around me
but I have no rights for myself …

no true friends or companions.
I should honour and worship others.
I wound my heart all the time
because I am foolish.

I fear even the hoot of the owl.
I flattered to survive.
O my heart, do not ache, do not ache.
You are my only stone castle.

The Watch

How can I live in peace
when rumours always surround me ...
such as forgetting I left my watch
in the bed you made last night.

I forgot about daily life and myself.
I forgot everything, every single thing
except you, my paradise.
My watch was left in your house.

My watch is ticking day and night,
running fast impatiently. Even if
I lived for a thousand years, the night
I spent with you would be worth far more.

Remember that precious night.
It made you so happy.
So keep my watch and treat it
like the handle of a golden spoon.

The watch strap is a gold chain
for the lovely young woman you are.
If I manage to spend another night,
just open the door, your hair dishevelled;

open the door with that scent of yours
and I will wish for the night to last forever.
None of the joys of this life
will be comparable to a night with you.

My only wish is for the dawn
to arrive as late as possible,
my heart timed to the watch
and beating fast.

In the night when you miss me,
simply alter the clock-hand of the watch.
And if my watch keeps going,
it will mean I am still missing you.

The Man Without a Name

Tell that man to come to the *dastarhan*.[1]
Why did you leave him sitting alone?
In uncertain times of wealth and misery,
people have shared food with you too.

Tell that man to come to the *dastarhan*.
There are so many contrary fates in our world.
When his country and people are in trouble,
your country and people might well be all right.

Don't look at him so negatively:
it is terrible to be left without a *dastarhan*.
Ask him whether he has a dream or not,
and where his home and fatherland are.

Maybe he has been forced out of his land,
for there is no sign of guilt in his eyes.
His tricky fate gives him no chance to get out
or to lament. He won't utter a word even if you hit him.

His resignation to his lot has made him hard
as stone. It is as if he has a lump in his throat –
he is so scraggy, all skin and bones.
Tell the poor fellow to come to the *dastarhan* –

it is too terrible to be without a homeland.
Just imagine if you were in his place,
would you be like a stray dog with no owner?
He looks around with anxiety in his eyes,

is such a pitiful sight when he stares at people.
My friends, maybe he is seeking some kindness –
this man without a name. Don't start boasting
about your own good fortune lest bad luck

[1.] *Dastarhan* – traditional concept concerning all the dining- and hosting-related practices and etiquette norms. Inviting someone to a *dastarhan* means hosting them according to all the norms of hospitality. *Dastarhan* is also a synonym for a dining table or a table cloth.

befall your people. Without passing
any comments on his homeland,
he listens to every word of yours attentively.
'Deprive me of success, luck and wealth,

my God, but O save me from the haunted eyes
of the outcast, from not being known by anyone
in the whole world, and from curling up in the back
of a house. Save me from seeing my country

only in dreams, from having no clothes or food.'
A yellow goose swimming on a lake has more dignity
than a knowledgeable person. Dignity
is for fools with no understanding or discretion.

Many might have butter. But the good man
who possesses inner riches lives in poverty –
how disgraceful is this! The enlightened
remain like snowy peaks in the distance –

while respect is given to governors, rulers,
wrongdoers who are blind to what goes on.
Tell that man to come to the *dastarhan*.
Tell the poor fellow to come to the *dastarhan*.

Speak Up

I have a secret that hurts my soul.
There is one night I will remember forever.
There is a debt I still owe to society.
There is a complaint I couldn't voice to the UN.

There is a silence like that in the burial shrine.
There is a truth I could not bring myself to write.
There is our ancient culture which has left no trace.
There are some householders who are unworthy.

There are strong men who wasted their strength.
There are unloved women never seen naked.
There are eloquent people struck dumb by policies.
There are invisible political fetters around us.

So that the dumb would not be without song,
we broke the fetters and now we are free.
Alas, though, the truth became weakened –
like alcohol mixed with water.

Everyone was worried about the truth.
It was written down in poems and songs.
But the truth of the truth diminishes
as time goes by, if not told in time.

A lot of truth is all very well –
yet if told late, it loses its value.
My friend, tell, do tell the truth
if you want its dignity upheld.

The Grudge

My life stopped me in my tracks –
as if my very existence was wasted.
For I can't help bearing a grudge
against the general public who are favoured.

I have a grudge against the unscrupulous,
against the soul-less who appear kind-hearted.
I bear a grudge against those who don't care,
who have done nothing for anyone.

Crows will be crows, my darling.
Even if they have golden tails,
they will then just be golden crows.
I bear a grudge against those men
who, like overfed lice and swine,
are rude to the servants sweeping courtyards,
desperate to marry a king's daughter.

I bear malice against goats that never lead
the flock to the right places.
And I wonder if the lamb-like people
will notice too late that they are standing
right in front of a slaughter-house.

I have an aversion to the stony-hearted
who consider everyone else stupid.
So many words have died inside me.
I carry on like a thief who is riding
a white horse and is going to be caught.

Translated by Patricia McCarthy

ULUGBEK YESDAULET
(b. 29.04.1954)

Ulugbek Yesdaulet is a poet and public figure. He graduated from the Faculty of Journalism at Kirov Kazakh State University (now Äl-Farabi Kazakh National University) in 1977, before going on to study literature and creative writing at the Maxim Gorky Institute of Literature. Throughout his life he has worked within media and creative arts, both regionally and nationally, before taking leadership roles within the following government organisations: the Ministry of Foreign Affairs of the Republic of Kazakhstan (1993), the Ministry of Culture, Information and Public Consent (1997), and the Prime Minister's Office (2000). He was the editor-in-chief of both major literary periodicals, *Ķazaķ ădebieti* (2002–08) and *Žūldyz* (2008–17). Since 2017 he has been the secretary of the Writers' Union of Kazakhstan. Yesdaulet is also a member of the State Commission of the Republic of Kazakhstan for awarding the State Prize of the Republic of Kazakhstan and the member of Constant Council of the Congress of Literary Journals of the Turkic World.

His poetry collections include *Ķanatķaķty* (Debut, 1974), *Žūldyz žaryğy* (Star-Light, 1977), *Altajdyŋ altyn tamyry* (The Golden Roots of Altaj, 1979), *Aķ keruen* (White Caravan, 1985), *Žūrektegi žazular* (Explosions in My Heart, 1995), *Zaman-aj* (Oh, Time, 1999), *Kiiz kitap* (The Sacred Book, 2001) and *Yntyķ zar* (Songs of Longing, 2010), along with his collected works in six volumes (2006–11). He is the author of the text of the anthem ('Zaman-aj') of Nevada–Semej anti-nuclear movement and of a number of popular modern Kazakh songs. His poetry has been translated into Russian, Chinese and Kyrgyz.

Yesdaulet has won a number of awards: the State Prize of the Republic of Kazakhstan (2002), Honoured Figure of Kazakhstan (2013), Alaš International Literary Award (2000), the Order of Ķūrmet (2001) and the Gold Yesenin Medal of Russia (2007).

The Stone Book

At the grave of my parents,
I placed an open book,
carved out of reddish stone.
Sometimes I sit in front of it,
aruaks[1] consuming my thoughts.
Under a clear sky,
with something to say to the stone,
I come and read the book.
Caught in the flood of a whirlwind,
grieving and suffering exhausts my heart,
then the candle of inspiration ignites,
and the sky itself reads the open book.
Night or day,
the Moon, Sun and stars
start to read,
centuries pass, yet still
they don't read to the end.
Wandering here and there,
darkening with rain,
white snow clouds have learned
to read from that open book.
Surviving fate's obstacles,
wintering on the graves
and spreading its wings,
this book wants to take flight ...

---

[1] *Aruak* – ancestral spirit. It is believed that *aruaks* protect the living descendants, thus they are treated with deep reverence. Kazakhs visit their ancestral graves to ask for guidance; they make vows in the name of *aruaks* and call for their ancestors' names in a battle cry.

Ulugbek Street

In Almaty there is a street called 'Ulugbek'.[2]
People were born and grew up there.
'Cheers to the fact the street was named after you,'
my friends and associates joke.

In Almaty there is a street called 'Ulugbek'.
Too few days to sweep up the leaves,
if Ulugbek is going to gleam like the street.
But the clouds did not abandon the head of this Ulugbek.

There is a street in Almaty called 'Ulugbek'.
A cool breeze calls you for a walk.
Its mood is as changeable as mine.
On some days it gets sultry.

Having been given his name,
I am close to this stargazer soul –
for the two of us, one street's enough,
after all I'm a street poet myself …

---

[2] Ulugbek Street – street in Almaty named after Mirza Muhammed Taraghay bin
Shahrukh (1394–1449), a Timurid ruler, astronomer and mathematician. 'Ulugbek' is a
moniker, loosely translated as 'Great Ruler'.

Don't Ask Poets the Time

Don't ask poets the time.
They just don't live by the clock.
No point trying to make them answer –
it only makes them look away.

The poet is a dreamer, straightforward as a child.
He lives without learning how to.
But he has learned how to immortalise time,
just so you can wander aimlessly.

What is our life? Dusk to dawn,
putting out fires to the end of our days.
Don't ask poets the time – it is eternity,
that's the whole secret.

Balbal's[3] **Song**

I entered my life –
I left it.
What have I created?
I awaited the star in the heavenly heights,
I cursed the muddy water.

I set out on my life –
I returned.
At dawn at prayer time
I offered your troubles to God
hoping he will help us.

I opened and closed my eyes.
I am a dead silent stone,
I have nothing to say to you.
Leave me alone.

---

[3] *Balbal* – anthropomorphic stone stela, installed atop, within or around a *ķorġan* (burial mound) in cemeteries.

Flow of the Gulf Stream

Happiness fades returning to your family home –
your father scowls at the door: 'If you can't
write letters home, then you're wasting
your time writing poetry for nothing!'

So cheerful and spirited, before sorrow froze his mind,
sea waves on a weathered rock face, weighed down by
unbearable cargo, staring old age point blank in the eyes,
ever since the day he lost his eldest son ...

White frost in the temples, and lowered lips,
permanent black cloud shadows under his eyebrows ...
How could this face once filled with lifeblood
transform into the Arctic Ocean?

'Birth of a grandson!' – the father
straightens his shoulders at the news,
his face lighting up, confirming,
there is still a warm current in the ocean.

Perhaps You Remember
the Winter Garden …

Perhaps you remember the winter garden …
it showered our shoulders with snow.
I kissed you, and I dream of this evening
again, having dreamed it a hundred times.

Perhaps you remember the winter garden …
enduring, kissed by frost,
elusive as vines
your lips – ripe grapes.

Perhaps you remember the winter garden …
I caught you up and kissed you again,
in a whirlwind of snow – incredible, and tender,
you laughed quietly with your fixed gaze.

You probably remember the winter garden,
the snow – how I rubbed your cheeks with it,
you laughed … wisps of smoke,
bare birches pierced the snowfall.

Perhaps you remember the winter garden …
how you lost a button. Both of us
searched for it in the depths of the snowdrift,
and with such trifles our troubles began.

You probably remember … Since, that's when,
without us noticing, we lost our happiness.
I left you in the garden. And now,
fate hardly ever takes me there.

Since then, I've had a lot of losses –
desperate ones from those who are insatiable,
criminally kissing those I don't love …
But you, do you remember the winter garden …?

Rainy Morning

Dawn barely opened its eyelashes,
as the sky pushed back the darkness.
Autumn rain knocks on the window,
and the willow knocks with its branches.

The heavenly river played –
but I still managed to find a way across.
My light, do you remember how it was,
how I knocked on your window?

Nature rages, makes a noise,
the river is flooding over again,
but I no longer seek out a crossing,
never more will I knock on your window.

How the wind moans, flying
directionless through groves and forests.
The rain is knocking.
The window is crying.
Or could it be me who is weeping?

Letter

I close my eyes to conceal their shining light.
This is love, glowing, inextinguishable …
Nothing you can do about it.
Maybe kind winds have brought us here,
winds dear as your departed breath.
Are these storms in the night?
At the window, is it the rain that knocks?
How wonderful – the time for happiness has come –
you found my door, even when we were apart.
O my love, try to live without sadness.
In the heat, water gleams golden beneath the Sun.
Do I hear your laughter ringing in from the distance,
or is it just past years that race through your fingers?
Do you pity those who have prepared so much for you,
there at the front with bright poems and speeches?
The Sun and Moon will lovingly crown you,
like a bright coronet of heaven's purest rays.

I Am in Love with Your Eyes

I am in love with your eyes:
transparent spring waters surfacing
from these clear eyes of yours –
I want to quench my thirst in them,
little lamps, shining and flickering.
I burn from their fires.

The whiteness of your conscience lies
in these raven black eyes of yours,
the purity of your soul.
I am developing a passion for your eyes –
a childish innocent passion.

In the richness of your eyes,
I see the roads you haven't taken,
longing, grief, desires,
the essence of you,
higher than the highest peak in the sky.

In the shining of your eyes
is a trunk bulging with spiritual mystery,
governing your heart and will.
Your eyes dissolve barriers and ice-blocks,
my coldness melts, tears fade.
A hundred times I die in the flames of your eyes.
A hundred times I fall silent, freezing.

Your eyes help me discover many things –
the symphony of *dombyra*[4] orchestras,
blizzards, brooding storms and melodies
of rain, of overflowing daydreams.

[4.] *Dombyra* – tthe most popular traditional musical instrument among the Kazakhs. It is made from wood and stringed with animal intestines. It comes in various shapes, with 2–4 strings and 8–24 frets, but the most typical is an oval shape *dombyra*, with 2 strings and 12 frets.

And when in your eyes I see a burning furnace,
flashes of lightning stir in me:
I set out with the road as my guide.
I set out at dawn to meet the dawn.
Though sad at how little time we have,
I'm soon restored and cheerful once more.

I can't say how often I have looked into your eyes,
and seen the lake of sadness evaporate ...
Because I felt joy, I could celebrate,
letting happiness take over,
I could let myself fall in love,
with you – with your eyes.

The Corner

The father punished the mischievous son,
since to spare the rod is to spoil the child.
'Stand in the corner!' he cried, with a
piercing yell, like the *batyr*[5] of old legends.

Begrudgingly, this frightened youngster
did as he was told. Although a small chap,
his expression was threatening, shoulders
occasionally trembling, little nose sniffing.

In every room there are four corners –
for him it was always the one of disgrace.
He thought to himself:
'I wouldn't have to stand in the corner,
if I was born homeless and free.'

This boy did not like corners.
This boy hated the corner.
One day he explains to his mother:
'When I grow up mama,
I will build a house with no corners ...'

I am with this little imp, but I don't know
whether it's bad parenting to forgive him.
Ah, how happy our ancestors would be,
to have been nurtured in a yurt with no corners.

---

[5] *Batyr* – originally a term for 'hero' or 'valiant warrior', roughly equivalent to the
European knight; nowadays the term signifies military or masculine prowess.

Woman – Washing the Monument

'There are some mountain ranges east of Almaty...'
An enchanting song needs language.
In the mountains –
there is a memorial to a certain poet.
The mountain ridge is reflected in his steadfast look.

The poet rises over the waves of blue undergrowth
and grey feathergrass.
Over his head are the nomadic songs of the cumulous clouds,
and beyond his breast the strained lines of verse,
as young poets strive to pay respects.

Gradually,
winter loosened its icy hold on the sky and the earth.
Spring's beauty appeared.
Now it cheered up the stone statue,
contemplating those who had managed
to remain alive and healthy before the spring thaw.

Having experienced the snow blocks and slush,
and days of inclement weather,
the monument's face was covered in cobwebs.
A woman appeared
and tenderly washed the stone body,
conscientiously creating a great lather with the soap.

The poet immediately turned into a white snow cloud,
as the woman sponged down his head,
as if muffling it up in white silk.
The world saw that the statue started to weep,
its eyes sobbing profusely with sequin-like tears,
which lay there like pearl works of art,
like precious objects,
as if from his tears one could
craft the absolute essence of all that is living.
And then, sadly, she kissed the sculpture –
perhaps she didn't get to kiss the poet when he was alive?

Twilight in the Cool Ravine …

Twilight in the ravine as the fresh wind forces its way in,
we two rattled and bobbed along in the bullock cart,
bowling down the slope homewards.

We travelled, hidden from view, along the
wide breast of the steppe so rich in stories,
our bodies growing numb in the biting wind.

The mountain tops were singed with flames,
the crimson disk of the Sun was setting –
Just when I noted this with interest,
my grandfather turned to me and said:

'My grandson, don't be lured in by the sunset,
when the Sun sets – it is the end of our day,
the great horizon goes farther than the eye can see
and we only live before it sets.

Time flies like a ferocious arrow,
destroying barriers.
That is why, grandson, before the dawn,
make sure to say what you have to say.'

With these words his voice quivered.
Struggling with his short breath,
his eyes reflected the red of the setting Sun.

Sadness lay in the eyes of the old man –
now wretched and broken down.
He gave one look back, sighing heavily,
yet still seeking the morning in the East.

Is There Power?

The artist diligently removes
aspects of the portrait
that clearly aren't working –
whether excessive or inferior.

He removes facial expressions,
the manufactured smile.
He removes the thin lines of cruel eyes
that hostile look.

He removes shell-like ears
that listen in to gossip and tittle tattle.
He removes the prattling lips
that do the gossiping.

Not many people in the world
are insensitive at heart.
Not many sucked evil
from their mother's breasts.

Is there not a power on high,
that can undo the tracks of these
cold hands, which inflicted
such wounds on you
to discredit you?

I Love Only You

I love only you, you alone.
I love your manners and habits.
From the heavy weight of this longing,
my heart grieves a thousand different ways.

On remembering your name, I secretly murmur it,
and my life becomes sweet as a dream at dawn.
It's only in experiencing the depth of your feelings
that I have been able to grasp the depth of a raindrop.

When you are silent, or give a glance,
I forget about the cruel world around us.
I am ready to bow down silently before you,
to sacrifice my own dear fate, for you.

Away from you I suffer – I'm all
over the place like a pot boiling over.
My heart flies off with aching wounds.
All I need is a word from you.

I love only you. Even though, my love,
I couldn't preserve your love forever.
Perhaps you will find it in the darkness,
and light the candle of my heart.

Hurry

It is no secret –
We hurry where we don't need to.
We hurry out on to the road.
Once we get there we hurry back.
We hurry in the morning in the nursery.
We hurry at midday to make a buck.
We hurry to point the finger at people's mistakes.
We hurry to commit the dead to the earth.
We hurry to get familiar to make bosom pals.
We hurry to say goodbye when we've said hello.
We can't find a mate, we're getting divorced –
We hurry to fall in love again.
We argue, we wander, we suffer,
We are constantly in flight, in a reckless fit.
Till our strength is dried up.
The soul is worn out.
The heart runs fast like a clock –
tick tock – we say, there is no time,
no time, no time,
casting all our blame on time –
till the question arises:
Where are we hurrying to?

Translated by Belinda Cooke

YESSENGALI RAUSHANOV
(b. 5.10.1957)

Yessengali Raushanov graduated in Journalism from Kirov Kazakh State University (now Äl-Farabi Kazakh National University). He held senior positions at the journals *Žalyn* and *Araj* (1978–87) and *Bilim žǎne eņbek* (1988–95). Currently he runs Žazušy publishing house.

His poetry collections include *Bastau* (Beginning, 1980), *Kelintôbe* (1984), *Šolpan žuldyz tuġanša* (Until Venus Rises, 1986), *Ġajša bibi* (1992), *Ḳara bauyr ḳasḳaldaḳ* (The Cruel Baldicoot, 1995), *Bozaņġa bitken boz žusan* (The Wormwood Grown in Dry Steppe, 2006), and *Perišteler men ḳustar* (Angels and Birds, 2006). His poem 'Ḳara bauyr ḳasḳaldaḳ' became an anthem for the young Kazakhs who rose up against the Soviet dictatorship in 1986, later named 'Želtoḳsan Revolt'. What is distinctive in Raushanov's voice is the way he absorbs Kazakh folklore naturally into his poetry, with ancient motives deriving from epic storytellers. His verses have been translated into Russian, Lithuanian, Ukrainian, Bulgarian, Uzbek, Czech and Kyrgyz. Raushanov is the author of the novel *Nůrdan žaralġan* (Born from Light, 2002) and the ornithological essay collection *Ḳustar – bizdiņ dosymyz* (Our Friends, Birds). The latter was published three times in 2006, 2007 and 2009 in Kazakh and translated into Russian, Uzbek and Kyrgyz. He translated a book of poems by Uzbek poet Khamza Niyazi, the medieval classic *Temir žarġylary* (The Decrees by Amir Temir, 2018).

He is poet laureate of the State Prize of the Republic of Kazakhstan (2006), the Alaš International Literary Award (1991), the Literary Festival held in Moscow in 1989 and the Lenin Komsomol Prize of Kazakh SSR (1990). He has also been honoured with the Orders of Ḳůrmet (2005) and Parasat (2017).

Human Memory Is a Mystery ...

Human memory is a mystery ...
                    its secrets are deep ...
They say that my grandfather was a saint,
                    and his guardian
was a sacred snake *Saryùjek*[1] – so the old men said –
it lay in a corner of his house,
having rolled up in a ball on the carpet.

They forgot about wars and discord,
                    but for some reason the whole
neighbourhood
remembered how the whistle of a snake
                    was like the wind piercing the sands,
and that if grandfather walked into a meeting of old men,
                    majestically carrying this creature on
his shoulders,
the snake perched there would appear threatening
to all the people who saw it.

You can condemn me and my story,
only on the day my grandfather died,
            this
majestic creature
        lashed its tail on the ground
                    at the loss.
Sometimes I wake
            and suddenly
                    I sense clearly in the dark – a snake
crawling towards me –
            it clings to me,
                    ardently wraps itself around me ...
            No way is it a ghost or a dream,
                    it is my history,

[1.] *Saryùjek* – a sacred snake, the *pir* (patron) of the narrator's beloved grandfather.

crawling, coiling around my body …
                            clambering up on to my
shoulder, till it wraps itself around my neck and crushes me …

'What do you want to say – speak!
                            What do you want to say to your ancestors?'
it asks me –
                    and my spirit
                            each time feels tormented,
and I always fear one thing –
                            that it won't be able to undo
its ring of knots,
                            won't be able to uncoil itself.
I have seen many in my life
                            who think of themselves as saints –
they all scattered when
                            I told them about snakes.
… and it lies in a colourful ball,
                            as before, only the coils are closing in…
I live and don't know…
                    don't know,
how to straighten
                            its back.

The Blast of a Siren …

The blast of a siren swept urgently through my heart,
     a diesel engine glided through with its calming honey
           night song …
From the blind light.
     A lonely tree distances itself,
frightened, it reels away.

     Here an obtrusive dream came
          true –
I travel and travel beyond what the eye can see …
I sort out my luggage, through the window I count the
          poles …
a few lines
     lay in my heart,
and I travelled on them
       like of the rails of my fate.

I even had to drag myself out like baggage.
       Through the window,
the summer night breathed, lights ran along the dew …
girls – fellow travellers
     half asleep, are unaware,
that I had joined the train later
       during the night in Žaṇaḳorġan.

Yes, it was the beginning.
       My holidays have always been like this, I have
           always headed out
       ventured and galloped – ahead of others …
       sometimes I lagged behind.
But the years passed,
        and in longing for my own heavens
I returned home once more …
Came here once more.

Still the same lonely tree
              grows,
still the same familiar rumble of diesel engines
as the road stretches out …
along lines of poetry accumulated on the journey,
I am myself once more
              as I return to the source …
Greetings, *auyl*.[2]

---

[2] *Auyl* – social-economical formation considered to constitute the heartland of the nation and a basis for an ethnic and cultural union of the nomadic community. Consisting of 50–70 yurts in the eighteenth century, it developed into its current permanent state of 'rural settlement' (of a minimum of 100 dwellers) when Kazakhs adopted a settled mode of life in the nineteenth and twentieth centuries. *Auyl* can also be used as a synonym for 'native land' and 'homeland', concepts revered by the Kazakhs.

Forty Days Have Passed
Since Winter Came

Forty days have passed since winter came.
For people and cattle an ordeal set in.
Birds flew away in golden houses,
in a multi-coloured state.

Only the raven celebrates singing in the dawn:
extolling of frost:
'Don't you believe
        that I was the khan[3]
so that all of you would freeze ...'
My word is law.
I ruled the world in the previous age

and all the birds served as my slaves.
I only had to croak and they'd die.'

And let the raven kick up a fuss or curse
        the world,
there's scarcely a soul who will believe
        him.

It's just a pity that autumn died
so early this year,
        that even the howling of the steppe
snowstorm
    day after day
        wept this misfortune ...
Today is the fortieth day.

[3.] Khan – title of a ruler in Central Asia, equivalent to a king.

1932. Kazakhstan Famine Year

'Here the people died'.
This black and wild mound
silently wheezes.
The world is wretched,
like in November,
and is deaf to the offence,
in spite of reproach
after reproach.
Only the sand covers up
the past misfortune:
River beds dried up amidst the weeds …
Cattle died from hunger
in this terrible year …
After the cattle it was
man's turn to perish.
The whirlwind lifts the sand …
You see there
the thick locks of a dead girl,
the sand's plantain
entwines them in longing,
all the while admiring her past beauty.
She was young.
She was alive …
A *žigit*[4] flew up to her on his horse
that watched snorting to the side,
his bit between his teeth …
and their hearts burned, as in a fire.
Golden words
rang of love,
the braid entwining her supple figure …
Plantain-grass …
Plantain-grass …
Plantain-grass …
Kazakhstan …

[4.] *Žigit* – generally denoting a 25- to 40-year-old male, the term can also be used as an honorific indicating bravery, endurance, fortitude and being true to one's word.

Tôrebek Lover of Rain

'I am bored of the *auyl* – how many times must I repeat it …?
It's boring having to potter about the steppe with a hoe,
to go to the trouble of feeding hens by hand,
to drive away mangy cats – from boredom …

I will move to you. The *auyl* doesn't rule me.
In the capital I will soon become like you …'
Every time he comes home to visit,
he comes out with this litany of complaints.

So, this spring he visits Almaty.
It rains unceasingly.
At dawn, Tôrebek gets up and like a shadow,
hurries to the station …

He
walks out onto the porch,
and laughs
like a child alone, and happy:

'The harvest crop,' – he says, –
'now it will be a hundred fold!
The earth will be damp,
The clover will grow thick …
Gre-e-at!'
He says.

Translated by Belinda Cooke

I Fell in Love with a *Peri*-Girl

I fell in love with a *peri*-girl[5]
called Twilight.
It's either death or pleasure for me, but I risk it.
She sits down quietly beside me,
brass nails hidden in her long sleeves.

I'm left pale in the middle of a feather grass sea.
The *peri*-girl is fading into the dusty light,
blood dripping from the tips of her nails
she scratches horizon in front of my eyes.

All the surrounding slopes ignite instantly,
red blood pulsates on the horizon.
As if I haven't seen enough grief in my life,
oh God, what does this blood mean? What's she up to?

The earth covers itself in a dark-grey cape,
the wind runs again like a naughty child.
Fragrant with musk, the *peri*-girl
approaches me saying:
'Only I can understand you anyway.'

The earth is calm,
the lake is in its place,
the sky is unscathed.
Only the heart is trembling –
sad universe.
I'm in love with the world with its brass nails.
What can I do with it?
Tell me, what should I do?

---

[5] *Peri* – in Islamic mythology, a *jinn*-like creature created from fire. It can be both
benevolent and malevolent, and female peri are considered to be the most beautiful
beings in the world.

Human

There are rumours that Kôrkembaj the lame
is getting married ...
His relatives are bragging about it,
getting ready for the wedding.

A bride has arrived
with a dowry rather small,
but a mountain of gossip.
Is it true?
Or just tittle-tattle?
– She became pregnant while unmarried.
– Uh, Kôrkemžan[6] is lucky to get anyone.

Shoes are not torn,
meals are ready in time – great.
Kôrkembaj the poor has become a man.
What more do you want?
He fixed up his knackered old house
built of mud forty years ago,
finally repaired that rusty old door hinge.

His guilty young wife's health is weak,
she gives birth in less than a month.
They need ķalža[7] but there's no livestock.
Kôrkembaj is confused.
A man from her side brings a ewe,
and saves the day.

The guest looks furtively at Kôrkembaj –
he has his own reasons for that.
A healthy baby-boy is cooing in his cradle,
The young mother sits next to him pale as a paper –
all she sees is the misty, boundless steppe.

[6.] *Žan* – lit. 'soul'; appended as a suffix to a name to express affection.
[7.] *Ķalža* – traditionally, meat of a fat sheep slaughtered for a woman who has only just
given birth; *ķalža* broth is believed to help women regain strength post-delivery.

... Forty days passed,
... the baby caught a terrible cough,
his body is hot as if wrapped up in fire – what a tragedy.
From dawn, Kôrkembaj looks for a roller bird to treat the baby,[8]
going up and down the hills in the neighbourhood.

The baby naps, his fists clenched.
Kôrkembaj calls his wife silently, gesturing
fearing to wake up the little one,
'*My fo-a-al*', his lips mime,
'My foal', he whispers.

The baby looks at the man,
both close and stranger.
... Soon he closes his eyes forever.
That's life for you.
... Kôrkembaj fell into apathy,
unable to grasp if it is reality or a dream.

Frustrated, he endlessly smokes and ponders.
The burial hill took away all the warmth from his heart.
He's still afraid to speak in a loud voice,
as if the baby will wake up from fright.
'*My fo-a-al*' he whispers,
'My foal'.

[8.] Roller bird – in ancient times, Kazakhs treated ill children with the wings of a roller bird
to drive out the malevolent forces inviting the ilness.

Foal

Whether you wallow in the grass,
excited, or laughing heartily,
your young world is full of hope.
It is in your possession.
Once upon a time, I was a foal like you,
because my mother was alive.
Can you imagine?

I was restless, always on the move,
I climbed to the top of the mountains.
One day the hairy hand of death
came down and in one fell swoop
pulled my rib …
Then laughed and grinned in my face,
'Be strong', it said.

Since then though
a certain pain gnaws at me –
powerless, I raise my hands to the eternal sky.
I've made a boat out of my rib
to deliver my mother's body to the heavens.

If she were alive
would my heart be ever cold?
… Would my flowers ever wither?
Why, since she's gone, my foal
I visit this *auyl* less and less?
Why is that, my foal?

So gallop freely while you can –
for one day a leash will be stretched
pulling you back.
You'll be crushed,
your heart longing.
Then you will go down stiff like me.

Desert. Dream.

I have a brother called Saxaul[9]
in the mottled desert of Mother Alģi.
It grows, sprawling its branches.
If you ask, people, how I am,
just look at my brother, you'll see me.

February comes with its white fur coat,
we've seen its frosty might.
There were times when not only sand,
people had to move away too,
but we didn't leave our birthplace.

Ķuralaj[10] comes full of life,
days are getting longer by a field grouse step,
time to put horses on lush pastures.
Days of July are lengthened by a partridge step,
bringing scorching heat and swelter.

December arrives with a fierce wind.
What a howling row it makes.
Give a man who can withstand it, patience,
which only we, the poor ones, possess.

The sky is stubborn again,
the boundless steppe craves water.
My brother, poor fellow, looks up
with an everlasting hope.

White clouds sailed grandly,
blue ones didn't give birth to showers.
From the mottled desert of Alģi,
my brother raises his hands to the sky.

---

[9] *Saxaul* – dry, prickly tree growing in the desert and semi-desert; a symbol of endurance.
[10] *Ķuralaj* – short period of rains at the end of May until 1 June.

From the mottled desert of Alġi
my brother reaches for heaven.
I hope that one day
I will see with my own eyes,
how his hardened, sinewy hands
catch a careless cloud
and pull it down at last.

Shadows Die at Dusk

Shadows die at dusk,
because they should die anyway.
A riverside darkens, it becomes pitch black,
as if it swallowed thick blood.

The steppe darkens too, as if soaked in blood.
Deaf universe,
let me listen to you too.
Like a widow in a black shawl,
a lonely birch tree gave its shadow to the earth.

Sorry, my brother,
I'm not the one to blame,
A silent green sprout sobs shaking its head.
I buried them and came back today,
but nobody expressed any condolences to me.

The *auyl* lies in a hollow next to a hill,
Why does the Sun stand still all in flames?
My grandmother is in my thoughts,
a war swallowed her husband,
a son and two brothers at once.

The Moon rises with a swollen face,
a road runs into the dense thicket.
… Tonight I won't be able
to sleep again,
dead souls come into my dreams.

My Drama

– Goodbye, – I said to the sands,
– Don't be sad.
Someday I'll come back,
if everything is fine with me.
I am the last poet of these parts
who grew up shoeing a horse,
and saddling a camel.

I'll leave.
The neighbourhood is shrouded in a light mist.
A wind is getting stronger,
forcing an orphaned *ši* grass[11] to lament.
Nobody goes to Almaty riding a camel,
dromedary – don't give me this look.

Today is the day of parting –
a black *ķunan*[12] is chewing on the bit.
For the last time I brought it out of the stable.
You are free to go now,
Go away, my own.

Everything floats before my eyes …
all is in fog.
The *ķunan* doesn't want to leave, circles around me.
Why is it so eager to make me cry?
There's more than enough grief in my heart.

Why does it torture me like an enemy?
I don't have tears!
There are none left to weep!
All gone.
– Damn you, get lost! –
I shouted, and the wind runs away with my
breaking voice.

[11.] *Ši* – perennial herb usually growing in the steppes and semi-deserts. It is used as a valuable green fodder and its dry stalks are used in the production of carpets.

[12.] *Ķunan* – three-year-old male farm animal, primarily a horse. *Ķunans* are believed to be sufficiently grown-up, and thus highly valued.

That's how I left.
Since then I've seen many types –
some slow and lazy, others fast and resourceful.
The day that has just gone often wakes me up
in the middle of the night
looking like a *ķunan* with a thick mane.

On the side of that Kelintôbe,[13]
a tall figure stands silently, seen from afar.
I can see a full harness and body,
but where's a head?
Why does it have no head?

Where's the head?
Surely it must be some joke.
Why is it running away from me?
I wake up in tears,
like a poor fellow
who lost his trusted companion
while on the road.

The saddle pommel is raised high,
hooves are pounding on rocks, causing sparks.
The black *ķunan* with the thick mane
is galloping across the ancient land,
headless …

[13.] *Kelintôbe* – (lit. a 'hill of a daughter-in-law') refers to the *auyl* in the Žaṇaķorġan district
of the Ķyzylorda region, where Yessengali Raushanov graduated from school in 1973.

Greyhound. Elegy

October came with its chill sunrises.
November forced willows to dance.
A yellow greyhound lost its peace
since its owner, the old man, passed away.

No more bowls for food, no food either,
no home – the dog had to dig itself a hole.
Charity and affection are alien
to the late old man's cruel daughter-in-law
and his silly son.

They drove the greyhound away,
throwing stones and shouting: 'Get out!'
What do people know about dogs?
The yellow greyhound went
to the steppe, to the place
where the old man was buried.

Thin as a skeleton, with great difficulty
it reached the grave,
it whined and whimpered weakly.
It scratched the base of the grave
all night long.

Its heartbeat slowed down,
the light in the eyes faded.
The bright red sunrise raised its head
with the blooded claws of its rays.

Even the stone was brought to tears.
I know there is a yellow greyhound
under the red bright heat of the sun
that dispersed the darkness of the night.

'Who are you?' – conscience asks,
in the weak voice of the greyhound.
Some thoughts gnaw away at me,
all night long.

I'm Not Thirsty, My Heart Is

I'm not thirsty,
my heart is
since my mother
passed away ...
My heart is thirsty.
There is a certain cloud in the sky
above our *auyl*.
It greets me every time I visit.

Mother's no more.
Hope has faded,
has gone out.
But there is a cloud,
it is mine,
that cloud.
It follows me
when I visit the grave,
it always waits there,
poor thing,
weary and tired.

It is hanging
right over my head,
swelling up in the zenith.
(Other clouds float past.)
– Mama, – I say
– It's me, I came ...
Only this cloud – this boy-cloud
can hear my voice.

– Mama, – I say
– Everything is fine,
I'm in good health.
You told me not to cry,
I don't.
I remember what you taught me –
how to behave, how to live right.
Why would I forget that?

I know, my balmy days won't come back.
My cloud struggles to hold in its inner rain,
steps aside to dispel its sadness
only to cry frantically in pain.

– Mama, – I say,
– Everything is fine.
I'm in good health,
Our traditions are safe with me.
I endure,
always did.
Always will.
It's the cloud that cries, not me.

The Žajyķ River, Ancient Era

Your coast is overgrown with coastal reeds,
crouching softly, crushing the grass.
I make my way, leaving your side.
Who am I, if not a desperate tiger?!
Only pride saved me that day,
when I was destined to die,
running from a disaster
during which my bones would be scattered surely.

An enemy suddenly attacked,
flags held high.
I drew them away from you and destroyed them,
to protect you from the horror of spilled blood.

When I come to see you in the morning,
I catch my breath from your beauty.
When I see you at sunset,
you turn like a gracious horse.
You are my soul, Žajyķ River,[14]
I'm devoted to you.

If you were an unbroken horse with a loud neigh,
still I wouldn't be afraid of you,
but would praise such strength
that could threaten the enemy.
But you put me in the fire,
with your purity,
your transparency
and your meek temper.

Looking at you from your shore,
I feel tears streaming down my face.
Powerless to explain to this cursed age
that a son is born not to mock
the beauty, but to protect it.

[14.] Žajyķ – also called Ural, is a river that originates in the southern Ural Mountains and
discharges into the Caspian Sea.

Thirty Years Ago

Thirty years ago,
one boy left for Almaty,
A genius, of course.
His whole world was poetry.
Since then his *auyl* named Kelintôbe
on the Mother Syr's[15] shore,
is looking for his beloved son.

This poet never returned to his homeland.
Someone took his name for himself,
a listless person, head always bowed –
Our boy was nothing like him.

Our boy wandered through the dew at dawn,
happy to roam through the steppe.
This one is sulky as a tombstone,
spends all days at the graveyard.

A sad-looking poplar on the shore
blossomed and lost its foliage year after year.
The boy who left his Kelintôbe *auyl*,
was lost in the end in Almaty.

A gloomy man with head bowed,
perhaps is looking for younger himself in vain …
O, the city of Almaty …

Translated by Rose Kudabayeva

[15.] Mother Syr – Syr Dariâ, a river in Central Asia; it originates in the Tien Shan flowing through Uzbekistan and southern Kazakhstan into the remnants of the Aral Sea.

SVETQALI NURJAN
(b. 15.12.1962)

Svetqali Nurjan (pen-name Ajt-Man) is a poet and literary translator. He graduated from high school in 1979 in the Žetibaj (Zhetibay) *auyl*, Maṇġystau region, and worked as a machine operator in the *auyl* of Úlytas, and as a horseman at the Ķúlandy farm. He subsequently studied at the Faculty of Philology of Kirov Kazakh State University (now Ál-Farabi Kazakh National University), worked for some years in Almaty at the *Pioner* magazine for youth (now *Aķželken*), and returned to Maṇġystau region, where he was employed as a cultural worker in Ķaraġaj district (1988–94) and has headed the Maṇġystau Regional Art Centre since 1995.

His debut verses were published in a collection of young poets titled *Auditoriâ* (Classroom) in 1985. His own poetry collections include *Aruana* (1993), *Taṇ ķauyzyn žarġanda* (When the Day Breaks, 2002) *Aj taranġan tùn* (Splendid Moonlit Night, 2008), and collected works in three volumes. Among his numerous translations are: *Áulieler áuezi* (Melody of the Saints, 2009), *Europa poèziâsy* (European Poetry, 2010), *Europa klassikalyķ poèziâsy* (Classical European Poetry, 2011), *Ķyryķ hikmet* (Forty Hikmets, 2013), *Dármensizder dáleli* (Proof of the Insecure, 2013) and *Taṇnyṇ laġyl žùldyzy* (The Ruby Star of the Dawn, 2015). His thirteen-volume edition of collected works is forthcoming.

He is a recipient of the Tôlegen Ajbergenov Prize (1989), the Daryn State Prize (1996), the Medal for Outstanding Achievements (2008), the Order of Ķùrmet (2017) and is a repeated recipient of the State Scholarship in Literature.

Almaty. Despair.

To Mŭқaģali Maқataev[1]

I haven't heard the ring of a poem for ages,
instead I scream inside unable to fit in to Almaty.
Where did my former carefree voice go?
Has it become lower so as not to fall from a height?

Can't understand the language of a grim-faced city,
I feel dirty inside the concrete bathhouse.
If I could have reached my steppe,
where the wind would fill my chest,
It would have healed my mind, but what can I do?

There is no way I can get there –
I'm imprisoned here,
and all my thoughts, my whole soul
are imprisoned too.

No poems are written.
No blood flows through my veins.
The graves of the living dead
are not good for the soul ...

Why should I wear the formal kaftan of life?
Shall I go and visit Mŭқaģali's last resting place?
There my soul can find a sound full of sunshine.
He will arise saying:
a 'true poet' has turned up.

He will arise, –
his soul wrapped up in lightning –
He will start to remember Tôlegen and Қasym ...[2]

---

[1] Mŭқaģali Maқataev (Mukagali Makatayev; 1931–76) – outstanding poet who enjoyed a devoted following among ordinary Kazakhs. He translated foreign literature into Kazakh, including Walt Whitman and Dante's *The Divine Comedy*.

[2] Tôlegen and Қasym – famous Kazakh poets Tôlegen Ajbergenov (1937–67) and Қasym Amanžolov (1911–55).

Then he will ask me:
What young poetic talent is out there? –
I will tell him about Ăbubăkir
and Bajbota.[3]

Then he will talk
about his own struggle to fit into life
regretfully exhaling his last breath.

He will read
his own verse written freshly in the afterlife.
This world will cry as it listens to his *žanaza* prayer-song.[4]

He will sit on the ground with crossed legs,[5]
talking his life-song,
but who knows how will he interpret my state of soul?

I will climb the hill to reach Keŋsaj[6] – the last stop on a life
path for many,
and after that I will lose myself, dissolving into a mirage …

'I spit in your face, the vanity world!' –
I said, and with excitement
put on a shirt made of feelings.

Leaving beside everything – a stone city and an empty house,
I will go to Keŋsaj, to be near Mŭḳaġali!

[3.] Ăbubăkir and Bajbota – prominent Kazakh poets Ăbubăkir Ḳajran (b. 1958) and Bajbota
Serikbajŭly (b. 1954).

[4.] *Žanaza* – Muslim funeral prayer.

[5.] Sitting cross-legged on a felt mat or directly on the ground was a traditional pose adopted
by men in the nomadic Kazakh society.

[6.] Keŋsaj – a cemetery in Almaty. Many of Kazakhstan's most prominent and famous
citizens are buried there.

Spring Song

Bird's song filled the whole valley in celebration.
A winding stream spread over the hollows.
Folding all joys to her breast,
an abundant and green steppe sprawled.

Snowdrops and tulips bloomed in the hills,
as if to say: 'Sing with your heart!'
I walked across these fields of flowers:
suddenly my chest was full of sounds like a spring sky.

Earth understood my soul, the sky spoke to me. I was
floating over the green ocean of space.
Countless images,
myriad melodious songs
were a feast for my eyes and ears,
and my voice joined them.

Now I know what it means to be a poet.
I want to untie all knots with my songs.
Would anyone guess what a miraculous state I am in,
with spring and downpours filling my soul?

Blizzard

Nothing is visible around – darkness interspersed with light,
thousands of *peri*[7] lit a torch of white snow,
but the snow is chased by the mad wind,
Unstoppable as a wolf, wanton and wild.

The ferocious wind snatched the spine from the earth.
The mischievous sea hits the steep shore with masses of water.
Such a cacophony …
It is like a hundred *baksy*[8] gathered together,
all playing the *kobyz*[9] at once.

It is as if unbroken horses are racing,
rearing up, dragging long lassos behind …
Phantoms shake their *tulak*,[10] made from
the skin of a white camel.

Snow-white *šubat*[11] is whipped with brutal force.
You have no patience so eager to taste it.
I feel that a storm is brewing in my heart,
ready to burst out and join the snowstorm outside.

Ten wolves and the leader of the pack
are getting wild outside,
their howling cry almost bursts your ears.
… I'm walking through the snowstorm without losing my way,
a white angel is illuminating my path with a torch.

---

7. *Peri* – in Islamic mythology, a *jinn*-like creature created from fire. It can be both benevolent and malevolent, and female *peri* are considered to be the most beautiful beings in the world.
8. *Baksy* – shaman, a priest of Tengrism said to possess unique abilities (e.g. clairvoyance, healing powers, access to the spiritual world). *Baksys* typically treated minor ailments with plant-based or other medicine and entered into trance states to heal more serious diseases. It is believed that they had *jinn* slaves helping them during divination and healing rituals.
9. *Kobyz* – traditional Kazakh musical instrument with a wooden body, two to four strings and a bow made of a horse's mane. It is the main attribute of the *baksy* during a healing ritual and is considered sacred.
10. *Tulak* – dried skin of cattle and other livestock animals used as mats and rugs.
11. *Šubat* – beverage made from fermented camel's milk, popular in Central Asia.

Autumn

Feather grass pastures are tired-looking.
Powerful autumn has come.
Birds fly away in search of spring.
Leaves-hearts whisper:
'We are yellowed by longing.'

Stone obstacles won't stop the birds.
A horse with a white star will neigh and wallow on the grass,
looking longingly at the sky.
A mountain range seems to have subsided,
because it doesn't have a bird's eye view.

Nature has its own troubles and blows of fate.
Dearest steppe, why do you neigh so much?
… Tumbleweeds are rushing flickering around,
they want to fly away with the birds too.

Hearing a mournful tune from the steppe – is a grief,
I'm a miserable man too, who lost all hope in autumn.
Spreading our arms in bewilderment,
we are longing for the birds' freedom, but are left behind.

Hollows are reddish.
Hills became brown – kissed by an autumn wind.
I was sad before in exactly the same way.
What else can the birds dream about in this life?
They are lucky to spend it in search of spring.

In Search of Five Weapons[12]

Who hasn't been tormented by dreams?
Listen, Steppe, listen, Woods.
I've lost my whip made of the skin
of a camel's neck.
It was artfully made, with a lead core
and a copper-trimmed handle.
It was a true *dyrau*,[13] you won't find another one around here.

It had a brass finish,
one of the mighty *kertartars*,[14] a real weapon.
Tigers, hissing like cats,
ran from its blows.
I will reward anyone who can tell me any news
by giving people *sùjinši*,[15]
if the slaves who run our country
have left anything in our coffers.

Listen, grave,
and the sand *ķorġan*[16] over you.
I survived good and bad times,
but I have also lost my sword.
It had a hilt covered with gold,
a steel blade decorated with ivory.
Wealth collected by the kings for a hundred years
is nothing compared with my sword.

[12.] It is believed that a true *žigit* had to have five weapons. (There is a Kazakh proverb: *Er ķaruy – bes ķaru*, which means 'A warrior has five types of weapons'.) Each type of weapon has special fighting properties, divided into: missile, bladed, cutting, thrusting and striking, with each classification comprising several varieties of weapon.

[13.] *Dyrau* – large whip with the core made of lead, considered one of the five major weapons of a Kazakh warrior.

[14.] *Kertartar* – also a large whip, used as a military weapon.

[15.] *Sùjinši* – Kazakh tradition whereby the person who brings good news is given a gift.

[16.] *Ķorġan* – a tumulus, a type of burial mound or barrow, heaped over a burial chamber.

It could cut a camel with ease
in one fell swoop.
Even an elephant will not have a chance.
A dazzling fire that could cut smoke in half.
It comes out of the sheath in the blink of an eye,
and Russians on hills and Chinese and Kalmyks in the steppe
lost their hopes,
fled with sobs from my Edil,[17]
retreated groaning from Alakôl,[18]
withdrew bleating from Marķakôl.[19]

But I was robbed of my sword by this mortal world.
I asked for help from the hills.
I sent out a cry from the sand dunes.
I called from the tops of the mountains.
Nobody saw my sword.
No soul was using it.

I had a longbow too –
a bowstring would bellow like a piebald bull,
fast as a white bird with a black head.
The mighty arrow flies weeping,
from a masterfully made quiver.
It wakes up mountaintops with its echo.
Becoming a ferocious cloud it wakes up sands too.
If you can hang your arrow on a sky before the sunset,
your enemies, standing guard,
will weep bloody tears in the twilight.

[17.] Edil – river Volga.
[18.] Alakôl – lake in Kazakhstan.
[19.] Marķakôl – lake in Kazakhstan.

This arrow's sound was the song of my ancestor,
with the stars raining and bolts of lightning flashing.
I look around, listening, for where will this arrow's whistle
come from?
Oh, my sacred White Spear!
Who forged you and made you ornate?
On the day of a major battle
I watered a spearhead with the blood of sworn enemies.
I covered my spear's handle with layers of velvet.
But in the caravan of time it is forgotten.
It was my enemy's luck.

If I look for my lost treasures,
with the *ķ̇uryķ*[20] hanging on my upper arm,
begging Almighty for help.
Nobody answers my plea.
This world's core, its religion, is eaten by worms,
only a *sajġaķ*[21] at the graveyard shares my sorrow.
To tell the truth,
I've decided to recite a song.

Although I hope for the best,
I'm afraid my shoulders will give up,
but my heart is still beating.
We are besieged by many,
but without my weapons my grit is nothing.
I've decided to stop searching for my club,
the one that took so many souls,
frightened so many enemies,
saddled itself with much sadness,
but its dignity was hundred fold.

I don't have a warrior's helmet.
My chain mail is torn.
Žüt[22] left nothing for me.
My shield is broken.

[20.] *Ķ̇uryķ* – light pole with a rope and a lasso or a loop at the end used for catching horses.
[21.] *Sajġaķ* – grave pole; in the past Kazakhs used a spear of a warrior as his grave marker.
[22.] *Žüt* – massive loss of livestock from starvation caused by harsh winter, drought or other unfavourable weather conditions.

I'm left only with my *bùtyrlyķ*.[23]
Thank God for that.
My hair was shaved off.
My temples hair cut short.
My knowledge is devoid of faith.
My traditions became void.
My spine is eaten
by worms.

Say it yourself, Kôk Tăņir![24]
If it's not enough,
dear Allah!
A human is Safi, a Chosen One.
Noah is the Prophet!
What has this life become?
We were looking in vain
for traces of our noble ancestors.
As soon as it became known
that I'm not in possession of five weapons,
enemies are ready to curse and swear.
They open the door of a mosque with a kick,
turning this holy place into a sabbath.

They drink *ķymyz*.[25]
Squeeze girls.
Choose wives.
They destroy everything that's dear for me.
They dig up the graves of my kin.
They humiliate those I respect.
Strangers trample upon my land.
When I cry they laugh mockingly.
Women miscarry – bad luck.
Tigers become cats.
Lions become puppies.
Pugs bite my calves.
O, God, let them be content with what they have.

[23.] *Bùtyrlyķ* – piece of mail armour protecting the crotch.

[24.] *Kôk Tăņir*– (lit. 'celestial Tengri') primordial deity in the religion of the early Turkic peoples; god of the sky, the only creator of the universe, often paired with the 'earth-mother', Ùmaj (Umay) .

[25.] *Ķymyz* – beverage made from fermented mare's milk valued in Kazakhstan for its refreshing qualities; it is a main drink for many occasions.

My black swan, on a white smooth lake,
beats its bloody wings
as if calling for bad news.
A white gull is carrion-eating along with crows.
A thoroughbred mount
is harnessed to a donkey cart.
I expect help from God,
but all I get is a bunch of mocking evil spirits
instantly, out of nowhere.
What a pain to remember the past –
my five weapons are nowhere to be found.

Evil spirits own everything.
The devil blinded everyone.
Who can a khaganate[26] trust under the black banner?
What do I expect from a respected brother gone mad,
from wise men, miswriting the history,
from the steppe whose coffers are looted by foes,
from cities, where men are destitute, women are barren?

But even so, let my country remain unharmed and well,
and not lose hope in our consciousness
that became free.
It will hang its five weapons on the belt,
and sit down again at the place of honour.
Claiming equality for all people,
it will speak of clever sons
who will be born
with their hair kissed by the Sun.
Best sons will emerge,
their forelocks combed by the Moon.
The night will ruffle the hair on
the sons' brows – deep thinkers
who will be brought by rivers to their shores.

[26.] Khaganate (khanate) – political entity ruled by aḳaġan (khagan) or khan.

They will come one day,
descendants of noble birth.
In my Fatherland,
they will be a continuation of the past.
These beautiful babies
are about to be born.
I'm ready to sacrifice for them
all my possessions material and spiritual.
And when it comes to masters and craftsmen that I know,
there is no benefit from them,
even if they resurrected seven dead,
shook the hand of the seven saints,
learned seventy doctrines
in seven parts of the world.

I couldn't find my five weapons,
although I searched among those who were in the know.
I tried to ask a galloping wind.
I asked the resounding whitish hills,
but didn't find anything.
I only wandered in vain.
After all these efforts I sing my songs,
I sing and listen as well
to the voices of five weapons
buried in the throats of *dombyra*[27] and *ƙobyz*.
If I die, I'll die at day, not in the night.

[27.] *Dombyra* – the most popular traditional musical instrument among the Kazakhs. It is made from wood and stringed with animal intestines. It comes in various shapes, with 2–4 strings and 8–24 frets, but the most typical is an oval shape *dombyra*, with 2 strings and 12 frets.

Soul's Lullaby

Your light is my shroud whiter than white.
I wish my dead body could be wrapped in it.
And your lips, Fair Queen, will read a funeral prayer,
saying 'My soul's lullaby – it's you …'

O, at that moment this world would have changed at once,
laughing with the sweetest sin in mind.
Eternity, you are wrapped in a light-shroud,
I would have read a song devoted to you.

Say – 'It's you …!'
wearing a flower on your chest.
Each of your eyelashes is like a bud.
There is a single blink between a lullaby and a funeral prayer,
if a person lives in dignity, angels will celebrate.

I will joyfully hug the Sky-Earth.
Even patient ones can't live without being thrilled.
The universe will find its long-lost song and beauty
in the crying voice of an angel …
So say to me: 'My soul's lullaby – it's you!'

Elegy

Sometimes black clouds wrap up the moon.
I come home silently, crushed in sorrow.
I go to bed tired as a dog and fall asleep.
And in my sleep, I dream of a racehorse …

I saddle it and ride through gorges and valleys,
jumping over mountains, stepping over peaks.
I'm riding faster than the speed of light,
I am a dream and my *tulpar*[28] is whiter than a dream.

O, what a ride –
a new song whirls like snow –
what sort of *tulpar* have I at that time?
And who am I?
Every soul has a reckless desire.
It seems that far, far away
there is another beautiful world waiting only for me …

I'm like a swan on water covered by snow,
I could have reached that white world to bury this woe there.
Why don't you gallop towards my everyday world sometimes,
the racehorse of my dreams?

[28.] *Tulpar* – a winged or swift horse in Kazakh mythology and folklore, like Pegasus. Every
major hero of Kazakh epic poems has a speedy *tulpar*, which grows fast and, through its
supernatural powers, helps the hero to succeed in his quest. Nowadays *tulpar* is used as
an honorific term for a horse

Last Breath

'Earth pulls you down.'
– That's your complaint.
The mind's duty is to shove you into a grave at the end of it.
Shouldering the grief of the whole world,
day by day you're sinking slowly into the ground.

Don't think that you are the only victim.
Not all wise men benefit from thinking.
From the very beginning, when they were sharing things out,
you should have chosen a load you could bear.

After your death, people will only celebrate you to show off,
they will put you in a sleeveless shirt made of calico.
Your heartbreak of the moment when entering the grave
will be shared by people who make light talk of it.

Everyone's pretending to be sad.
Startled and noisy they hurry to the graveyard.
The grave opens redder than a red mouth,
and swallows you like an insatiable beast.

You'll probably get a place in hell or heaven.
We've heard nothing on this subject from the other side …
Your soul will fly away like a white cloud,
when your body tires of all torment …

So what's the way out for your mind that has eaten you like a worm?
A wise man with a song for a friend will think about it at dusk.
Only nature will lament for you –
your white cloud will turn into a sobbing black one.

Sergei Yesenin in the
State of Drunkards

Yesenin,[29] you were killed by order of Bronstein.[30]
You wrote 'Land of scoundrels'.[31]
I count to myself again all your sins –
haven't poets been criticised enough?

You had another sin – you loved Russian peasants.
Your next – you loved sausages too.
You hung around in noisy *kabaks*,[32] like a hawk you had
them to the full –
But it's not your fault.

Of course, you smashed the faces of five or six people.
They deserved it.
You ignored the cries of five or six girls –
But they asked for it, didn't they,
leaving their doors open?

You went to the jail, hit its door with your head,
Your case took a bad turn ...
Very often you lay drunk in the mud,
next to false patrons and predatory snitches.

Russia is your Fatherland, but it is a slave to the others.
You were put on trial as an 'anti-Semite' ...
Will I enrage an old man myself
for saying these words out loud?

[29.] Sergei Yesenin (1895–1925) – one of the most popular Russian poets of the
twentieth century.
[30.] Leon Trotsky, born Lev Bronstein (1879–1940) – Russian revolutionary, Marxist theorist
and a Soviet politician.
[31.] 'Land of scoundrels' – a poem by Sergei Yesenin completed in 1923, seen as a critique of
Soviet rule.
[32.] *Kabak* – Russian tavern.

Where are 'The white nights'?
Who blackened his night with dirt?
Maybe it wasn't the dirt, but a poet's blood?
Yesenin, that night you were beaten to death,
by a tall tsar and a short bald man's[33] city.

Sergei, you survived thousands of fights,
but if the fatherland is against you, will your strength be
enough?
Rogue tramps masked their shit,
they battered you to death in Hotel Angletere and then hung
you up …

It is interesting that people love their hooligan poets,
Angry Peshkov[34] didn't like it at all.
My brother, don't be offended by me,
What have I done apart from knowing something?

Oh, Sergei, it's a pity that you didn't get to our *kabak*.
There was a great wine, pure honey.
But you went into the taverns of vultures –
did they kill and devour you there?

If you were near old Leo, your father-in-law,[35]
nothing like that would happen to you.
But the moths were drawn to the Light at that time,
and the Creator was their benefactor.

Hayyam[36] and Hafez[37] were slaves to pure thoughts.
You were not able to enter their garden.
But, all the same, you didn't drink the grief
of Ķůl Ķoža Ahmet,[38] master of speech and joy.

[33.] Short man – refers to Lenin (1870–1924).

[34.] Peshkov – refers to Maxim Gorky, born Aleksey Peshkov (1868–1936); Russian and Soviet writer, founder of the socialist realism literary method and a political activist.

[35.] In early 1925, Yesenin met and married Sophia Andreyevna Tolstaya (1900–57), a granddaughter of Leo Tolstoy.

[36.] Hayyam (Omar Khayyam; 1038–1141) – Persian mathematician, astronomer and poet.

[37.] Khwaja Shams-ud-Din Muhammad Hafez-e Shirazi (1315–90) – Persian poet, known by his pen name 'Hafez' or 'Hafiz'.

[38.] Ķoža Ahmet Âssaui (Kozha Akhmet Yasawi; 1093–1166) – poet and religious figure, who influenced Turkic peoples in adopting Sufism.

Rejoicing like the bud of a red flower filled with blossoming light,
you would break up with the devil.
Not letting Satan's poison back into your blood,
you would experience the best of pure drunkenness.
You turned your eyes to the East, looking for Shagane[39] too.
You left Chagin's[40] side.
You couldn't enter the world of truth,
walking on your thorny path.

In seven places you are a poet destined to die.
Your truest poem was never written,
but your soul was noticed by Allah,
and I will tell you why:

Eternal nightingale, sing well from the garden,
arise, there's no place for you in the grave.
At the end, you were sent to the heaven for *kaffirs*,[41]
purified by your own blood.

Sadness rules in places where no one likes poems.
Will I have the same fate?
… But it's likely you are getting drunk now,
soaked in Light,
in your true Fatherland next to the truest poets.

One can't be angry with the deceased,
one should pray for the deceased.
There is my prayer for you:
If we meet in the true poets' feast,
I wish you recognised me as well.

In this feast, Sergei, I wish we entered heaven.
What else can one dream about?
And then, becoming *fannah-filakh*,[42]
let's immerse ourselves into the aether!

[39.] The poem 'Shagane, oh my, Shagane!' by Sergei Yesenin was dedicated to Shaganeh Taliyan, a young teacher from Batumi, whom the poet met in the Caucasus in December 1924.

[40.] Pyotr Chagin, Yesenin's friend.

[41.] *Kaffir* – non-believer or infidel in Islam; in Kazakh colloquial speech also a synonym for 'dishonest', 'ignominious' or 'cruel'.

[42.] *Fannah-filakh* – Sufi term meaning 'immerse oneself in Allah'.

Sign

I won't suffer and I won't sigh
while there is magic light
descending from above –
mighty tree called Night.
Heavenly sphere.
With its stars looking like full buds.

With its stars looking like full buds,
they tempt me,
they touch my soul,
depriving me of peace.
Hey, my friend, why are you standing there blank?

Hey, my friend, why are you standing there blank
instead of climbing the mighty tree?
You are bound hand and foot with your earthly concerns,
instead of thanking the Creator for his gifts.

You bound hand and foot with your earthly concerns,
but don't harbour anger in the heart.
Kùnekej-sky[43] is constantly changing her style,
she wears the Moon like an earring of light.

She wears the Moon like an earring of light.
Kùnekej-sky is singing a sad song of parting.
Do you notice, how the night world is swaying?
Her *săukele*[44] is swinging like a bright flower.

Her *săukele* is swinging like a bright flower,
Your heart will drink light from that flower.
Magic Light is calling to a faraway place …
Who's soaring there rustling their wings?

[43.] Kùnekej is a heroine of Kazakh fairy tales, distinguished by her beauty. The poem
compares the sky to her beauty.
[44.] *Săukele* – richly decorated bride's headgear, the most expensive element of her dowry.

Poem about Nobility

Hey, you, wretched Nobility,
we consider you almost an angel
but today I'll find a fault with you for sure –
I'm in a demonic mood today.

The reason is – I saw the devil
in your eyes too.
As soon as I discover that,
all my patience is lost.

This devil in your eyes
soiled your minds.
He saddled you first, then asked:
'How are you?' – mockingly.

He ripens a whirlwind in your chest –
sometimes he tries to tickle you.
Your patience, an unfortunate one,
runs out in the blink of an eye.

You can't be an example after all
for an honest tomorrow,
and you quickly join the ranks
of a global crime ring.

You could have avoided crimes,
You have a sacred grief – God's gift,
which doesn't fit in the belly
of your boundless lust.

The very blood in your veins
will scream and curdle from disgust,
and a little bird in the heart
of your shame will yell too.

The screams of the bird in the heart
will make your ears bleed,
to the canine lustful growls
deceit will cling with all its might,

so it won't be left behind;
asking help from Satan,
it wants to have its own share
in the bloody global devilry.

A fierce winter all around –
even spittle comes out abrasive.
Everything pricks like a hedgehog
when you're so very cold.

The long-white-bearded snowing sky
cuts the face with its ice particles.
Nobility, frost chained your spine
leaving you rigid.

Then you're going to scream,
praying to the world for mercy.
You worshiped the spirits of your ancestors –
but they all died of cold and frost.

Nobility, you are guilty
of a global crime.
In this shameless world
you'll be left howling to the sky.

Though you're howling to the sky –
the lustful canine growls
will never let you go,
grabbing you by the throat.

After that, we'll also howl to the sky,
tired of desperate thoughts.
A huge blue dog-lust stands
urinating into the Moon.

Life

*This mortal world is in front of me – naked
sticking out its tongue it revealed its face.*
– Mūķaġali Maķataev[45]

Who am I? –
an image of a walking skeleton,
Hot blood injected into an animal-like image.
I realised quite late that I came to this world,
stuck to the saliva of canine lust.

But what would I do if I knew?
Nothing.
Many of the devil's seed passed one by one.
If you thought to stay well and sound,
keeping out of sight of a dodgy night –
it's an empty hope.

Although I was born because of
canine lust,
I can't bark like a dog,
I will live – I said with human words.
I opened my eyes –
hypocritical laughter,
hot hugs,
a temptress named Life had already
got to me.

My newly opened eyes saw a disastrous image.
Words can't describe it.
A song would die trying to do so.
Completely naked,
taking off all clothes,
it was dancing around with its tongue
shoved into my shame.

[45.] From the poem 'Shamilge hat' ('Letters to Shamil'), translated by the National Bureau
of Translations.

I cleverly closed my eyes:
not having time to say: 'Go away, evil spirit.
Leave me be.'
I wanted to ask Allah for his help and sympathy,
but my tongue wasn't able to say *kălima*.[46]

This false reality that flashed
through my mind, confusing me,
immediately extinguished the fire of a fantasy.
I wanted to be a melody, a window broke.
I wanted to be pure,
but the raging voice of life smashed this dream too.

It sprinkled dust on Grace's eyes,
made footcloths out of Beauty's dress.
Even if I kept my eyes closed, the world smelled like dirt,
and rough sounds drilled into my ears.

I wasn't afraid of its anger.
Well, in a pinch …
it will raise its index finger.
So I thought and, unable to resist,
I opened my eyes,
but she's ready to take her clothes off …
O, what Lechery!

[46.] *Kălima* – a phrase from the Qur'an about one's commitment to Islam.

Steppe. Night. Magic. World View.

Having painted every sound with the thickest paint,
night and magic fell into each other's arms.
The sky-cat licked cloud-cream
from the milky surface with its moon-tongue.

Shooting stars sound like a broken string,
or like salt being sprinkled over liver.
When a black-blue Night is making itself ready to fly like doves,
a breeze from flapping wings reaches its face.

When an orphaned *jinn*[47] sighs close to me,
without making a sound,
I protect myself by reading Abaj:[48]
Although the steppe is silent as if out of breath,
falling into apathy –
yet I cannot find peace.

As if someone is calling me silently to go outside,
I'm agitated, talking to myself:
'Who did I allow to steal my golden time,
when I was picking stars from the garden of the Night?'

I took this question with me to the sky.
This feeling is inherent in tales and legends.
I wanted to pick the stars and eat them like berries,
clinging to the branches of the huge tree-sky.

---

[47] *Jinn* – in Islamic mythology, an intelligent spirit created from fire (as opposed to angels created from light and humans created from earth), invisible to humans. *Jinns* can be male or female, Muslim and *kaffir*; they can be born, marry and die. They appear in different forms and move at great speeds. It is believed that non-Muslim *jinns* can possess human beings and do harm, whereas Muslim *jinns* serve a *baksy* to heal people and fight evil *jinns*.

[48] Abaj Ķùnanbajùly (Abai Kunanbayev; 1845–1904) – the most influential of all Kazakh poets, also a composer and philosopher. He is considered to be a reformer of Kazakh literature on the basis of enlightened Islam; his works also reflected the European and Russian cultures.

Seven stars of Ursa Major –
Do they still remind you of the *ķobyz*
with its cracked body?
It seems that the cloudy Milky Way's track
directs us towards an unknown dwelling place.

If you touch the *ķobyz*'s string,
Ķypšaķ-sorrow and Oġyz-sadness[49] will wake up.
A mighty *jinn* mocks an orphaned *jinn*
And dances over my *ķobyz*-melody.

The Night covered everything with its cloak.
The steppe is asleep.
The mountains lie in oblivion.
Even the Moon whose light was streaming
from above is dead now,
its melting wax has stopped.

It seems I climbed up following my dream,
but I came back to my senses,
descended suddenly to the ground …
But then I begged the sky:
'Night-dove,
Don't fly away taking my luck.'

My eyes see everything.
My soul – in agony,
My body exhausted
I felt the tramp of horses' hoofs along my spine.
Sorrow subsided.
Jinns run away from the sky.
With the call to Allah
the dove-sunrise was landing …

---

[49] Ķypšaķ and Oġyz (Kipchak and Oguz)– confederations of Turkic people in the Middle Ages.

Azure World. Longing for Spring.

Azure world –
It was my unquenchable desire.
I missed my *ḵanžajlau*[50] at sunrise.

I'm bored of winter.
It's been getting on my nerves for a long time,
but an azure light flashed in my eyes.

It didn't shake my gloomy looking place,
but this light became a fire that licks winter's hem.

Bringing a caravan of tulips in its tow,
spring will reach a place of paradise tomorrow.

A nightingale of happiness landed on the roof.
Azure world is leisurely building its home.

Like a modest girl's face blushes from pink to red,
dawn comes rising over the mountain tops.

Ḵunans[51] race like arrows on the hills, *dônen*[52] get impatient,
not a horse, but a heart is riding a song.

A laughing stream rejoices running down the hills,
following the Sun, falling a thousand times.

Azure world – a place where happiness settles.
The sand will keep the mysterious secret to itself.

The mirage's honey is sticking to its lips.
The mound basks under the rays of the Sun.

[50.] *Ḵanžajlau* – high season at a summer pasture, when Kazakhs hold horse races, weddings, celebrations, youth games and visit relatives and friends.

[51.] *Ḵunan* – three-year-old male farm animal, primarily a horse. *Ḵunans* are believed to be sufficiently grown-up, and thus highly valued.

[52.] *Dônen* – term for four-year-old male horse. *Dônens* are considered mature enough to become stallions; also, mature *ḵymyz* is called '*dônen ḵymyz*'.

The Moon – a witness to all secrets – is getting paler,
still hangs in the sky that didn't sleep all night.

After that ...
one girl who guarded the sheep all night
goes up the hill cold and tired.

Well, I'm crossing the pass on a white horse,
and everyone looks back at me in admiration.

I hear the sad song of the girl, the sounds get quieter.
The horizon is dipping its hem in the Sun's blood.

The Azure world generously sings a single song –
then, deeply moved, it sighs with a hint of guilt.

I will put hobbles on a white-maned horse and go up the hill.
Like a butterfly I will disappear among flowers.

Ķyzemšek Hill[53] is covered by a blue cape,
I can see an image of a whitest beauty on the sky –

Lying on my back –
my fantasy is on fire again.
I bite a blade of grass,
close to losing my mind ...

... But for now, everything is only a pointless dream.
Fierce winter still mixes its anger with devilry.

It conceals all behind its white curtain –
A wind sweeps away sweet visions in an instant ...

[53.] Ķyzemšek Hill lies in the West Kazakhstan region. The literal translation of its name
would be 'a girl's breast'.

But spring is coming nearer with the sounds of birds.
Each song pours from its throat with magic.

With its song-melody, with a heaven in its soul
joyful life roams this steppe ...

All my prayers and pleas were not in vain,
look, ice floes cracked all night.

From early morning today, we show bravado –
the mountain is sewing a rainbow curtain.

Azure world ...
At last it is upon us ...
Azure world ...

Translated by Rose Kudabayeva

GULNAR SALYKBAY
(b. 15.05.1963)

Gulnar Salykbay is a poet and literary translator. She graduated in journalism from Kirov Kazakh State University (now Ăl-Farabi Kazakh National University) in 1986 and has worked for various mass media organisations. Currently she is the editor-in-chief of the national TV channel Ķazaķstan (Qazaqstan).

Her first poetry collection *Bir žūtym aua, ķyzyl kùn* (One Breath of Air, a Red Sun, 1990) was published in 1991 to great acclaim in the literary community. It was followed by *Žan* (Soul, 1995), *Aspandaġy aŋsarym* (My Beloved in the Sky, 2001), *Tùs* (Dream, 2010) and *Keširiŋder kelgenimdi ômirge* (Forgive Me for Coming into this World, 2012). Gulnar Salykbay's poems are known for their reflection on the depths of the human condition; her passion and linguistic experimentation mark her as a strikingly distinctive voice in contemporary Kazakh poetry. Her verses are included in the numerous national and international poetry anthologies. She has translated a book of Marina Tsvetaeva's poetry and her own poems have been translated into several languages; two volumes of her poems have been published by the Ethnic Publishing House of the Republic of China in Beijing.

Gulnar Salykbay is a poet laureate of the State Prize of the Republic of Kazakhstan (2014), and the Poetry Prize of the nationwide contest dedicated to 150th Anniversary of the birth of Abaj (1995).

The Sky Can Capsize Out of the Blue

The sky can capsize out of the blue,
mountains can shed tears once in a while,
a stormy sea can lose its way
and beg the mighty cliffs for help.
So what? Life is good anyway!

Eyes clouded by fog
so thick, light unable to pierce it.
You're left at the mercy of the night,
covered by the dark cloak of doubts.
So what? Life is good anyway!

The heart trembles on a love's leash,
trying to escape, to be free.
Guided by a soul without a hope
where they will end? In the abyss.
So what? Life is good anyway!

Blame the Moon for not being the Sun
falling from above like tears of the night.
Turn your back to the sky
and end up as some meaningless clod …
So what? Life is good anyway!

Adagio

Days die,
nights sing you a lullaby.
You look around,
to find a way out –
but like a river without its bed, you can't flow.

Days die,
nights are looming.
But you're still daydreaming.
You cherish the past, but
aren't ashamed to forget easily.
Closing your eyes and ears,
you turn yourself into a lonely island …
Nothing comes in, nothing out.
You shut close in on yourself.
It's painful, but you won't die.

Months are flying,
stealing all dreams –
you're not ahead.
You're not behind.
Out of breath, you try to do enough.
As for me, I can't catch you.

You are so far from me now,
spinning around the Moon, I guess.
One day you are sad,
another day angry –
like a voice discarded by its owner.

Like a stream that dreamed to be rain,
like a wind not free to blow,
you are always hiding,
unsure of yourself,
but still like an unruly storm.

At parties – people corner you,
in your head – dark thoughts punish you.
You don't fall.
You don't cry.
In your sorrow you won't ask for help.

When hope leaves, doubts set in.
What is there to find?
Who's there to please?
In the past you had your wings,
no way you can sew them back.

If you don't trust yourself,
you're like the earth without the sky.
Defaming or hurting others
won't help –
you're digging yourself a grave.

The sky will cry,
and fall on your head –
quenching your thirst,
calming you down. You'll feel good –
but will befriend no one.

The Sun will rise,
grief will disperse.
You'll be yourself again,
recovering strength.
Still against the world.

But you'll question yourself as ever,
full of regrets, sadly sighing …
Time has no shame,
happiness no limits.
But you still can't get it.

Waiting for You Is Like
Adding Pepper to Honey

Waiting for you is like adding pepper to honey,
like asking a smiling midday to wait for the Moon.
Waiting for you is like placing an ice cube into the fire,
and being whipped by memories.

Waiting for you feels like being a blind cloud, lost in the sky,
or feeling nothing at all, but pretending to smile.
Waiting for you is like begging for emptiness,
breaking like a flower's stem under the sparrow's weight.

Waiting for you is like spraying water on the sand, such a waste!
opening the door and facing a bogeyman instead of a friend.
Waiting for you is like looking in the mirror
and fleeing from your own reflection in disgust.

Waiting for you is like trying to light a candle made of ice,
wearing a necklace of shiny crystals of salt that burns your skin.
Waiting for you is like crying alone
feeling the taste of your tears on a sunny day.

Waiting for you is like having a charmed life on the seventh sky.[1]
But I'll never have a chance to fall as rain.
Waiting for you is like fighting a shadow.
You won't lose, but what is the point of it anyway?

Waiting for you feels like being lost inside yourself,
or being hungry, and dreaming about bread.
Waiting for you is like turning into a white statue,
with a face either crying or laughing.

---

[1] 'On the seventh sky' – or 'on the seventh heaven': the highest heaven in Islam. The phrase means 'to be in bliss'.

Waiting for you becomes an art of expectation,
I tell myself everything will be great.
My eyes are getting tired, but I'm waiting,
until all the colours of the world will slowly fade.

I'm waiting for you, no lies and doubts.
Who will refuse such happiness? Kidding I'm not.
I'm waiting for you till my soul is dethroned.
Because you are me and I am you.

It Is You I Was Looking for, But in Vain

It is you I was looking for, but in vain,
hoping that everything will light up one day,
when I finally meet you.
Everywhere I went, I checked all roads.
I wanted to look from above,
but my wings were clipped.

I've been waiting for you like for the drab tiredness of an
                                             autumn garden.
Like an empty golden throne awaits for a king.
My thoughts, pure as silvery drops of a summer rain
when I've been waiting for you.
But you were always ahead like a swirling mirage.

I've been waiting for you like the steppe awaits a shower,
impatient like a child craving for sweets.
Thoughts of you my only companion –
I was walking for hours, killing my feet.

Days passed, sunsets were born
while I was waiting for you, blaming time for my pain.
This woman coming by your side.
How can she bear such happiness?

What a Joy to Meet the Spring

What a joy to meet the spring –
and cry from happiness.
Forgetting that autumn came with its sadness,
but still loved by the Sun.

What a joy to meet the spring –
to fall under the spell of this bloom.
To get lost before entering
the thick forest of common sense.

What a joy once more to see a handkerchief
that wiped crying eyes.
To ignore all rumours that will follow me tomorrow,
and forget about you at last.

What a joy to sit on a chair
facing the sea,
learning to treasure every hour
before joining the madness of life.

What a joy to step into a stream
that can take you away,
to accept the craziness of this world
and continue to live.

What a joy to see young foliage
greeting its first sunrise.
To feel the unending pulse of the street
and hear its voices and laughter.

What a joy to smell a bunch of tulips,
picked especially for you.
And then be cooled by a light breeze
following you tenderly on the road.

What a joy to meet the sea
and float on its salty waves.
To trust no one and nothing at all,
but be joyful anyway …

If I Fall Asleep,
Don't Wake Me Up

If I fall asleep, don't wake me up,
Be yourself, not the echoes of others.
Don't look for me when I'm gone,
You will know when I want to be found.

Meet my evening with your sunrise
Be a song that will tremble my soul.
If I'm old, make me glow like a full moon,
Trust yourself, leave the burden of doubts.

You can move to a different planet,
Always searching for a happier place.
But wherever you go, don't forget me
Otherwise you'll forget yourself.

Don't be surprised to see me standing apart,
Far from any crowds or streams.
Be my friend that I'll never lose,
Like the earth catch my falling dreams.

Don't pity me if I go astray,
You won't scold me for that, will you?
If I'm found in a thousand years,
Everything I wrote will open your eyes.

Blame me if I'm not at loud parties,
Blame me for my past.
One day I'll nest in your heart
With my song written after the rain.

Penelope and Me

We are just few whose dreams still survive,
Brighter than the Moon,
Hotter than the Sun we are.
For some we are long dead,
For some we are still alive –
Penelope and me.

All warriors are busy with bloody battles,
They fall and rocks become their eternal pillows,
Clouds pour their last drinks.
We wait –
The last leaves tattered by the wind,
But still clinging to the tree in autumn –
Penelope and me.

We're the palaces where only hearts dwell,
We're ready to host the happiness there too.
We don't have regrets, we're busy weaving,
Our glances are not for the others,
We're just looking through the windows –
Penelope and me.

Umbrellas Float Along the Street

Umbrellas float along the street,
covering our faces.
I don't know how old is she,
what century she came from, what age?

'Everything has been forgotten:
my succulent rice, my joyful life known to others.
Now all I can do is wait,
I was born to wait forever', she says.

Her forgiving heart and her old coat
have lost their vivid colours.
Hunched and faceless, she stands
by the road – heart on her sleeve.

She's not interested in weather,
she ignores blossoming Almaty gardens.
A loaf of bread is in her bag
and letters left unposted.

Nobody would recognise her now,
sorrow itself, wiping her tears away.
The road is muddy, people drunk –
will no one notice her somehow?

The Sun is looking in the clouds
for the beloved Moon, no hope for them.
A woman out of this world watches me,
her gaze burning my back.

She's standing there like a dead hope –
revived somehow but forgotten.
There's a silent question in her eyes –
I didn't look back, what can I tell her?

What could be better than this day!
Everything awash in this drizzle.
In the end I will become her umbrella
to protect her from the rain, at least.

My Soul – My Leaves – Are So Cold

My soul – my leaves – are so cold.
My body – my tree – is so numb.
Sun's sleepy eyes half-closed –
watch me, but don't warm me up.

Life for me is staring into the abyss,
disappointed and lost.
I'm cold, then I'm burning
I'm laughing, then I'm in mourning.
Always in trouble, that's typical me.

But once in a while my soul –
my leaves are stronger than iron,
the most honest tears from night eyes,
my song is coming …

To Restore Peace of Mind,
Look at the Sky

To restore peace of mind, look at the sky.
Be fair to yourself, be honest.
You feel like a pale moon in the midday?
Dry your tears, you'll find your way.

Yearning will come followed by hope,
These flowers of hope will console me.
Then doubt will knock on my door,
With laughing disdain to destroy me.

What does life want from me?
How can I fool myself?
Sharing my secrets with a deaf rock,
I stroke its cold forehead ...

Forgive Me, Good-Natured People

Forgive me, good-natured people,
for wandering through this boundless space!
Forgive me
for what I am too,
for coming into this world.

Forgive me
for being madly in love,
waiting for a spring gust of wind.
For my life spent bending my back,
doing some useless things ...

Forgive me
for loving you all,
for wanting to see you in the best light.
And after that to burn all my possessions,
scratching up the ground in grief.

Forgive me
for trusting without any reason,
for my shining luck.
For throwing away needlessly my youth
like some old things and junk.

Forgive me
if I can't recognise in time
the meanness of the ungrateful.
For not caring about endless holes
in my shabby old towel.

Forgive me
if I misunderstood some of you,
and was left a bit disappointed.
Forgive
my heart and my poems
for all their cherished dreams.

Forgive
my views for being only my own,
for dreams never coming true.
My worn dress, its colours faded,
my senseless business too …

Forgive me
for waiting with bated breath.
For times when I was wrong.
For my hidden tears
not shed, but poured
straight into my heart.

Forgive me
for secret wounds
never bandaged and never healed.
Forgive for holding this pen
that is never satisfied with itself.

Forgive my book that will be finished
without telling the whole truth.
Forgive the beat of my heart
expecting some wonderful news …

Forgive me
for being a person
who doesn't like to be in the spotlight.
Forgive my abandoned shore,
if you possibly can.

Forgive
my unwritten words
and me being still alive and well.
Forgive my loving eyes –
looking straight at you.

I Scattered Myself Evenly

I scattered myself evenly
down the street.
I heard sounds of happiness on the phone.
It made me drunk.

Without it, life is a lie,
it becomes an orphaned beauty.
It dawned on me.
In snowless winter I laughed
becoming a birdless summer.

Like the source of a shadow
no one is visible around,
and I followed my heart …

Even the Sky Didn't Suit You

Even the sky didn't suit you as a place of eternal stay.
Come to me,
Don't be shy, come, the lonely Moon.
Let's gaze at the lonely-lonely stars,
They twinkle, born to become shooting ones.

Come, the lonely Moon.
Who needs your struggle?
Earth is lonely, sorrow is lonely too,
You know that …
If the crowd laughs, they show their stupidity,
Let's show them their loneliness.

Trouble runs away from me, black clouds from you,
One day they will leave us after sipping bitter tears.
It is clear that you will never reach your Sun.
And I will be left half-way, robbed by someone.

A Soul Will Cry on a Rainy Day

A soul will cry on a rainy day,
Is there anything more priceless than a soul?
Your heart will wander down the street,
Cherishing traces of a dream.

Joy and sorrow will make peace.
A far-seeing heart will burst into tears.
Unbroken luck that bolted from its master
Will then mess with your head.[2]

A soul will cry on a rainy day,
Is there a kind person who can console it?
A tree in pursuit of fashion will wane
If it doesn't have leaves to enhance its beauty.

As if all earthly disputes had died out,
A peaceful melody would come from a teardrop.
Filling your chest with sweet pain,
Taking you to a world of beautiful sadness.

… My mind was defeated by you,
Will my voice reach you now?
You are close to me like a rainy night,
You are far from me like a rainy night too.

Translated by Rose Kudabayeva

[2.] There is a saying in Kazakh: 'Let luck nest on your head.'

MARALTAI RAIYMBEKULY
(b. 29.04.1969)

Maraltai Raiymbekuly (Ybyrajymov) studied fine arts at Žambyl State Pedagogical University named after Ķoža Ahmet Âssaui (Kozha Akhmet Yasawi). Raiymbekuly worked for numerous mass media organisations: he was editor-in-chief at the newspaper *Kentavr* (2007–08) and senior editor for the TV and radio corporation Ķazaķstan (Qazaqstan) (2008–12). He went on to become deputy chairman of the Board of the Writers' Union of Kazakhstan (2012–18) and since 2018 has been the deputy director of the National Book Chamber of the Republic of Kazakhstan. For a number of years, he headed the Žas ķalamger section of the Union, working primarily with emerging talents in literature and supporting them in their careers. He is also a member of the Board for Youth Policy under the President of the Republic of Kazakhstan.

His poems have been published in literary newspapers since 1987, but his first collection, *Aj-Nùr* (Moon-Light) did not appear until 1996, for which he received the Prize of the Kazakhstan Union of Youth. This was followed by *Aj* (Moon, 2001), *Asau* (The Proud, 2014), *Tarpaņ* (The Unrestrained, 2014), *Ķaratau ġazaldary* (Songs of Ķaratau, 2014) and *Kentavr* (Centaur, 2018). He is acclaimed for creating otherworldly images out of the most banal surroundings and trivial events, and he has greatly influenced younger poets for the ambitious and unbroken spirit of his verses.

Raiymbekuly has won many prizes: the State Award for Youth Daryn (2000) for his book of verses *Aj*, the Alaš International Literary Award (2014) for the collection *Kentavr*. He is a three-times holder of a Grant of the President of Kazakhstan (1997–99).

471

Self Portrait

Like Solomon, who shared his sorrow
with every living creature,
I indulge my sadness composing songs.
Like a fading world I languish,
finding nothing to ease my soul.
Unable to gather my thoughts,
I feel that time is passing me by.

Like one unable to find a companion
in the depths of conscience and in the abyss of sorrow
I feel empty, for I have done more harm than good.
I'm like the Taj Mahal whose treasures were robbed.
My soul has landed on the heart
of a beauty. Just look at it.
I am dragging my body back from the grave
I am scouring the earth for my soul.

There's a flower barely surviving
beneath April snow.
Its petals are full of visions, as am I.
In a world where visions sustain us
am I one who has been deceived?

Like a desert plant I put down deep roots.
Could my verses save me from death?
For good or bad, who am I? What have I achieved
in almost thirty years of life?

Is there a place for me in the world
and the thoughts that I've expressed in verse?
I can only tell the truth,
which even my friends and foes acknowledge.
Between this life and what comes after
I will have left my mark –
like red ink dripping into milk.

My *ḳobyz*-heart[1] is shaped like the moon.
If a fly brushes against its strings,
it's enough to make it throb.
You who believe, your eyes turned
towards the Ka'aba,
you whose spirit is pure,
look at me now and tell me
whether I'm true to myself.

[1.] *Ḳobyz* – traditional Kazakh musical instrument with a wooden body, two to four strings and a bow made of a horse's mane. It is the main attribute of the *baḳsy* during a healing ritual and is considered sacred.

Disoriented

O great Žajyķ,[2] you are my delight,
I am your lost and wandering ibex.
When I see the Sun rise in the East
I look, frustrated, towards the West.

O great Žajyķ, you're like an ancestor's belt,
hanging loosely as he moved with grace –
one of those who communed with *aruaķs*,[3]
his scarfed head as tall as a mighty tree.

Aķ Žajyķ like a belt, you let me slip from you.
No one has ever pampered me since –
I'm like a camel's calf who has lost his mother
and suffers from it for the rest of his life.

Still, a suffering man is nothing new.
O Žajyķ, my one and only,
your tides glitter like beads, in which the music rages.
But am I worth more than Ķaztuġan?[4]

I am no better than the great men before us,
those disparaged by the ignorant conqueror,
who did not perceive what Yķylas's[5] *ķobyz*
was saying in Sùgir's 'Bozingen'.[6]

[2.] Žajyķ – also called Ural, is a river that originates in the southern Ural Mountains and discharges into the Caspian Sea. 'Aķ Žajyķ' (lit. 'white Žajyķ') is an honorific term.

[3.] *Aruaķs* – ancestral spirits. It is believed that *aruaķs* protect the living descendants, thus they are treated with deep reverence. Kazakhs visit their ancestral graves to ask for guidance; they make vows in the name of *aruaķs* and call their ancestors' names in a battle cry.

[4.] Ķaztuġan Sùjinišùly (Kaztugan Suinishuly) – a fifteenth-century *žyrau* warrior, storyteller and poet.

[5.] Yķylas Dùkenùly (1843–1916) – Kazakh composer and virtuoso *ķobyz* player.

[6.] Sùgir Ăliùly (1882–1961) – composer and *dombyra* player (*kùjši*), a pupil of Yķylas. 'Bozingen' is one of his most famous *kùjs* (traditional tunes). The story behind this *kùj* has been narrated in multiple variations, one of which is about a female camel (*bozingen* – lit. 'white female camel') who parted with her calf; the *kùj* is her mourning.

My song and my valour are the best of me.
My only aim to give a voice to my sorrow.
My heart will never howl towards those alien forests,
as beneath this Moon, I tread my native earth.

My great Žajyķ shares its innermost feelings with me,
just as it did in my forbears' high-spirited days.
… I will return to you one day,
like one whose tale has a happy ending.

Baķsy[7]

Hey, birds, I look at you and see
your innocent souls soaring in praise of Allah.
I have a *jinn*[8] within me that makes me shake with rage.
Even Ķaķaman[9] would run away in fright.

The *baķsys'* laughter rings out like an innocent child's,
the rustling of a *peri*[10] in their walk.
When playing the *ķobyz*, they reach for the Moon,
shining their light into the night.

If I die, my hope will shine with a dazzling light.
(I will perish knowing that hope never dies.)
Reborn, I will walk again across this world
and grow alongside the flowers of the field.

Was it autumn or spring, I can't remember,
when a girl who kissed me became a song?
She will always be there, waving at me
from the sky's abyss with blue veils.

[7.] *Baķsy* – shaman, a priest of Tengrism said to possess unique abilities (e.g. clairvoyance, healing powers, access to the spiritual world). *Baķsys* typically treated minor ailments with plant-based or other medicine and entered into trance states to heal more serious diseases. It is believed that they had *jinn* slaves helping them during divination and healing rituals.

[8.] *Jinn* – in Islamic mythology, an intelligent spirit created from fire (as opposed to angels created from light and humans created from earth), invisible for humans. *Jinns* can be male or female, Muslim and *kaffir*; they can be born, marry and die. They appear in different forms and move at great speeds. It is believed that non-Muslim *jinns* can possess human beings and do harm, whereas Muslim jinns serve a baqsy to heal people and fight evil *jinns*.

[9.] Ķaķaman – *jinn*, a patron (pir) of Kazakh *baķsys*. It was common for a *baķsy* to address Ķaķaman when performing healing rituals. He is believed to be a giant, a benevolent leader of the *jinn* army who serves the *baķsy* to help people in their troubles.

[10.] *Peri* – in Islamic mythology, a *jinn*-like creature created from fire. It can be both benevolent and malevolent, and female *peri* are considered to be the most beautiful beings in the world.

I'm still in love with that girl,
perhaps I'll love her until the end of time.
There's a serpent circling around the fire.
Could it really be my *pir*,[11] my guardian spirit,
closer to humans than *jinn* or *peri*?
In whom can I place more trust?
With a *baksy's* cry I raise both hands to heaven.
No *aruak* or angel replied.

Hey, serpent, with silver belly and golden scales,
if I don't dream about you for a few days,
I really start to miss you.
Only you understand my pain.

Powerful serpent of dazzling gold,
your crown is precious, your throne priceless!
If you can say, tell me, O master of verse.
Why, in this world, is gold so sad and cold?

[11.] *Pir* – patron, holy spirit who oversees and protects the living; every craft has its *pir*. It is also a term for powerful religious figures in Sufism.

Balbal

I am only at ease when I play my *ķobyz*,
and then my fate changes.
Our hearts are related, our sorrow is common.
My stone heart thrills whenever I see you.

Although our hearts are different,
they weep and bleed together.
My fellow spirit with agonising soul,
my stone heart weeps whenever it sees you.

O, *Balbal*,[12] you belong to the earth, but I do not.
This is a mystery, like those enshrined
in *ắbžat* .[13] When I see you,
my soul soars into the limitless sky.

Azrael[14] frolics beside me
when sometimes I walk on the earth.
Was I the only one, heaven-born but mortal,
who turned his death to a feast?

Devious girls of twilight
slithered into my arms like snakes.
Three nines[15] is the punishment I'll be content with.
Don't make me responsible for another's death.

[12.] *Balbal* – anthropomorphic stone stela, installed atop, within or around *ķorģans* (burial mounds) in cemeteries.

[13.] *Ắbžat* – Arabic alphabet; in the poem's context it is used as a symbol of enlightenment, since Islamic education was considered prime schooling for Kazakhs for many centuries.

[14.] Azrael – angel in the Abrahamic religions, identified as Angel of Death, responsible for taking the human soul away from the body. In Kazakh folklore he is occasionally represented as personified death.

[15.] 'Three nines' – punishment in traditional Kazakh *bi* judging system. It was handed out for petty crimes: a convicted person had to pay three nines, e.g. three horses, three camels and three cows. For a homicide one could be condemned to death.

Who can change my fate?
You'd like to know about the grave? Well, there it is.
I would have crushed my foes mercilessly,
but there is no foe as mighty as a lion.

The Sun God blesses us with its grace.
Though I was expecting a greater light
to reconcile mankind to Iblis
with the blessing of the Kok Turks.[16]

On the grey stone there are spots of red:
is it your soul weeping
in the embrace of Heaven?
Or is it my blood dripping
from the embrace of Heaven?

O, *Balbal*, my brother!

[16.] Kok Turks – (lit. 'celestial Turks') a confederation of Turkic peoples who established the
Turkic Khaganate (552–659 AD) and the Second Turkic Khaganate (682–744 AD) in the
Altaj Mountains and expanded their territories throughout Central Asia.

Punishment

Accepting everything as decreed by Allah
I have worn out my soul with suffering.
When the birds return, my heart sounds its bugle call,
in the grip of its blood red destiny.

Bugles and trumpets resound so loudly
that every king is overthrown.
Every poet searches for Abel
in the black heart of Cain. They shed bitter tears.

What does my restless soul yearn for?
I flee from the fire I've started myself.
As if I were Cain who murdered his brother,
I struggle to find some peace.

Bugles and trumpets resound so loudly –
you think you're alone in missing those times.
On behalf of a thousand kings, in the name of Allah,
true king, Abel would question Cain.

The Whore

What can I do, if my fate is evil-eyed?
If commoners judge me, what do I care?
I have never met another like you,
a woman of the night.

A starlit night reveals the secrets of the universe,
I have immersed myself in the pleasures
of such a radiant night, and I confess:
I was prejudiced against you
and every woman on Earth.

You lay in my arms exposed,
a source of shame to my guardian angel.[17]
The Moon observed us through the window.
It is love. It begins in hope, and ends in sorrow.

[17.] In Islam, angels are also called *al hafathah*, which means 'guardian angels'.

Centaur

I am a proud son of the steppes
riding horses. O my beloved,
when my enemies brandished swords,
my flowers were severed.

Don't say my brow is more deeply furrowed.
Why do I suffer when I look about me?
Falcons hunt for sparrows.
No geese are heard across the lake.

We say: A wonderful spirit came from the sky.
Our ancestors fought with enemies
for the sake of a piece of land.
Noblemen died defending their dignity.

When I learned to interpret ancestral songs
like Kùltegin,[18] I couldn't sleep.
Beyond the borders of my land
my culture's still unrecognised.

What was the point of glorious days
when forbears conquered half the world?
If one man tramples another
the age itself must suffer.

My dream doesn't have to be sad.
When a bold son is born, he will look like a human,
but, with the unbroken heart of a steed,
he will untangle the secrets of history.

[18.] Kùltegin (Kul Tigin; r. 685–731) – outstanding military commander of the Second Turkic
Khanate, formed in the seventeenth and eighteenth centuries after the liberation wars
against China. He became famous as a brave soldier and participant of many Turkic
military campaigns.

Those men as proud as mettlesome horses –
I don't dream of ancestors today.
If I inherited my heart from them –
why doesn't it whinny then?
My devastation torments me.
What song does my *kobyz*-heart sing?
Suddenly, as if in a fairy tale,
a mane is growing down my back

and, miraculously, I gallop,
my hoofs pounding the rocks.
Hurling myself, like lightning, up to the heavens,
my golden hoofs shine like the moon.

Inspired, I let out a roar
and call upon my ancestors.
Facing the East, I draw my bow.
May God bless me. May all end well!

Eyes and Words

I often work late at the Writers' Union office and
feel unfamiliar eyes staring behind me from the hallway.[19]

I feel the eyes staring at me
I hear the voices behind my back.
Golden-hoofed stallions
gallop beside me.

Why can't they slow down a bit
or is it me that can't keep up?
And then, suddenly, the lament
of Sùgir's *kùj* whinnies in my mind.

My heart is filled with anguish
when I recall the past,
and how Mahambet[20] thirsted for revenge.
Kôkbozat[21] came down from the sky
and wept on the foothills
of the poet Abaj's[22] song.

Where is the Aḳbozat?[23]
The wretched sky!
A foal galloped to the Writers' Union hall
and now it is all lit up.

[19.] The Writers' Union of Kazakhstan is a literary organisation established in the 1930s. The author has worked for the Union for many years.

[20.] Mahambet Ôtemisùly (1804–46) – Kazakh poet, a major figure of Kazakh Romanticism, also known for his leadership roles in rebellions against Russian colonialism. This activity is believed to have resulted in his treacherous murder.

[21.] Kôkbozat – original Kazakh word refers to a blue-white steed and also to one of the stars in the Little Bear constellation. When the poet says 'Kôkbozat came down from the sky', it conveys the image of a star-steed, combining those two Kazakh meanings.

[22.] Abaj Ḳùnanbajùly (Abai Kunanbayev; 1845–1904) – the most influential of all Kazakh poets, also a composer and philosopher. He is considered to be a reformer of Kazakh literature on the basis of enlightened Islam; his works also reflected the European and Russian cultures.

[23.] Aḳbozat – lit. 'white steed', also a name of a star in the Little Bear constellation.

I will stay here as the guardian
of our poetic inheritance.
There is no other friend to support me.
The posterity of Ķambar ata[24]
musters here in the dusk.

You can hear them neighing,
all night they paw the ground.
They kick, bite and fight.
Why are they not at peace like humans?
Why don't they act like friends?

I remember Săken. I recall Săbit.
Why Ķadyr didn't drink and Mûķaġali drank too much.
Ădil is missing. Ămirhan[25] died burning in throes.
How ghastly this nightmare is!

I feel the eyes staring at me.
I hear the voices behind my back.
Who knows? Perhaps the eyes belong to the dead.
Perhaps the words belong to the living.

[24.] Ķambar ata – folkloric figure, a herdsman and patron (*pir*) of horses and horse breeders.
[25.] Săken, Săbit, Ķadyr, Mûķaġali, Ădil and Ămirhan – references to important literary
figures from modern Kazakh history: Săken Sejfullin (1894–1939), Săbit Mûķanov
(1900–73), Mûķaġali Maķataev (1931–76), Ķadyr Myrza Ăli (1935–2011), Ădil Botpanov
(missing since 1996) and Ămirhan Balķybek (1969–2014).

Still Life

There's a pen lying on the table
and, beside it, a piece of paper.
There's a lamp – switched off,
And here's the Qur'an – the unchanging Qur'an!
The Sun had risen, as if it would never set again
or if it sets, as if it would never rise again.
There is also a beautiful yellow flower,
I should have mentioned it first of all.
If the grain of the universe turns to dust
when a flower becomes a bird,
what is the pen's or the paper's offence?
The Qur'an is lying beside the watch.

Master

To You,
who scattered the stars and sewed in the Sun
and who, in the endless universe,
gifted life to humans,
all praise to you, Allah!

You,
who let me live,
whose kindness knows no bounds –
wherever I look,
I see you.

I can only express to you
the sorrows I endure,
to you who light up
the heaven and the earth.

Mountains and steppes,
oceans and seas –
all things are in harmony …
with Allah's decree.

The meandering waters,
the splendour of lakes,
the raucous croaking of frogs …
My mind absorbs them all.

Snow and ice can look like sugar,
what wonder there is!
It only takes one glance
for the stones to chat among themselves!

The hint of a breeze across the steppe,
a mirage beyond the plain,
a flower's scent: that's all it takes
to make me think of you.

You are my cradle –
my dream and my desire.
You are the one who presides
over life and what comes after …

(Prepare yourself, if you're not ready.)
You are magnanimous, the solitary one.
Whether it is breathing or not,
all creation needs you.

You are my sustainer,
I call out loudly
that I'm happy in you Allah
even if you reduce me to a speck of dust.

You are the creator.
No poet's words
will ever describe your grace,
no artist's skill.

You alone sustain me
but when will I find peace?
My heart is pounding,
repeating your name in awe.

You are the one who illuminates
eighteen thousand worlds.
In truth, I love you,
my God!

Recognition of Muhammad

O, my lost home,
I pledge to you the morning dew,
I pledge the setting Sun,
it is I who bids the whole world
to kneel down.

If my race were ever endangered,
I would exchange my pen for a sword.
Their blood is my blood.
I would be the first in battle.

I was born the same day
that the warrior Muhammad died.
Without me, who else
would heal your soul?
I am the one:
the true poet,
my birth foretold by Muhammad.

Farewell to the Earth

The Earth is covered in blue mist
my star is not visible from here.
I shall visit it myself one day
when spring flowers blossom.

I know
I will have my wings by then.
The aether will make me forget my troubles.
I will fly through it, this is what I was striving for.
I will leave behind my mortal body,
always so hungry for life.

O, my poor head,
be grateful.
You tasted honey, you tasted poison,
though you were always full of troubles.
It is not seemly to be a poet
if you were born on the Earth
a Kazakh, and
are too fond of drinking.

O Earth! A green star,
you can wash your eyes with tears.
Leaving you for a distant realm,
it seems unlikely I'll see you again.
Though drunk, I spent little time with you.

Moon

A bottomless world, but if your depths are full,
I'll send my soul's light to where there is no way back,
when the moon is full and the soul sighs,
and when my tawny shade stumbles.

Like the Moon, I'm a living creature –
her body resembling a flower.
We have found each other,
yes, but it is still ending badly.
I used to think of her as myself,
as if she were a gleam in my eye.

When the Moon is full, I invite troubles.
Left alone, my soul aches.
I saw from the full Moon's tides
that my breath is on fire.

If an innocent love condemns you
because of a sin I am unaware of
kiss the Moon on my grave.[26]
Pray to the Moon in the skies!

In the depths of midnight
a star falls, disturbing sleep.
Whose star is it?
One day we'll be as one,
joined together
by one umbilical cord –
the one that connects
the Moon in the sky
to the Moon in my grave.

[26.] Kazakhs, as do many other Islamic communities, use a crescent moon symbol as a graveyard marker.

At a Bar

Listen up, my friend,
my good, kind man,
look after my heart, get a cure for my soul.
For God's sake! If you buy me a drink,
you won't be any poorer.

My life depends on a single drop.
It is you who is deciding my fate.
Who knows, perhaps
we might get hitched
and be best friends forever.

Hey there, holy one,
the kindest beauty,
who knows what sorrows I've endured?
How could I harm you, when I've cried all night
and lost myself in the Milky Way?

Like a fool I've wasted my youth
and haven't accomplished a thing.
I have no friend standing by me
to threaten the Heavens with his fist.

Hey there, holy one,
be the kindest friend to me.
I know a wretch like me won't fool you.
You're an angel covering your peaches
with those two wings of yours.
Tell me, does Paradise exist at all?

Translated by David Cooke

TANAKOZ TOLKYNKYZY
(b. 2.11.1977)

 **Tanakoz Tolkynkyzy** is a poet and journalist. She graduated from Abylaj Khan Kazakh University of International Relations and World Languages (1999) and Robert Schuman University, Strasbourg, majoring in international law (2000), funded by way of the Presidential Scholarship *Bolashak*. She has worked for numerous mass media organisations, and is currently a producer at the national TV channel Ķazaķstan (Qazaqstan).

Her debut poems were published in the nationwide journal for children and youth *Pioner* (now *Aķželeŋ*) in 1988, when she was eleven and won numerous literary contests for young poets. Since then she has been published widely in Kazakh literary periodicals and secured her reputation as a striking emerging writer. Tanakoz Tolkynkyzy's first poetry collection *Biz – taulyķpyz* (We Are from the Mountains, 2001) was followed by *Saģynyp žùrmin* (I Miss You, 2008), *Ajtķym keledi* (I Want to Say, 2010) and *Sùjemin* (I Love, 2014). Her verses are regarded as fine examples of contemporary Kazakh poetry for their daring yet genuine expression of the most intimate feelings common to many Kazakh women, a topic that, until recently, was not common in mainstream Kazakh poetry. She has translated Spanish poet Justo Jorge Padrón's collection *The Dreams of Hell and Exile* into Kazakh (2014) and edited the first anthology of Kazakh poets in Spanish and Azerbaijani (2017). She translates verses from French.

Her awards include the State Scholarship in Literature (1998) and the Dmitry Medvedev Russian Presidential Literary Scholarship (2008). She is poet laureate of the international poetry contest Debût dostastyģy (2008) and of the Šabyt International Festival (2002).

When I Lean on Your Shoulder

When I lean on your shoulder,
a sudden frenzy breaks out and dies
in my heart. O my darling,
let us stop this rage of beating hearts.
Let them not make a record of noise.

When I lay my head on your shoulder,
my soul unlocks as if at royal gates.
My poor heart hides its pulsing beat,
my eyes try not to heave a sigh.

I am mesmerised by your innocence.
You are a model of honesty.
I forgive the betrayal of the world
when I lay my head on your shoulder.

My Sole Desire: To Die

My sole desire: to die.
My sole wish: to see only you.
Here I am roaming, aimless,
and you don't even know
where I am wandering.

I am desperate to leave …
I want to kiss …
I want to change into a cloud.

Sitting on top of death, I want
to hug someone really tightly,
then to pour out all my tears.

I want to run away, run far away
to unknown places, and put out
the fever in the fire inside me.

Let me die. For heaven's sake.
Let me die. I don't need earth,
air, the Moon or Sun –
if I can simply see you.

Forgiveness

I forgave those who pulled their triggers
behind my back. I forgave those who betrayed me.
I turned off the darkness with my light
and I doubled the Sun's rays with my forgiveness.

I forgave those who envied my talent,
who didn't look up to the Sun as they matured.
I forgave the wicked with their vile lives,
those who slandered the honest,
and who found spots even on the Sun.

When asked to paint the darkness,
I copied the white lights in the dark.
Many ill-fated people burn themselves
yet heaven can accommodate all of us …
I vow never to play dirty to fight the darkness
as I want to help the world to stay bright.

Why Did You Get Me in a State?

Why did you get me in a state?
I entered your world drunk and came out sober.
My heart that loves you is my enemy.
I am a total disaster.

I flew off, becoming one with your clouds,
thorns of sorrow pierced my eyes;
even the birds brought grief
as I turned into an enemy of myself,
worse than the enemy of mine that you now are.

I forgot I had been born as a bird to fly
when I became the bait for your trap.
No treatment could cure me.
Now you are the poison I drink to heal myself …

O let me release the wind of grief,
let me set free the verse of my grief.
I beg you, just stop a while at my ailment,
stop a while at the fire you yourself lit.

Prayer

When a person I trust most betrays me,
please teach me to be strong.
When the senses take over my emotions,
please teach me to see my feelings
for what they are. When a car covers
my white dress with splashes of dirt
from the street, please teach me not to curse.
Whenever I flatter myself, teach me
not to lie to my child. When my wishes,
in all their innocence, are assumed wicked,
please teach me to be patient.
Whenever I see a disbeliever, please
teach me to see the God in him.
When days turn gloomy, teach me
to sleep like a baby. When nights
are stormy, teach me to leap to the Moon.
When I fall totally in love, please teach me
to stay silent. And teach me to live
without Sun in my body, which is like a sunflower.
Better still, teach me to live totally
without Sun. When the world is merciless,
teach me to be merciful. Whenever
I get injured, teach me to heal the wounded.
Teach me to believe in individuals,
to overcome my Self. Please teach me
to look as a saint on this immoral world.
When what seems to be a good word
is hurtful, please teach me
not to react. And when feelings
become tainted, teach me not to weep.
Whenever my gentle soul is hurt
by other sensitive people, please teach me
to forgive. When the pure world
is darkened by the innocent, please
teach me to get angry at myself,
at no one else. When the person closest
to me does not listen to my troubles,
please teach me to love him.

Teach me to lose.
Teach me to back off.
If you wish to change my fate,
I beg you: teach me to bow my head.
Please …

Dusk Has Fallen …
Farewell to the Day

Dusk has fallen … farewell to the day.
Dark night is stretching its wings
and I desperately need a friend,
someone who would invite me out
in the small hours. All poets think
they are the greatest and will make
an important mark on the world.
When a restless night keeps me awake,
nobody is there to call out to me.
When I want just to knock on a door,
no one is there to warm me up
with a cup of tea. I need a friend
when I am down, someone to soothe
my aching heart. At home, I have
four phones … when dawn breaks
I will throw them all away –
don't ask me why. When the alarm clock
goes off, I think it must be my loneliness.

You Will Leave

You will leave. Gossips will have their say.
The wind, my restless spiritual friend, will stay …
You will leave. Those who are jealous
will also disappear … The Sun will remain
with its rays. You will leave,
and your life will follow you.
Your verses will stay fighting for their lives.
You will leave. My fate will lose its meaning,
the wind will lose its sense. The Sun
and the rain will lose their senses too.

We Don't Need
any Lamps or Lights

We don't need any lamps or lights,
and you are seated there as usual, so polite …
I am reading my verses to you
while you are reading my soul
and staring at me. My verses
move a million hearts, but alas
they don't touch yours at all.
While I was ordering coffee,
then drinking it, you scanned my body
and drank it all in. Someone smokes shisha
while I smoke my grief. But the world
won't change … You came
and the streets wore light floaty dresses.
I would like autumn to come and undress me.
The same scene again. The café on the left bank.
See me off, but please put my coat on.
Not my fault it is spring. Let me kiss you
just on the face, as if by accident.

Try to Cure My Poor Soul

Try to cure my poor soul.
I can hardly get from one day to the next
with my heart so longing for you.
I am afraid of meeting you face to face.
If you get on the tram unexpectedly,
where will I be able to hide?
Should I alight and pretend
I haven't noticed you? Should I forget
my daydream in which I longed for you?
So worried and confused, I wouldn't be able to work out
what these feelings were: good or evil,
yet I would fight and fight to get rid of them:
in vain … I tried to pretend
it wasn't me who loved you,
who kept searching for you,
and I wished I could burn up like ash.
Why did I play with the magic in your eyes
and quibble with love?
Are you a thief of strong feelings?
Why do you stand at the back of my mind?
Time cannot heal – and my fortune
is in the tip of my nails.
O try to cure my poor soul.
I can't get by from one day to the next
and even though my soul longs for you,
I am terrified of meeting you face to face.

Nothing Worse than Silence

Nothing worse than silence.
Ask me why it is cold today,
but don't remain silent, say anything …
Say how you love me,
how you are in a state of joy,
weeping …
blazing …
Say you are burning with love.
If you can't speak, just ask:
'God, what shall I do?'
If you can't utter a word, just cry …
And let the morning dew talk of love,
let a sob weep about love…
let a resentment talk of love
and let the others talk in vain.
Let the spring articulate love
as long as it doesn't talk in a simple way.
Let the spring dominate.
May your bones, instead of your soul,
speak of love, and may your chin
that trembles speak of love.
May the bridge of your *Adaj-dombyra*[1]
speak of love, even with its strings snapped.
And may the town square talk about
the love that has been waiting for us.
Let the weeping soul talk of love.
Do not remain silent.
Shed your tears instead …

---

[1] *Adaj-dombyra* – refers to a particular type of *dombyra*, a two-stringed traditional Kazakh instrument, one that is widespread in the western parts of Kazakhstan where the Adaj tribe reside.

The Elegy of You

1.
You are devouring me like a beast.
Even if you killed me, you would remain
the one and only love of my life.
Confide in me instead of departing,
and I'll put an end to your troubles. Just call me.
Even a surgeon's knife wouldn't kill me.
I can't live without you, no matter what.
I am told that I deserve to end up ruined.
But O dear, how can it be that loving
is the same as dying – and being buried
in a plot of land … my living life left
as a donation for alms. Yes, love and death
are the same … You had better not touch
this strange death of mine.

2.
I can't half-love.
When I love, I'm on fire.
I resent all those
who can't feel jealousy.
I will never share you
with anyone else
and since I am forced
into this, I feel pain.

I can't half-love.
I get burned if I'm in love.
When two soul-mates meet,
there should be a wedding.
If you are shaking
somewhere in the shallows,
I'll take you like a wave,
tearing apart your soul
to leave you wounded.

I can't half-love.
I'll knock myself out
or walk with no signposts –
since it doesn't suit me.
Let rains sing their songs.
Why can't you understand
this is how I love:
in hearts I leave no joy,
only sadness.

3.
I smell of mint.
Its scent warms me up
when my soul is chilled.
Whenever I walk through crowds,
those who are lonely recognise me.

I smell of mint.
Many ladies would approach me
if they knew how –
since lonely autumn souls
always search out one another.

You are my special scent,
mint, my dear aroma,
for time is going by
and you will be in my last breath,
the tree I rest under, when I'm broken,

pure as when I first inhaled you,
pure as my passion. And if,
just if it is possible to live
without you, my beloved, then,
dear God, let me believe this
before this autumn ends.

4.
I swapped my fate for trusting,
a curse for blessing
a gossip for silence.
In order to save myself from weeping outside your doors,
memories I swapped
for heartfelt apologies.
Don't make me cry!
Insults I banished.
Doubts swamped in mud
I swapped for clear water.
I swapped myself for love.
I swapped my crying soul
for the deafness
that patience brings.
Sorrow I swapped
for poems.

The Hurt

You have wounded my heart
and now you want it to tell you the truth.
A fragile flower can grow through stones
once it knows somebody loves it.

If a stranger sends a basket of flowers,
my heart starts beating excitedly.
Such a blessing: to feel one heart
needed by another fearless heart.

I am saddened by such tiny things
as millet seeds, but flowers make me
think ... so I'm not struggling for nothing.
I long sometimes to die ... or to fly
once I know somebody loves me.

I Am a King

I declare I am a king,
for my loneliness is that of a king
and my love is of money.
I realised all of a sudden
that the swan I saw
was an owl. And now, listen!
It is not my soul crying,
but the creak of a hinge,
rusted and dried.
Nobody knows the truth inside me,
although people offer me
ninety different versions of myself.
Who, I wonder, destroyed
my heart's own garden?
I declare I am a king,
for my unhappiness is that of a king.

The Burden

My heart is weighed down by a word.
My most precious hopes have deceived me.
And now no one can steal from me
because there is nothing left to be lost.

When a real sorrow eats into your soul,
you keep yourself to yourself, all alone.
True happiness and a meaning to life
are found only when all is lost.

My heart is weighed down by a word.
This single pain eats my heart out
until it is hollow, and I have nothing
to regret in taking my leave.
This is life's reality, my dear.

Translated by Patricia McCarthy

ALIYA DAULETBAYEVA
(b. 14.11.1977)

Aliya Dauletbayeva graduated from the Faculty of Philology of Halel Dosmŭhamedŭly (Khalel Dosmukhameduly) Atyrau State University. After working in the media for several years, she is currently an editor at the Atyrau People's Art Centre and director of the Ruhaniât Public Organisation. She founded (2016) the young poets' club, Fariza Žŭldyzdary, in memory of Fariza Ongarsynova, with the aim to nurture young talent in the region.

Her first poetry collection, *Sol bir săule* (The Light I'm Striving For, 2014), was followed by *Žandauys* (Cry, 2017). Her poems were included in the *Aķberen* (The Sacred Gun) volumes of young writers and *Žanartau* (The Volcano), and are also published in the anthology *Ķazaķstan-Resej* (Kazakhstan–Russia). Being a lyrical poet, she relies on the ancient traditions of epic *žyrau* poetry – uncommon sources for the poetry of the relatively young generation whom she represents – but searching for a modern language and new imagery. She authored such epic poems as *Aj astynda bir kôl bar* (There is a Lake Under the Moon) and *Orbŭlaķ*, dedicated to the legendary 'Orbŭlaķ battle' between the Kazakhs and Dzungars in the seventeenth century. She translated verses by Rainer Maria Rilke and Qadriya Temirbulatova into Kazakh, as well as the plays *Noises Off* by Michael Frayn and *Antigone* by Jean Anouilh.

Dauletbayeva is the winner of the international festival Shabyt dedicated to the 100th anniversary of Bauyržan Momyšŭly, as well as a laureate of a number of other poetry contests, including the poetry festivals dedicated to the 350th anniversary of Tôle *bi* and to the 550th anniversary of the Kazakh Khanate. She is also a laureate of the International Šyġys Šynary Poetry Competition.

I Have Been Feeling Strange Lately

I have been feeling strange lately,
my laughter often framed by sadness.
The universal restless whisper
no longer disturbs my state of mind …

Like a wound-down clock,
my patience stops in solitude.
Drained by suspicion,
my cursed days pass,
failing to achieve their one desire.

Amidst the empty laughter of friends,
you can't distinguish one voice from the other.
Will anyone ever pity my dream?
Can anyone understand my soul?

I conceal my confusion, head well down,
in these days that move along haltingly out of step
with these times where I block out thoughts of eternity
in this restlessly meditative, colourful world.

Could it be that my soul's voice reached distant lands?
Could this have caused the sky to explode?
When lightning strikes it doesn't burn.
Tell me, where does your patience come from …?

Do not kill me, p-l-e-a-s-e …

You Are the Gloomy Night, My Love

You are the gloomy night, my love,
frowning at me from the far distance –
my wretched feelings weakened, I have
only my single wing to reach your arms.

So that I strive towards you … burn from your fire.
So that then … and then … choking, I catch my breath …
you burned like that, you gave yourself to be loved,
scattering and spreading the sparks of your soul.

You lured me into your arms, my free bird.
I swore to myself that I wouldn't trust you, but failed …
There are hundreds of cures in the world
but am I willing to recover since you are my disease?

To hell with my greatness – I walk about in tears.
Today you are the song that made me weep.
Who said joy and pain are opposite spheres?
Look here and you'll see there's just one step between them.

You are the night, my love, the mystery –
you wash my eyes, as if with rain.
Could I mindlessly submit to your power?
Am I to blame that my mirror broke?
Tell meeee …

Time Drips from the Palate of My Sweet Poison

Time drips from the palate of my sweet poison.
August breaks off beads from my patience,
desperate for the restless fairytale you tell,
and the beautiful legend voiced by autumn.

You are bored of everything, and I am bored …
We did not believe the heart's whisper,
blind to the locked pearl of August …
as it circles, ever, round and round.

August, August heads towards autumn …
Our passion would be so much richer
if we could only tap into its secret, your gaze,
always flirtatious, mine pure longing.

I can't move closer or further away.
I can't help loving you, and I can't forget you.
No one promised not to deceive me.
No one promised not to make me cry …

Why kick up such a fuss, like some traveller
stuck on the shore, late for his ship?
The world is crazy enough already.
Let's be smart in the future...
OK? …

Now I Have No Mind

Now I have no mind …
Why would I need one?
I can live life without it.
I like your laugh.
That's why I miss you.

Your laugh after all
lit a fire in me.
My only fault is
my own weakness.
I am grateful to fate
for making me love you.

Without you,
past days have no appeal.
O, my fate, will you elude me?
In the midst of a crowd
you deprived me of my will,
caressing me with your eyes.

If loving you is a crime,
what can I do?
Let them decide
on my punishment,
only don't interrupt my dream.

I have no mind right now.
Don't ask me
what time it is … what day …
Having lost my mind,
I have given myself up to your will,
not listening to myself …

Untitled

I was feeling uncertain.
Who feels sorry for anyone in the world?
My life is a bag of holes.

It is absolutely true.
Why don't you believe me?
Thoughtless days are coming to the end
as I head towards the sunset.

Poisonous sediment builds up in my arteries,
and I became fond of the devil.
I made a fool of someone.
Someone made me cry.

Years of mulling over the past to discover
it's not real. See the suntanned girl,
her thick eyelashes – letters written
with no reply.

We called on the name of mercy
but with no humanity.
Lost in the sighs of lamentations,
we can no longer be deceived.

It's only my eyes that laugh.
Don't say that you think it's me.
The truth, known to me alone,
is in my poems only.

God Creates Poets

To be a poet, look to God.
To be a man, yourself.
Moments of sadness, trivia,
offer the illusion of calm.

I am my own worst enemy.
I lost my peace of mind,
heavy as a dog's life,
stuck with its lot.

My heart is exposed,
swaying there powerless.
How can you understand
such passion and futility?

Sadness is close to my heart.
Has anyone noticed this?
I am not the very last
among the broken poets.

I grieve as I fall alone into the
arms of night. My dead
poetic creation lies
in swaddling clothes, engenders
prayers on the repose of the soul …

I Am Sick Because of You

I am sick because of you … but how are things with you?
You wound my heart a hundred times, a hundred times you fix it.
I wanted to walk without freezing, without burning with fire,
but God knows how, some troubles overtook us.
I'm sick because of you … but how are things with you?

There is nothing but calm
in the direct gaze of your eyes.
Maybe that's why I got carried away so quickly,
mesmerised with sorrow in your eyes.

And now, my life has become storm-tossed
I bend like a reed in the wind.
Meeting you, has caused lines to spin in my head –
my life has become increasingly complicated by this.

My life was difficult enough without you,
and there is no one to share this with,
yet autumn is so cold, and I have only a single late hope that flowers.

I realise, like a fool, my love,
my suffering comes when my mind is on hold –
that's exactly how it is, chattering away, chasing mirages …
I do not want to love.
Yet I love.

How Are You, My Silent Love?

How are you, my silent love …?
What is it like walking without me, without sadness, without
the dawn?

I fell in love with your essence, it seemed unique,
but the wind blew so cold from your side.

You think, anyone is asking how I am?
My mind here tormented by longing.

This set look of yours is without hope.
This look of mine is full of passion.

What was I hoping for from you, my love?
What you gave me was only sadness.

If only I hadn't seen your eyes, hadn't seen them.
If only I felt thirsty for a different ray, a different light.

If only I walked loose-tongued, drunk with some
happiness, having got rid of you forever.

If only a flame leapt in your blood from jealousy …
What can I do – I have no strength to fight you anymore.

Hey, my witless love, how are you?
What's it like walking without songs, without the sun,
without the dawn?

Why Didn't My Fairy Tale End?

Why didn't my fairy tale end?
Why does my lonely soul feel sorrow?
Remain out of date … transformed to a mirage …
Leave … and I will live without you.

Leave … and without you I'll get dressed up to the nines.
Do this … and all my suspicions will melt,
I will place you on a pedestal. It may even lead to a poem,
a meaningless fantasy concocted by me.

Don't look for me … Don't call.
Don't pin the flower of hope on your chest.
Unable to return love offered makes us strong.
Our feelings are used to being done out of our share.

Our feelings are used to the challenges
of crashing to the ground from that high pedestal.
Suddenly I liked your laugh …
Is that my poem I hear weeping …?

It must be my poem is forcing me to regret,
guarding my soul from heartless days.
Go away. Don't look back.
I have decided to live my life without you.

Do this …

Truth Has the Privilege of Being Placed in a Prison

Truth has the privilege of being placed in a prison,
even my personal truth.
My horrors don't come to light.
No one sees what I get up to.
Anyone who opens up my private prison
is certain to choke there.

I have a private prison, it is my truth, my love.
Embittered by grief I don't invest in idle talk.
Those people you see shouting slogans, cries of hooray,
how often do you see them floundering on the rocks?
When my poem falls like a careless foal, it scratches,
my worth is less than that of a crow.
Then … then having smiled,
I draw my wretched curtain which hangs there
– a prostitute, her honour in tatters …

When I was sharing my dreams with the wind,
thinking of the homeland that sings lullabies to those who
have none,
thinking of my grandfather whose people endured so much
thinking about my baby's unknown future as all this ended,
and at last, being preoccupied with the world,
it's my people who have imprisoned me,
judging on the best of the best
and the worst of the worst,
as all alike.

Translated by Belinda Cooke

The Language of Abaj

I speak the same language as Abaj[1]
How harmonious and beautiful it is.
Because the universe chilled me
with sadness, I became a poet.

Unaware of what I may have lost,
or the grief I have made for myself,
my errant days went by
spending nights beside the *balbals*.[2]

Brought up in a foreign land
I cannot speak of it without anger.
Back then, I lived like an orphan
trying in vain to find his mother.

How could I ever forget the sorrow
of days when poison and honey
were mixed: the inside of one cheek
bloody, the other filled with butter.[3]
Like a winter tree, my spirit is naked.

Oh, my mother tongue,
I am sobbing. I sank down
on my knees before you today
and the joy of your lost darling boy
spreads through the *šaṇyraķ*.[4]

---

[1] Abaj Ķùnanbajùly (Abai Kunanbayev; 1845–1904) – the most influential of all Kazakh poets, also a composer and philosopher. He is considered to be a reformer of Kazakh literature on the basis of enlightened Islam; his works also reflected the European and Russian cultures.

[2] *Balbal* – anthropomorphic stone stela, installed atop, within or around a *ķorġan* (burial mound) in cemeteries.

[3] The phrase 'the inside of one cheek bloody, the other filled with butter' is used of a person who is sorrowful and joyful, poor and well provided for at the same time.

[4] *Šaṇyraķ* – upper dome of a yurt; its image is considered to be a symbol of unity.

Looking up at the sky,
I am hoisting a blue flag
to demonstrate my Turkic origin.
The ice has melted
within my anxious soul.
Support and bless me, magnificent Abaj.

I Have Invented You

I have invented you
for the sake of a song,
and so that I may not die
or disappear
in twilight's evil hour.[5]

When I am tired
of everything
there is one thing only
I hope for –
to soar like a songbird
up to the sky.
And so, I made you up.

My imaginary darling
I had to create you.
For this transgression
I bear no shame.

I have invented you.

[5.] Twilight is believed to be the hour when evil spirits, demons and *jinns* are active. Sleeping was not allowed at twilight because, according to traditional beliefs, evil spirits might harm a sleeping person.

Back to Ķaroj

To Mahambet

We came in the spring and again in autumn,
here where Mahambet lies, who yearned for justice;
and as we probe his life's story
we follow his footsteps.

Who can speak of all that he aspired to
in this deceptive world?
Admiring his boldness, our days pass by –
I would like to stay here forever, a guardian of his shrine.
But, *Baba*,[6] I'm not noble enough.

Whether it is winter or summer,
ancient Ķaroj[7] always looks severe.
Hunkering down, beneath its splendid dome,
are hidden torments once inflicted
upon the Kazakh people.

And so,
with my son, I am here today
to understand the lessons you teach, *Baba*,
and to acquire, if I can,
some share of your persistence.

[6.] *Baba* – term for ancestor. In the context of the poem, it refers to Mahambet Ôtemisůly.

[7.] Ķaroj – place where Mahambet Ôtemisůly (Makhambet Otemisuly; 1804–46), a Kazakh hero and leader of the rebellion against Russian colonialism, is believed to have been murdered.

Unconcerned with Reason

This is how my verses go –

unconcerned with reason,
they are all a pure invention
that has no truck with truth
or even belongs in the world.
Having no bone to pick
with others,

       or wanting
to make their presence felt,
I'm not even sure
I get them myself,
though ever awake,
they will not leave me.

Suppose one day I imagine someone …
I can't say he's real
but won't say he's not.
A rational man
would never accept him –
some figment possessing my mind.

Unseen by anyone else,
he has his claws in me
and never lets me go.
With no visible strings
we're tethered together.

Whether you do or don't know him,
what does it matter to you?
I can't say I know him myself –
this mystery man, the stranger,
the subject of my poem.

Translated by David Cooke

AKBEREN YELGEZEK
(b. 24.01.1980)

Akberen Yelgezek is a poet and public figure. Although born in Almaty, he was raised in Mắdniet *auyl* of the Šùbartau district in the Semej region, where he graduated from school. He went on to study at the Faculty of History of Ăl-Farabi Kazakh National University. He has held senior positions in a number of administrative and arts organisations, including: Department of Internal Affairs at the Administration of the City of Almaty (2001–03), Kazakh National Academy of Engineering (2003–04), the Centre for Informational Analysis in Almaty (2004–08), Ăl-Farabi Kazakh National University (2009), Atažùrt publishing house (2009–10) and the Bôbek Centre for Human Development (2010–11). He established the weekly literary newspaper *Kentavr*, the website http://ult.kz and the Ķazaķ ădebietin ķoldau Public Fund. Yelgezek is currently the first deputy chairman of the Writers' Union of Kazakhstan.

His poetry collections include *Kôleṇkeler kùbiri* (The Whisper of Shadows, 2009), *Ġaršy* (2014) and *Šeksizdik syrtyndaġy šam* (The Light Outside Infinity, 2014). His poems are distinguished by strikingly unusual images and surrealist expressions deriving from dreams and the subconscious rather than reason and logic. He wrote the autobiographical tale *Bolmaġan balalyķ šaķ* (The Childhood that Never Happened) in 2014, to great acclaim of the literary community, the work providing a key insight into the majority of his later poems. His verses have been translated into Turkish, Azerbaijani and Spanish languages and included in several international anthologies. He has translated the poetry of Dmitry Merejkovsky, Guillaume Apollinaire, Ivan Bunin, Vladimir Vysotsky and Varlam Shalamov into Kazakh.

He is a winner of the Serper Prize of the Kazakhstan Youth Union (2006) and the Daryn State Youth Award (2010), as well as of Altyn Ķalam Public Prize (2010).

On the Night of the First of June

Black birds – like black drops,
swoop down low.
Tedious people, an eye without lashes,
a hospital groan.

Dust of the battlefield, dead horses,
spirits of war.
What a picture, someone mutters,
God, make him stop.

I notice with the eye of my soul
how a sigh flies off.
Quivering it shakes and disappears,
a rainbow of darkness.

What will calm you? The music of light?
The colour of scales? The shadow of the Moon?
On the testament pages
someone forever crumples the dreams.

That's enough. It is summer already.
The wind whispers in greeting: 'Go to sleep …'
slowly and colourfully, the smell of spring
departs with an echo …

Radio-Mystics

Splinters bursting from someone's throat,
somehow, with the dawn
in the little room there is an altar of words.
The night is dressed in a veil.

Is this burst of air
just an ordinary voice?
The rain absorbs minds.
The door left open, with a quiet question.
There is the echo of a carnation ...

Torn from somewhere there is the shadow of music,
a note of the supernatural world.
It falls with the sharp fragments of plots,
the cry of the enchanted lyre.

... here I am, it says, in living form, right before you,
a bottomless shooting gallery of sounds.
God is known to us again with his lips.
Quietly he whispers from the radio waves ...

Night Elegy

Night pierces the veil in the quiet room.
We still haven't been born as a sonnet.
Our thoughts are like autumn on that shore.
They dance over the poet's grave ...

It's as if we haven't been born with endless pain.
We speak to the God of sweet moments.
This room is the flat note of silent embraces.
Or do we just weep like the living?

Could it be that we haven't even met one another,
in the incomprehensible nuances of sadness?
This room is the indistinct drop of the pen.
Only the tenderness of grand crescendos can drive us wild ...

One can simply pass through by the light of a wax candle,
at the risk of disappearing like a shadow.
Yet, in these surroundings where they can't find us,
why do we still have such bitter longing ...?

Like a Black Shadow ...

Like a black shadow lying on the page,
like a white light waking early in the morning.
At some point I might become a magician,
but I remain naive and stupid.

To flame like the horizon in the east,
I learn and forget about pain.
Night rocks me with a tender current,
and the soul endlessly laments.

Like a grey stone stain gathering dust along the road,
I change my weakness into strength.
With an incomprehensible, alien monologue,
again and again I kiss my hearing ...

Balcony. I Stand,
Smoke and Weep …

Balcony.
I stand, smoke and weep.
Someone whispers to me 'Write!'
'Like the day, I know nothing, I am
simply a shadow of the great soul …'

But night with its great eyes,
looks at everything, everything …
Don't breathe!
Only little children know how to
with such starry tears …

And I am a child. Father is there somewhere …
He is right before me. He is alone.
Tell me, who am I? There is no response.
Tell me who you are, black smoke?

And my life before Him is like childhood,
and I am such a strange child.
And sometime someone will come for me,
to return me to the sky, to my native home.

Translated by Belinda Cooke

Nightmare

Their meaning obscure, I dream of sleek black ravens
whose croaking fills me with doubts and dread.
They have built their nests in my hair.
Like poisonous words, they've dripped into my mind.

They swirl around inside my head,
dragging my brain with them in ever-tightening circles.
In my dreams I'm weeping
and find a house that was never built.

I have begged for others to come to join me,
where my past lives subsist.
I imagine brothers who've never seen me.
Glancing at ravens in the yard
my spirit-dove scavenges food.

In the dark house inside my head
my family resides. They live just as they used to –
my father and mother, my brother,
I can see my grandmother too.

How I would love to cross that threshold,
but can't. The suitcase I carry becomes a black dog.
The dumb wind moans
as if it were whipping around a pylon.
I seem unable to get past it.

There are people there who watch me struggling.
I wander around leading my dog,
forever tugging on his leash.
Tearing around inside my house,
I peek in through the window.
There's no one else paying attention.

My father sighs, also, when he's drawn to the window.
Heading nowhere, I could leave it all behind me.
I seem insubstantial.
I'm a shirt flapping in the wind.

I sigh in a place of many tombs.
My lamp flickers. I shudder awake.
The room is dark now ...
I am feeling my way around the walls ...
Has the room become a suitcase?

Autumn City. A Rainy Evening.

Outside my window life is a fight for survival.
What does any of it really mean?
Should we rage like wild beasts
until our eyes are burning green with envy?

Outside my window there's a grey street,
its three eyes blinking: red amber green.
Whenever we drink, let's raise our glass
to the muse of wistful thinking.

Outside my window engines roar,
exhaling poisonous fumes.
Their tyres are printing angry words
onto the asphalt road.

Outside my window there's dreary rain,
and the clack of women in high heels.
If autumn could send me a verse on a leaf,
it would bring me some relief.

Outside my window there's a world of mists,
and beyond it distant planets …
How I hate the stench of money.
There's someone jealous squinting at me.
Look at his eyes. They are so green.

Euphoria

One day, out of the blue, I flew away as an angel.
Sprouting wings, in the midst of sighs,
I corkscrewed up into the sky, bewildered by height.
Weeping profusely, I cried aloud to the blue around me:
'If there was a remedy for my sick heart,
I'd soothe the Moon with kindness
and wrap my arms around the Sun!'
And with that thought, I flew up higher
beyond the realms of Hell.
Proclaiming its freedom, my spirit soared.

I would never again know such joy,
when, like a bird, I flew beyond myself.
Next I saw a shimmering garden,
my mind touched by the sweetness
of its light. Was it the paradise
described by the prophets? Was it really heaven?
If so, I would gladly go there.
Forgive my apostasy, O my God!

How I yearned to enter.
I saw more beings with wings like mine,
swarming into paradise.
They were close friends, family, acquaintances,
communicating through thoughts.
No voices were heard.
So I tried it myself and spoke
to a snake with a beautiful crest.

Was it a woman? I had no way of knowing
who or what she was,
whether accursed or wretched,
with only a crescent moon to light it.
I learned that I had no right of entry
when an angel whipped me
back to Earth.

Since then
I have been afraid
of my body lacking wings …

536

Crossword

My intuition grappled with the mystery in my mind.
The night sank towards the horizon.
Who feels sorry for my black moods?
Someone heaved a sigh inside me …

I approached the world with my heart.
Some noise took over my mind …
Where did I come from, where was I enclosed?
I pitied my Mother …

Then … I approached the sky,
and frightened all the stars …
I put off my mask, revealing my face.

My lashes flicked the air.
They do not know what patience is.
Where do my thoughts come from?
Where do they go?
Where is the sky that words pour down from?

I approached the Moon … it did not move …
I can't make sense of anything.
Someone is writing a verse on the sky,
completing the crossword in my mind …

Eye Orbit

Human skulls resemble each other.
– Ernst Muldashev[1]

Trying to find an immortal world,
I look for a place inside the mirror
where stars are singing in pure delight.
There's a full Moon in the sky

that doesn't sigh for its past.
Like a tribe discovering paradise
I look at my face in the mirror
to see if it is lit by grace.

As yet
the future is still to be written.
The scribe has lost his pen.
The tangled veins of the world
are yearning for light.

As darkness spreads
across it, the flickering stars,
like eyes, light up the steppe.
My spirit scours empty space,
for the mythical land Shambala.

The eyes of the dead are black holes.
They stare at me, they frighten me.
In a world of cracked mirrors
I am lost to find myself.

---

[1] From *Where Do We Come From?* by Russian ophthalmologist and author of several books on metaphysics, Ernst Muldashev (b. 1948). Translated by the National Bureau of Translations.

My *Ḳobyz*-Soul

When disparate thoughts hesitate between
day and night, and I'm plagued by doubts,
wandering through pitch-black forest,
the holy voice of the *ḳobyz*[2] seeps from my soul.

It's as if each sound in the universe
has come together in a solitary place,
where I can imagine shamans dancing
with the ancestral spirits.

A guardian
of the holy places, it reveals to me
my inner music, its sad refrains striking
to the very heart of the blues.
It makes you understand how unimportant
the world is, a tiny ephemeral place.

In the blink of an eye majestic music
brings back to life so many past ages.
The wispy grass ripples like an endless ocean.
till all at once you are brought down
to earth again by the mysterious power.

Sadness whirls around you
like the howls of a tigress,
and the world you know is swept away
in storm. All the village graves
are drawn up into the air, the voice of *ḳobyz*.

---

[2] *Ḳobyz* – traditional Kazakh musical instrument with a wooden body, two to four strings
and a bow made of a horse's mane. It is the main attribute of the *baḳsy* during a healing
ritual and is considered sacred.

Unveiling the sky's ultimate truths,
as puffed-up clouds battle for a tiny space.
When a cold breeze whistles, the stars
all round call to us from their far domain.
Look now and see how overwhelming it is,
when spirits land on the earth in throngs.
The voice of the *ḳobyz* will sing forever.
Blessed by God, it pours forth its notes like rain
and pierces the heart with sadness.

But don't let the devils learn about it.
Its strings were spun from my heart.
Its chilling songs must never cease
for even so much as a day.

In a Mist

Born from my grief and sorrow,
the steppe is veiled in mist,
an angel, also, is walking through it.
A heavenly light drops from its wings …
I am too impatient to stop for it
with time's light seeping away.
I hear the cry of a baby
born amongst the wormwood,
its pungent odours can't escape
beyond its petals.
Nor can the words escape the mouths.
In thrall to doubtful thoughts,
the brains are being cleaved.
A terrible scene lies before me,
There is the pale mist
with the eyes wide and troubled,
and a Kazakh *auyl*[3] in its depths.

I am becoming as one with it,
reduced to its blindness.
A fractured light shines upon me.
The fog is blind and with it me …
I say *Me?*
I do not differ from the mist …

---

[3] *Auyl* – social-economical formation considered to constitute the heartland of the nation
and a basis for an ethnic and cultural union of the nomadic community. Consisting of
50–70 yurts in the eighteenth century, it developed into its current permanent state of
'rural settlement' (of a minimum of 100 dwellers) when Kazakhs adopted a settled mode
of life in the nineteenth and twentieth centuries. *Auyl* can also be used as a synonym for
'native land' and 'homeland', concepts revered by the Kazakhs.

A Little Man

On the outskirts of town,
where the rubbish gets dumped,
it is a steaming summer day.
Drunkards sing and jump from the canal.
Avoiding them and their curses
an abandoned child crosses the road
whose life was blighted before it began.

Begging for bread,
his face is that of an old man.
And yet he is only a child,
no more than seven years old.
He has a chronic disease, this orphan.
His chin is trembling, shaken by sobs.

This child and others like him
show our society for what it is.
If by chance a nickel *tenge*[4]
happens to fall into his cap, he thinks
it will cure him of his illness.
He plays with his stick
like a musical instrument;
and even when his songs don't rhyme
it thrills you to hear them.

For whom is he searching
in a cruel world?
His song impresses no one!
Strolling on, his body is wretched,
his mind's troubled.
The passers-by are indifferent to him.

[4.] *Tenge* – the modern currency of Kazakhstan; historically, silver coins used as a currency.

Today is the same as every day –
there are rubbish heaps and the air is stuffy.
Drunkards groan along their way.
The little man pretends
to play a tune on his stick
and quietly weeps.
Good God! It sounds like a flute!

Alone

In the infinite universe
Earth is a tiny lonely star
and on the surface of this star
you are lonely and so am I.

Why is the world so lonely?
You are sociable and so am I.
A spider creates its intricate web
to snare some innocent moth.

Copper is lonely and so is lead
as all the atoms are.
A bird is alone
and every Poet too.

The heart is single, so is the brain.
A cigarette burns alone.
The lonely moon stares down,
into your cunning face.

All things are on their own.
Even God is.
Death and honour are lonely.
The meaning of life
is like the struggle
between the moth and spider.

A Drop and Stone

It was not a real night today,
the Moon was peering proudly.
Lying on the stone, the raindrop
whispered to the wind.

Is it a teardrop?
No, that's an illusion.
What an interesting play!
I am also unreal –
The stranger's fake thought.

Born of sadness, the tears in my eyes
were not sad.
The raindrop on the stone
was like faint lightning –

and the hair dye with its fragrance
is also a cunning lie.
The teardrops are heavy stones.
The stones themselves
are huge dark drops.

I know that night is not a night.
It's a pulse of veins.
I am also unreal –
I am a grave in which
my thoughts lie buried.

It seems that soon there'll be no tears …
that the agreement will not hold,
that the stone will remove his dark coat
and all at once stand up …

It wasn't night at all,
the last word was heard.
Missing the illusions,
I'm lying inside the drop …

Translated by David Cooke

NAZIRA BERDALY

(b. 5.07.1980)

Nazira Berdaly is a poet and journalist. She graduated from Sarykemer rural school named after Nyǵmetolla Kiikbaev in the Bajzaķ district of Žambyl region in 1997 and went on to study at the Ǎl-Farabi Kazakh National University (graduated 2001). She began her career as an editor at the Ķazaķ Radiosy (Qazaq Radiosy) radio station and national TV channel Ķazaķstan (Qazaqstan). She was a TV presenter at the same channel, as well as at Astana channel, and gained some popularity among the audiences. She is currently head of the Taņšolpan Arts Association at Qazaqstan.

Her debut poems were published in *Aķ žol* regional newspaper, and later were selected for a collection of work by young writers of the region. Nazira Berdaly's first poetry collection, *Žaņbyrly tùn* (Rainy Night) was published in 2001 and was followed by *Sùjgen žùrek* (The Heart in Love, 2009) and *Aru ǎlem* (The Beautiful World, 2014). She is an author of the lyrics for some popular songs, such as 'Sùjgen žùrek' (Loving Heart), 'Aņsarym' (My Beloved) and 'Ôzim žajly' (About Myself).

Berdaly is a winner of the Literary Prize for Youth named after Tôlegen Ajbergenov (2004) and was a recipient of the State Scholarship in Literature appointed by the First President of the Republic of Kazakhstan Nursultan Nazarbayev (2014).

When You Ask Me Where I Am

When you ask me where I am
I could ask myself the same
as I think about life and verses.
Laughing and making the most of my days,
I've not been away at all
or not in the way that you imagine,
determined not to lose sight of myself.
For who's impressed by histrionics
or even cares if I succeed?
If I keep my failures under wraps,
the hidden powers ground me
or else I'll borrow wings
to fly away somehow.
Don't let on you are disappointed
or tell the world how tough it's been.
Rinse off the dust you've accumulated
and don't forsake your dreams.
Don't bore those nearest to you
with the torments of your soul.
When you accept what lies before you,
it doesn't mean you'll be alone.
So let detractors mock me
my secret muse will be my strength.
I wasn't away as you had feared –
alive perhaps
only in my private sphere.

It's Autumn Again and the Trees Are Golden

It's autumn again and the trees are golden.
A new term has started. The TV schedules change.
Though all the sound bites say the same,
I hope for better things.
Smiling, I ask for news about you
as soon as day dawns.
Like an autumn leaf, my soul is trampled.
Even you were trampling it,
When you wished me well.
Still young and writing poems,
I don't know what the future holds.
Is autumn leading me on again
towards its spurious spires?
One strike of the match and I'll explode
as day after day I dither
at every fork in the road.
Just passing through,
like a seasonal guest, I crave
no more than a friendly welcome.

The Red Dress

I didn't wear it today, that red dress.
Though who will not be drawn
to the woman wearing a red dress?
Or am I like a crimson flower
that no one dares to pick?

Rightly or wrongly, we're struck
by the beauty wearing a red dress –
enticing her lover,
destroying the grudgers.
Her red dress –
it's like her dazzling world.

And all my life how I tried
to be the one who led the field
and be the envy of my rivals,
those days I basked in red sun.
But when it set, a twilight came
that left me unregarded,
dragging on the black dress
of silence and gloom for days –
so many regrets and sombre thoughts!

My black dress!
As the poet Maḳpal[1] sang,
I might as well be hidden
inside a black box. But now,
black dress, I cannot bear you
for soon the day is coming
whose light is white not red.
Burning the past in vibrant flames
I'll quench what's left
in blackest rain.

[1.] Maḳpal Žŭmabaj (Makpal Jumabay; b. 1985) – contemporary poetess-bard.

Sluicing out my mind,
I'll repossess my life
and slip on a dress
that's white and gleaming –
white dress, white hope, white dreams!
Can any soul be pure
before it wears a white shroud?

Rain

Where did you come from, rain?
Refreshing my garden, you make me rich,
delivering news of spring,
its solace mixed with sadness.
Your pitter-pattering music
is like the joyous sounds
of a homely celebration,
evoking also tears and doubts.
I remember the days of my youth
when I would splash playfully.
But why do you take me back,
stirring my muse, my passionate heart?
Desires pool like puddles.
With clouds adrift across the sky,
banks and gulleys overflow.
The rain is warm, the raindrops dance.
The spring sky is brightening.
How I have loved it all!

On the Train

Away with the fairies,
my food and drink abandoned,
the train's hypnotic clatter
had taken over my mind.
With nothing better to do,
I counted every pylon,
peering through the window
as the train thundered on.
Years, fleeting years,
why did you forget me?
A station hurtled past,
where it seemed I had stopped before,
as I tried to decipher blurry signs,
houses, steppe, gardens –
in one a greenhouse glinted …
There were faces there
that seemed familiar.
Night fell and I wondered
would I ever get off this train,
and who was that waving?
Had she been delayed?
Unable to guess her name,
I stared and stared –
a friend from school, perhaps,
who'd let me down?
And then, suddenly, a solitary oak …
I had a companion with me,
but didn't share my secrets.
That wraith in the corner –
was it a boy who gave me flowers?
Another shape emerged
that might have been my mother
who had come to see me off
when I was seventeen,
hiding the tears in her eyes –
till there we were reflected
in drops of crystal water,
my mother, my father and me …

How carefree I sat beside them –
my mother pouring the tea,
my father blithely chatting.
For such perfect moments,
stored in the mind forever,
I must surely live,
thanking one who made me.

A Beauty in Mourning

The night is like a woman in mourning.
Her eyes are closed, her arms inviting.
A moth flies out of the night
on flickering wings towards the light.
The woman's eyes
are glistening, yet no tear falls.
Is it the fault of the moth
that it is fated to search for love?
The moth is like the heart,
accepting nature's law.
One is happy in love.
Someone else will suffer.
The heart is cut to pieces.
Love is dark as night
but night, absorbing our desires,
will leave you craving more.
The beauty who mourns
is lost in grief …
The fluttering moth
can scarcely live
unless it seeks the light.

Overwhelmed by Joy, I Return to My Land

Overwhelmed by joy, I return to my land.
Decked out in its loveliest dress,
it greets me: Come to me now, my child.
Its looming hills are welcoming arms.
In a warm embrace it hugs me,
its green slopes drawing me on
towards the sky's playground,
where clouds, like mischievous
children, have free rein all day.
The Sun kisses my face, it's like a mother.
The silky breeze takes care of me
as gently as my *žeŋge*,[2]
who in the city waved her hand
towards a sky I could not see.
The mountains, the lake, the garden –
they are all familiar to me.
Having yearned for them so long,
I'll wander far and wide.
My motherland, you gave me life
and nourished me with rain.
Now that I've left, you're like a mirage.

[2.] *Žeŋge* – an older brother's wife. In Kazakh culture girls have close relationships with their older sisters-in-law, who become mother figures for them.

This Is Where My Heart Is

When day draws over the night its white *žaulyķ*[3]
and the dawn chorus is at *con brio*,
and the Sun pops up to peep through a window,
smiling warmly at you …
That is where my heart is!
When lightsome breezes ruffle your hair,
when torrents batter the roof of your house,
the drenching rain that God has blessed,
when flowers carpet the thirsty land
That is where my heart is!
When the slopes are fragrant with fresh growth
and crickets sing their summer songs,
when neighbours greet you on New Year's Eve
and snow gleams on Christmas trees …
That is where my heart is!
When the trees know that autumn's here,
they'll sing my verses to every ear.
When the leaf falls, grieving, from its tree,
take care of it, please, retrieve it …
That is where my heart is.

[3.] *Žaulyķ* – head covering worn by women, typically of white fabric; hence, another common
name for a woman is *aķ žaulyķ* ('white *žaulyķ*').

Spring Can Really Hang You Up the Most[4]

When it came this year, spring did nothing for me.
I had no time for songsters chirping.
My frozen heart languished.
Buried like bulbs, my feelings groaned
beneath the weight of snow.
Who cares for seasonal birds
and springtime on the shore?
So what if I haven't spotted a gull.
It's spring in the city. Big deal!
It bucks you up or it doesn't.
City. Spring. Night.
Its stars are familiar and fake.
Its cacophonous songs go on and on.
When I stepped out on the balcony
I said to myself: It's spring
then tore up the tulip I'd planted …
And when night falls it's just as bad.
I'm ill at ease. The sky is cold.
I try to play the recorder
and improvise a 'Song of Birds'.
It leaves me cold, joyless.
My verses, too, are lifeless,
the images vague as shadows
glimpsed on distant slopes.
Could any spring on earth
be so devoid of grace?
Let me waken up again.
For so long I yearned for spring,
but not, alas, this one.

---

4. This is the title of a famous song by Fran Landesman.

Another Day ...

Another day has closed its curtains
as night sneaks up and taps the window.
I'm all alone in a silent space.
When the stage curtains are drawn apart,
we are all the actors,
the singers, the poets ...
We play the parts of wise men.
We play the parts of heroes.
We act as if we're stars.
We pretend we're close to each other.
In tower blocks, in spacious flats,
we only exist because we rent them.
There's a cold meal on the table,
a pot, a plant ...
And if you miss me, just come over.
Tap on the window
instead of the night.

My soul's an empty playhouse
where all have now departed –
the lights turned off,
the makeup removed.
And so, once more ...
Goodbye!
Till another day and night arrive
and the dark wins out again,
reducing me to bare walls
that hem me in like a coffin.
Excuse me, please, I beg you,
for being so tired of my role.

I Lie to Myself When I'm Alone

I lie to myself when I'm alone,
I lie too when I meet with others …
My sorrow has landed a knockout punch.
Even when I'm near you I still can't love you
but worse than that I cannot hate you.
How can I blame my heart
for feeling something?
To cross my sorrow's black sea
I undress myself without submitting,
but you, stay by the shore.
Even if you have turned my joy to sadness,
and my firmness into sand
I will forgive you
and still want to see you,
longing for the brightness and warmth
of a new day dawning.
I never knew that the silence of night would win again.
Because my dream deceived me,
because you have stayed on a different shore
I will forget you.
Oh my sweet sorrow!
My cruel, strange … and familiar sorrow!
I will not stroke your hair like a breeze,
I will not enlist false hopes against you.
I will not battle against your torments
in order to find some happiness.
I will go away and leave you standing
barefoot, on the pebbled shore,
singing desolate songs.
I am swimming far away.
You will lose me.

Doubt

A small blue flame is heating the white enamel kettle.
My poet's soul has never been understood.
There's a glimmer of light and loneliness
in the quiet kitchen.
At half past one in the morning
we are together
but still alone.
My sadness slides across the window.
On the sill there's a jug with a dried carnation.
It's the 8th of March, the sorrow of Women's Day.

Still my *mankurt*[5] city remains –
It doesn't change for winter or spring.
It is always the same in the afternoon.
It doesn't change for evening.

It is never hot. It doesn't freeze.
I can never feel anything here.
Even that red carnation died.
Not so much a bright ray
but a sadness that fell from the sky.
I feel let down by you and the flower.

In the eyes of the spring
I am a lake of tears full of sin.
When the Sun rises will we disappear?
We are fleeting as spring, as meaningless.
Do you feel that we are strangers?
Do you think we'll manage to stay together?

[5.] *Mankurt* – person who has lost connections to his or her historical and national past.

Now That Autumn Is Here

Now that autumn is here
I should let you go –
now that the sky is dark
and my sorrow has deepened.
If you are not mine,
however jealous I might be,
would I have shot you,
if I had a gun?
Would I have caressed you,
if there were even the slightest chance?
No, you are not mine.
I accept it and let you go your way.
Again I hear that song …
No, it is merely the song of rain dropping.
What kind of torment lies before me?
Were I to fall today
I would only raise you up.

Autumn

It is autumn.
I am at the airport
and feeling anxious.
What am I supposed to do,
when your plane flies in?
Why did we meet anyway
if fate doesn't keep us together
and your flying away
is the only thing that's certain?
Unsettling autumn.
Meaningless evening.
When you first came smiling,
my sadness passed away.
My whole body trembled.
Why did I hear
the melody of happiness
when your flying away
is all that's certain,
if your homeland isn't here,
if you are always bound to leave?
Why did you stare into my eyes?
Did you notice how beautiful they are?
I know I will spend years without you,
thousands of endless empty days.
Each time I hid in your embrace
it could have been for the last time.
I grew warm
but have turned now into a tear
that hangs on the tip of your eyelash.
It should have all been different.

Translated by David Cooke

BAUYRZHAN KARAGYZULY

(b. 17.10.1982)

Bauyrzhan Karagyzuly graduated from the Kôkšetau Kazakh Teacher Training College named after Žahan Musin and then went on to study at the Petropavl Kazakh Humanities College named after Mağžan Žùmabaev (Magzhan Zhumabayev), and the North Kazakhstan University named after Manaš Ķozybaev. He worked for *Alaš* university newspaper (2003–04) and *Astana* journal (2005–08), as well as for the National Academic Library (2008–11) and *Žas ķalamger* a literary journal for young writers (2009–12). He was head of the Ädebiet portaly internet project under Kazcontent JSC (2012–18), and has been the Advisor to the Minister of Culture and Sport of the Republic of Kazakhstan since 2018.

His poetry collections include *Žùmbaķtasķa žauğan kùz* (The Autumn Was Pouring over Žùmbaķtas, 2011), *Ôŋ. Men. Tùs* (Reality. And/I. Dream, 2011), *Žùrek kitaby* (A Book of Heart, 2014) and *Topyraķ demi* (A Breath of Earth, 2016).

Karagyzuly is a winner of a number of national poetry contests, including with *Älemge ájgili Astana* (World-Renowned Astana, 2010) *Žyrym saǵan, atažùrt!* (My Songs are Dedicated to You, My Fatherland, 2011) and *Ķazaķ eli, bir auyz ajtam saǵan* (I Have a Word to You, My People, 2011). Likewise, he is a poet laureate of the Sejdolla Bájterekov Award (2010), the second degree diploma (2006) and the Grand Prix (2008) at the Shabyt Festival, and has been awarded the Ķazaķstan Patrioty Medal (2011).

Lullaby

This night sounds like the voice of tired hope,
a favourite of space – a round face, hair flicked up.
It felt like it called us somewhere …
When I hear its voice I think of God
and my heart cries as horses cry –
without tears.

This night – is probably an essence of my roads leading nowhere …
There, where I always consoled my soul with lies …
This night – is the jaded ghost
of an aged Dream, worn out with longing for death.

Why can't I fall asleep?

This night – is the home of words dancing
to the eternal music –
This night is sworn patience –
It is truth.
It loves the light,
It will die from the light.
It comes from the light,
it goes into the light.
Hush, black night,
sleep well.

Earth

Earth,
I'm afraid of a false sorrow …
Of a night without prayers,
Of blind words …
Of the dark eyes turned into the grave,
Of the innocent tears that washed guilty lashes …
Of an unrepentant mind.
I'm afraid of all this,
Earth!

God's thoughts are raining from the sky,
the kindness of his most pure thoughts is pouring.
Yes, it is true,
we are orphans, thrown to the Earth,
drunk with Nothing,
or drunk with the light of mercy.
We are forgetful specks – wandering aimlessly.

Earth,
I'm afraid of myself …
Of angry patience.
Of false feeling
hidden beneath my gossiping voice.
I'm afraid, Earth …

Look –
The rain is passing by,
where does it go?
Fate passes …
Look,
One drop fell lit by the light …
One life plopped and collapsed.
Earth …

The Lost One

I
You called all beings human.
You said that you can find something that doesn't exist.
When you are bored with everything,
come to me,
come to me, the Lost one.

The day when you are frightened of yourself, afraid to run
away from yourself,
you will turn to the sky, showing it respect.
The night when you despair of your loneliness,
come to me, the Lost one.

I saw a friend in everyone, only good in everything,
but this mortal world is full of treason.
I've seen, my dear, tears running from blind eyes,
come to me, the Lost one.

Look directly into the sad eyes of those
who enquire about us.
When you're crying completely alone,
run away from all that is 'the god'.

The robbed feelings, a heart cheated
will eventually see a dawn …
I'm waiting for you, a lost life,
come to me in the end.

II
I wasn't the only child of my father,
I felt my mother's kindness from afar,
I was the Lost one.
I wouldn't say that I'm completely alone
among the crowd who believed in one God,
loneliness visited me as it visited you before … but I'm tired.
Really tired, my dear.
Hey, is there anyone who can really understand a soul?

That's why I'm drunk and eager to pick a fight.
That's why when I run into myself
and from myself,
I become pure, hang beads of light
on my heart and look for you,
the Lost one.
That's why ...

III
When you are in trouble,
shadows avoid you ...
When you are in trouble,
it is nice to watch the birth of the gracious Moon,
forgetting about the betrayal of time.
Alien to everything,
you sit alone, sad and tearful –
how nice that is.
As if a load had fallen from the shoulders,
you peer into your life from the balcony
and it peers back into you –
what a precious thing –
and you trap bitter sobs in your throat,
sadness swells, you clench your teeth, put up with it,
then fall into the silent cry of your soul.
When the blackest night pats your head,
you can't hold back any more and start to cry,
how nice that is.

IV
With time pouring from his eyes,
the Lost one asked:
'Is religion needed? Or God?'

Ah, you are back to yourself I see,
Now your words need some warmth,
and you need yourself.
If you don't exist,
along with your feelings,
what's the point of them?
You returned, returned to yourself, the Lost one ...

Look through the eyes of your heart,
have you seen any travellers
at the far end of your soul,
their foreheads glowing, kissed by flowers?
Have you seen these travellers,
who circled the entire universe and their own fate,
inhaling the smell of rain?
Have you seen these travellers,
the Lost one, or not?

So what was your wish?
You should know in your gut.
And your heart would hurt for a long time …
When the night will spill on the mournful steppe,
a knife will be put to your throat
by the purest question of honour –
your own eyes' ashen spring.
On its shore spreading like the thickets of reeds,
a graceful light will grow in the flames of prayer.
If one word flying from your mouth
turns into a teardrop,
your thoughts may be guilty.
But your fate is not sinful.
Don't spill time from your eyes.
Don't walk away from yourself now,
the Lost one.

V
The Lost one,
come, let's drink together tears of the night,
so your soul doesn't disintegrate,
let time awake sadness.
That's interesting.
Don't obey ignorant people
who don't take you for a human being.
Let's give thumbs down on power, my friend.

For centuries we were deceived,
for centuries we were wandering,
the Lost one.
Today, eternal and unwise,
our voices are reborn,
Abaj.[1]
Long live this echo,
resounding for another thousand years ...
A reborn mountain – that's the fate of Sisyphus.
Right, let's leave it ...
Let's protect our feelings, so beautiful
and tender like the wings of a butterfly.
We won't let the words cry,
we won't let our Spirit crash.
And this spirit is the poet.
From the very beginning, it was God's oath,
the Lost one.

VI

The Lost one,
you are the one to blame.
You liked the unlikeable,
you pushed innocent souls out of sight.
And now,
words that spill from crazy lips
made your heart cry ...
But then sorrow comforted it,
that is a paradox.

Leave it ...
The truth is – this path is not ours.
Why are you in such a hurry for the unknown, my friend?
Is your wandering life worth it?
In this mortal world,
is your gullible spirit worthy?

[1.] Abaj Ḳůnanbajůly (Abai Kunanbayev; 1845–1904) – the most influential of all Kazakh
poets, also a composer and philosopher. He is considered to be a reformer of Kazakh
literature on the basis of enlightened Islam; his works also reflected the European and
Russian cultures.

Is it worthy at all?
Your soul,
Your honour,
Your mind …
Your dream …
My precious,
understand,
your dream is life.
The Lost one,
with your trampled soles
why are you in such a hurry to achieve glory?
I don't understand.

When Meeting with Syr Dariâ

This *Dariâ*[2] – is a dear legend of my people,
my land's true heaven, its major artery.
It is my artery as well.
Spirits of my ancestors,
dreams of my children flow from it with sadness,
like a sound of *Ķorķyt's ķobyz*[3] ...
smartening up like a hyacinth,
trembling like an inspired singer,
it flows gliding,
in sad slumber ...
It flows tormenting a fierce demise,
it flows teasing, a choking death,
it flows silently – emerald green life flows.

Epochs flow from my artery.
by the oath of the Almighty,
with the affliction of fate,
blood dripping from its eyes,
tears dripping from its words,
the history of mankind flows sorrowfully ...

Oh, this mortal world,
my revenge flows angrily
with the head cut off by Queen Tùmar,[4]
whose wise heart was born for honour.
Thoughts of a young *Alaššyl*[5]
flow from my artery.

---

[2] Syr Dariâ or Syr Darya – a river in Central Asia flowing through Uzbekistan and southern Kazakhstan into the remnants of the Aral Sea.

[3] *Ķorķyt's ķobyz* – Kazakh national musical instrument believed to have been created by a legendary poet and composer of the eighth/ninth century, Ķorķyt. Legend holds that he lived and died on the banks of Syr Dariâ.

[4] Queen Tùmar or Tomiris – a queen who reigned over the Massagetae-Skythian people in parts of modern-day southern Kazakhstan, western Uzbekistan, Turkmenistan and Afghanistan. She defeated the invading armies of Cyrus the Great in 530 BC, killing him in battle on the banks of Syr Dariâ.

[5] *Alaššyl* – member of the Kazakh liberal-nationalist Alaš Party, which established, in December, 1917 Alaš Orda, the autonomous Kazakh government.

His cherished goal was honed by nobleness,
his honour was honed by lightning.
Like a red ghost, choking on its sobs,
my sorrow flows too,
what can I do ...
My artery – Syr Dariâ flows,
its clear waters running calmly
as if to say let Kazakhs have it all,
as if to say let their faces shine.
Let the injured Aral[6] be full again –
says my river – my artery.

[6.] Once the world's fourth largest lake, the Aral Sea is a site of a major environmental disaster. Due to extensive and destructive irrigation projects in the Soviet era, Kazakhstan has witnessed the virtual disappearance of the lake.

A Night When Words Acquired Their Wings

Make a wish. Wish it to yourself. Ask yourself.
Eternity is born every moment within yourself.
Let your lost thoughts
come back every moment,
let them blossom
so sparkling words
can spill from your eyes.
Another world will be born in your heart.
A new smiling day will be born inside your wish.
Wish it to yourself.
Wish yourself pride. In the Night of Power.[7]
Let your doubts form shoots
when they ripen.
You can create another world
with one teardrop,
and the truth can be read
by one teardrop.
Oh, let then a thought fly from your palm,
let words fly from your palm, *taġdyrlas*![8]
From now on
God won't give us any advice.
He did before, making an oath to time.
And who is honest now?
Who is dishonest
among those who wrote?
Everything is written down,
so read yourself.
In the Night of Power
do not let your earthly needs govern you.
Only the Song descends to earth
from the sky on this night.

---

[7] The Night of Power – Laylat Al Qadr, traditionally celebrated on the 27th night of the Ramadan, is revered as the holiest night of the year for Muslims. It commemorates the night when the Qur'an was first revealed to the prophet Muhammad.

[8] *Taġdyrlas* – those who share a common fate, bound by destiny.

If We Look Through the Eyes of Premonition

If we look through the eyes of premonition …
I'm on my way.
Maybe, I will run away from you, the future,
but why do I hurry so much to see you,
why am I in love with you? I don't know.
I would know when I wash my face by the sound of longing.
I would know when I am in luck;
when justice sparkles in people's eyes,
when love spreads its wings with voices born out of kindness;
I would know when scorched envy turns to ash
and flows away as river waters,
and the evenings when this river turns into a life-giving source;
when evil will be trampled upon and buried,
while on the burial mound white flowers grow.
Then I will know how lovely you are!
How beautiful and charming!
When I think about you, all around me is filled with music,
with the sounds of *kùj*[9] settling on the eyelashes.
I miss you, the one that shares all my troubles,
my dear friend – the Future!

[9.] *Kùj* – musical genre (composition) based on a story arc, created for and performed on a number of traditional instruments.

Apathy

I

'Twilight is reading poems to the past again,
Many people are gathering words from the streets.
Tomorrow a hope will faintly appear from the east,
Next year's snow is crying in spring.

And when it comes to you – all day you have dreams,
and all night you're lost in your thoughts.
You pretend that you don't understand
the sadness of the wind,
when the Moon is born from the flower's root…'

II

Our fingers touched, and that touch has become –
the shrine of a newly created world.
You're in love. The universe isn't the same anymore.
Your feelings become the truth.
What a miracle it is.
What a change.
To roam every second
through the whole life of the universe,
to listen to its inner voice.
Death is a lie. Life is an eternity.
Where did we wander before this happened?
My love, pearls of joy are bursting from your lips,
rubies of hope are pouring from my eyes.
Space dissolved. A rupture in time.
Happiness. I'm happy, my God!

III

Well, I'm sleepless again.
Ready to forgive everything and say goodbye.
Did anyone approach me? I'm alone.
Children play in space born from my blood.
Ancestors read their blessings …
As for me, I'm smoking,
a window looks innocently at the outside world.
And the outside world looks at the grave.
No, maybe I experience grief
mocking the grave?
Who was it – came to mind?
I feel a smell of sagebrush.
When I remember the brown mountains,
I'm close to tears, but the day that is past can't come back.
All this is unbelievable
to a green flowering bud drawing out memories from the old
branch.

Me

… He passed away. But he didn't die.
P.S.

The wind of the Qur'an blows from Qibla …
Only the blind can see it,
Only the mute can read it,
Only the deaf can hear it,
Leaving behind all the talk of this mortal world.
Not bothering anyone.
To be honest,
he's not himself.
He is a wanderer.
He is Someone's love,
who was tired of kisses between the soul and body and
turned himself into words.
He was madly in love with Someone,
then forgot everything.
Or he didn't.
Or maybe, in some timeless space
he has read his own *ayat*[10] in a different book
and now he's seeking consolation
in his own repentance.

* * *

From the tears that rolled down from the flower's eyes;
From the laughter of the leaves of a young birch in spring;
From the babble of green grass in June;
From the song of the leaves dancing in the colourful autumn;
From the sobbing ocean;
From the weak hum of space,
past and present connected with each other,
They cry and laugh,
They laugh and cry.

[10.] *Hayat (ayat)* – Qur'anic verse.

Joys of this world are smiling in the tears
Fears of the afterlife are trembling
in the laughter.
This is interesting.
What's lacking?
Who's he looking for?
What's next?
Will he miss Someone later?
Maybe his yearning is false ...
False ...
False ...
Sometimes he runs away from his own thoughts:
when a frowning dawn is born on the East,
when the tender Sun kisses the edge of the Earth,
or
when the wind whistles in the red evening's plea,
or
when the darkest night sighs shuddering,
worships Him again,
but his adoration probably is shaken?!
Bismillah ...[11]
If he only understood the meaning of life
he would have remembered everything again,
and if after that,
he would have made a poem out of death
and read it silently,
angels would have descended from the sky
and kissed him on his lips ...
Alas!!!

[11.] *Bismillah* – the opening word in the Qur'an, meaning 'In the name of Allah'.

Have You Ever Woken Up in a Fright?

Have you ever woken up in a fright
from the voices of stars?
O, mankind, devoid of your pride,
it seems you died before being born.
Oh, mankind, devoid of your pride,
it is not a disappointment, it is just the state of your mind.
Why is your mind devoted to God
so tired?
You are in a hurry to achieve the magic
of radiant words.
You dig deep into a word,
and the universe seeps into your eyes.
Your affliction is grave. You didn't recover.
Feel the secret of everything,
Do you know, Light of my Life,
that you are everywhere?

Shadow of Time

When I wasn't turned yet into dust,
I felt loneliness exactly like you.
This world of light was created in one breath,
When it connected with Me.
This sunrise kissed my forehead,
When I was coming to life in an autumn sky.
And reaching the face of the Creator.
At that moment I met with life,
Oh, my life, full of self-loathing.
You will read a song dedicated to me
When saying goodbye to a beautiful death!

F. Dot.

– Drawing strength from the Holy Spirit
I was looking for honour from words, radiating sunshine.
What will I get if I make a life laugh?
– What will you get if you make a life cry?
– Drop it, this talk about life …
Is there anyone who wasn't wandering
trying to find the right path?
– Oh, this summer night, bored and exhausted from all the gossip,
grunts, noise …
– You are probably tired of too active, resourceful, frivolous,
nimble ones?
– I pity children whose hopes are already frozen by the heat of
cold words …
– I'm looking for a noble path …
– What will you do with it?
– One day you will crack from loneliness …
– Your heart will return to the dust,
And you will find yourself in front of God.

No Time

I'm 'not' here too,
There's no time for us to think.
I'll tell you how the ground sighs,
probably, it will interest 'You':
We silently count the coming days,
with everyday hustle they will pass in vain.
I'm alive and well, my kin are in good health,
one can say,
Thanks, God, for that ...
I'm not the one to speak against the faith and put on airs
before the Creator,
grooming sadness and looking after sorrow.
You will understand this,
or maybe not, I won't be offended.
clinging to my thoughts like a bindweed
I will feel empty ...
What is a thought?
I think within it.
It played among its own peers too;
it worshipped Someone too,
it sparkled like stars in its own way ...
What is a thought?
A 'Star' dropped from my inner universe
and found the congenial Light.
A congenial Light that reconciled every moment
could be a sparkle of a genius, still unborn.
I'm thirsty.
In a drop of a future autumnal rain
will we notice the eye of fate,
million times smaller than a speck of dust?
... I'm not reckless, idle.
I won't get crazy and trade my consciousness.
Thanks, everything is just great,
But why do I torture myself?
Why do I suffer silently so much?

Dialogue with the Author

'We'll end up in the ground,' – you say,
'Everything is futile …
I'll die' – you say,
but you don't.
– Death is being lost, who said that?!
– You did.
You understand, you know what happiness and misfortune
mean.

Sorrow is crying in your eyes,
your words are frowning,
you pretend to laugh,
but inside recklessness scratches 'the surface of the Moon'.
We'll end up – not on Earth.
– The Earth itself is the grave.
– Infinity …
… You pretend not to believe it,
you know everything but pretend to be ignorant,
you see everything but pretend to see nothing …
Or you really
don't see …
Or you really
don't know …
P.S.
Happiness goes in a circle
against a human heart.
Time goes
anti-clockwise.

VOID

To measure a volume of regret,
I would think about my past life and songs.
They flash past in my memory.
When I sigh, free of thoughts,
I would say ...
crying out loudly
without any reason ...
Well ...
I'm happy for now.

Are you tired of friends who made you laugh?
Here's the reason! Cry!

We are crying.
You are whiny ones too ...
Cry.
The moment you cry – it is a thousand times better than
saintliness.
Cry, cry – saddling your heart with sorrow ...

All children are the greatest whiners.
Cry.
We cried when we were in big trouble,
we cried when we fell in love with the beauty,
what happiness.
Well, cry for life,
we didn't come begging.
Cry.
That's an order of the Creator –
He's an emperor of the crying spirits.
Time is like a cabbage,
it is multi-layered.
But it has only one root.
We are souls born out of its tears,
we all come and leave in one moment,
one moment. Life is empty.
There's no one.
Cry!

Translated by Rose Kudabayeva

YERLAN JUNIS

(b. 7.11.1984)

Yerlan Junis is a poet and literary translator. He graduated from the Dulati Taraz State University in 2007 majoring in Persian. He was subsequently employed at the literary newspapers *Kentavr* (2007–09) and *Ķazaķ ădebieti* (2009–11). He is currently editor at the Žetisu Almaty regional TV channel.

His first poetry collection *Žyr-perzent* (Verse-Child, 2001) was published when he was still at school. His subsequent collections include: *Kieli tùnderdiņ dùġasy* (The Prayer of the Sacred Nights, 2011), *Ġausar* (The Heavenly Spring, 2014), *Hauas* (Insight, 2013) and *Ùmit žyrlary* (Songs of Hope, 2014). Yerlan Junis's lyrical verses are highly regarded by his literary peers for the unexpected surrealist images and the sincere, yet elegant expression of human emotions. He has also translated a number of world classics from Russian and Persian into Kazakh.

He has won a number of awards and national and international poetry contests, including the Grand Prix of the Shabyt International Youth Festival (2006). He was awarded the Daryn State Prize in 2014.

In the 'Gúlǎnda' Bookshop

Almaty.
September.
Evening.
Bookshop.
'Hey you, don't look at your watch!'
I understand, his family's waiting for him …
As for me, I prefer to stay indoors.
Life in the city is a non-stop party,
but the city's flowers lost their smell …
The street-wise scream mindlessly,
having a good time …
Here quiet wisdom resides silently.
Proud wisdom lies
inside the book –
bored of itself.
One day I will turn up here as well –
as a paperback …
I feel it.
You, a bookshop owner,
understand
that I will come here anyway.
Oh, then you'll charge a mint to sell me to the girls.
But for your kindness today
you will get my mother's blessing!
Bookshelves are supple
like a beauty's waist.
It's hard to bear the weight
of old men.
I hold books in my hands
lightly and carefully –
like a respectful daughter-in-law holds *kese*[1] while serving tea.
My desire and passion are pure
as I caress the book's pages.
I feel the breath
feel the very heart
of each word.

---

[1] *Kese* – traditional Kazakh bowl used for serving tea.

I feel how time itself melts,
simmering slowly
at the edge of the heart.
Fiery epochs melt in the thoughts
of the lonely one, standing at the edge of the crowd.
Wisdom,
silence,
calmness,
can only scream on page.
Old men wasting away from idleness
start teasing me:
'Such a fool, such an idiot –
this boy won't calm down
until he joins us!'
But then they become sad
as if they penetrated my proud thoughts.
You didn't manage to save anyone from falling into an abyss
and turned into the abyss yourselves.
But I love you, old men,
like I never loved anyone before.
I wish I learned from you how not to die –
how to die I can learn by myself.
Don't have many on my wavelength –
my father meditation, my mother sadness.
There's God's breath in everything!
Maġžan[2] and Yesenin[3]
continue to live in me,
Borges and Éluard
don't know me yet!

---

[2] Maġžan Žùmabaev (Magzhan Zhumabayev; 1893–1938) – one of the most influential Kazakh poets, member of the Alaš Orda Party. Accused of being a Pan-Turkist and Japanese spy, he was persecuted and ultimately shot in March 1938.

[3] Sergei Yesenin (1895–1925) – one of the most popular Russian poets of the twentieth century.

As for Hafez[4] –
He is like a *naġašy*[5] to me,
I'm ready to steal from his poetry anytime.
Maulavi – a mysterious beauty
that crushes you effortlessly.
Wild creatures,
wanderers,
how do they fit into the quiet book
of yesterday?
Song-breeze blows, legends are on the move –
till they are forgotten –
But even the forgotten ones
are more important than life.
Almaty.
September.
Evening.
Bookshop.
I close the door from outside.
Loneliness awaits me there.
I'm its only friend …

---

[4] Khwaja Shams-ud-Din Muhammad Hafez-e Shirazi (1315–90) – Persian poet, known by his pen name 'Hafez' or 'Hafiz'.

[5] *Naġašy* – maternal relative. It is believed that one has three groups of relatives: maternal relatives, paternal relatives and in-laws; maternal relatives are considered to be the most supportive and caring. According to Kazakh tradition, a *žien* (nephew or niece) can request any three things in the latter's disposal and the *naġašy* has to oblige.

Loneliness

Are there any lights up ahead?
If not, stop, I'm getting out.
I will drink my sorrow
and eat my troubles
in the pubs and bars!
Maybe I'll be met
by a cheerful, smiling good-looking face!

My friend, the master of ceremonies
will loudly announce: 'The Poet has arrived!'
He'll honour his guest pouring wine
red as the girl's lips – shyness
in the waitress's eyes – mine will light up meeting hers …
'No regrets!' will flash through my mind.
Silence is noble, words are cruel …
My friend the master of ceremonies
will yell out the hits: 'Orphans' and 'Godfather' …
The universe bellows in unison
all the lonely hopes, thoughts and dreams.
The universe can't write exactly like me
and I can't compose like the universe.
But I could write,
I wrote.
I am guilty of causing tears to flow.
The world's grace comes from honour,
the world's power comes from shame.
Hey, you lookers – read a poem,
otherwise, inner passion
will die in vain …
If poets are afraid of something
the beautiful girls will head there at once.
Just cut that out!
Switch off the lights!
I lost weight.
I wrote.
I worried.
I got lonely.

I fell in love,
sorry, I'm bored –
bored with everything, my friend!
I drunk my heart's blood
to the very bottom.
A pint of tears followed,
and all the while they call me:
'The greatest poet.'
Though I didn't believe them!
So no more drinks for me!
Take me away from the bars
to the long winding roads!
Are there any lights up ahead?
Is there any loyal heart?

Blink and I Miss You

In the blink of an eye of a star
I managed to miss you,
In the moment you left my side,
I managed to miss you,
Between two wing flaps of a butterfly
I managed to miss you,
Waiting for the first city lights
I managed to miss you,
While the falling drop said goodbye
I managed to miss you,
While the match thought: *I will burn*
I managed to miss you,
Trying to escape my thoughts
I managed to miss you,
Thinking about my next word
I managed to miss you,
While a flying bird attempted to land
I managed to miss you,
Before disappointment struck
I managed to miss you,
Trying to relieve you of troubles
I managed to miss you,
Putting your burden on my back
I managed to miss you,
Stepping from the train to the platform
I managed to miss you,
Before I understood everything
I managed to miss you,
Refusing to miss you at all,
I managed to miss you.
Don't tell me love is dead
better just kill me!

If You Watch the Rain Long Enough …

If you watch the rain long enough –
A whole day would fit into the space of one raindrop:
… I never tried to offend fate,
because I was ashamed before God.

The day will drip on to the earth with raindrops –
turning into a reflection of the dream:
… I didn't question wicked ones about their wrong-doing –
I was ashamed in front of the righteous.

I matched my feelings with every raindrop
and poured them into my heart;
… I forced my eyes to run away from beautiful women –
I was ashamed in front of my beloved.

Nature entered my dreams at dawn like an angel,
and left me a wonderful gift:
I never raised my voice talking to those younger than me –
I was ashamed before my elders.

Terrible failures after wonderful starts,
reminded me often that we are mortal:
… I never lied to my poems –
I was ashamed in the eyes of the future.

Sometimes I Think …

Sometimes I think
that I really exist in this life,
probably as one of
the leaves,
specks of dust,
raindrops. Or maybe
only as a simple book character.
Tired a bit probably,
and confused,
but nevertheless
a constant admirer of life,
embracing hopes, dreams
and yearnings,
flying with cherished thoughts
to every century.
Oh God, how boundless is the mind,
your imagined walks, talks and sights
they all become so real, that
sometimes only real love is missing …
No, I might be a bird or a flower –
sometimes I recognise myself,
sometimes I'm a total stranger.
Or maybe I'm just an image
in the dream of a beautiful woman,
or sadness in the soul of my beloved.
Probably I still exist in this world,
even in its backwoods and wilderness.
Maybe a flash in the eyes of a charmer
– yes that's me,
my lovely's heart skipped a beat
– it could be me.
Maybe there is a place for me in society,
but for how long? Years? Days?
Sometimes I feel a real urge to live –
does that mean that I really exist?

I want to learn the dreams of
sad people,
saints,
travellers –
get to the inner truth of their thoughts.
Hey, people, tell me
that I exist in this life surely?!
I don't know where I am from,
where I was before.
Did I build a palace for the Sun
or a fortress for the Moon?
… Maybe I'm a poet,
born when the universe sighed,
who knows?

Lily Flower Said:
'I'm in Love with One Girl'

Lily flower said: 'I'm in love with one girl.'
'OK, love her!'
Only loving hearts are owners of this world!

Lily flower said: 'I'd love to see this girl.'
'OK. Let's see her.'
If we don't see her the world will surely turn to dust.

Lily flower said: 'Give me to this girl
                                    as a present',
OK, I want to give a flower to a beautiful girl too.

… I gave her a flower and the girl said:
'I love you!'
Oh God, what am I to blame for?

These Eyes Are Like Family to Me

These eyes are like family to me
these lips are dear to my own flesh.
The first time when we met
with our souls intact,
and hearts fresh,
is still in my memory.
Our night of shyness is alive in my heart.
Do you feel that?
Do you know that?!
Your eyes … I remember their sadness –
like an unread poem.
These hands are like friends to me,
they embrace part of me!
You asked me not to be late,
but I kept my distance
and didn't come at all.
Your thoughts became my neighbours,
your words – my friends.
My love, since then –
roads lead to nowhere,
homes turn their backs to me.
When people like something,
they don't run away from it,
but I took flight,
and now the world is evil to my eyes,
a stranger to myself,
I am my own foe.

Save My Heart

Save your heart,
save my heart,
in this turmoil,
when life is hard!
Day needs a heart,
night needs a heart,
you can forget about it,
but a flower needs a heart too!
Guard your heart,
guard my heart.
If you don't love,
don't think that others won't.
Protect your heart,
protect my heart,
it's hardly beating
as if sensing trouble.
Listen to my heart,
listen to your heart.
Don't call me into the abyss,
don't make me sink into sadness.
Feel mercy for your heart,
feel mercy for my heart.
The heart belongs
to the realm of beauty.
The heart is a true poet.
Save your heart,
save my heart,
Oh God, give eyes
to those whose hearts
are blind!

Have You Noticed the Whims of the Universe?

Have you noticed the whims of the universe?
For a gentle flower, everything is gentle,
nothing else but flowers around it –
let the flower think so.
Its tenderness, whose fault is it?
For a simple rock, everything is rocky,
even a blackcurrant is a rock for it.
We fought so hard saying 'We aren't rocks!'
till our young hearts were bleeding.
Stand tall so the others can be on top,
be in love so the others can love too.
Don't make an earthen jug out of a rock,
to pour the tears of the whitest flower into it.

Tears

Clouds of my past
forgiven by my vulnerable feelings
float above me.
I've learned how to stand tall
from my own teardrop.

The mirage of my childish passionate dreams
was trembling over the steppe.
It was the time of spring rains.
I remember how my first tear dropped –
full of fate's bitterness.

Oh, I could have guessed then
that the world will change
and my song too,
and that will be the high price
I pay for everything in life:

This world was completely different,
before tears spilled from my eyes.
One teardrop became a black night
born from the white light.

Drip ...
The earth shuddered...!
The nature of the ground has changed:
Flowers and birds were born anew.
My heart wasn't the same anymore.

If I knew then
that words would transform as well,
and choose their own way.
That's how I learned to stand tall
thanks to one teardrop of mine.

After that …
mountains shed tears too,
and steppe cried.
Nobody asked why they're crying,
the reason was known to no one.

But they changed too.
With my changed song
I stand guard,
so no tears would be spilled
from anyone's eyes.

Since those clouded years
I tasted other sorrow.
Now I don't cry anymore
over years stolen.
Do not let me shed tears no more,
heaven!

To You, To You …

To you, to you, I'll come before the dawn,
wherever you live: in the mountains or in the valley.
I'll open wide your window and leave
a mountain flower on your pillow.

To you, to you, I'll come before night,
before the city lights go out.
I'll cover you with a white blanket
and leave a wild flower on your pillow.

To you, to you, I'll come ahead of myself,
ahead of yearning and ahead of patience,
even if I won't hear my name from your lips
even if I won't see my reflection in your eyes.

To you, to you, I'll come ahead of sorrows,
ahead of these cruel years,
misfortune, your fate, and heartbreak,
loneliness and coming close to tears.

I'll come ahead of any hope or dream,
before being thrown away like an unwanted gift.
Before old age and a young life withering,
ahead of strangers who don't understand you.

I'll come to you ahead of tears shed,
ahead of all retreats and defeats.
I will turn into an angel protecting you from
Day, from Night, from sadness and tears.

Even if hard times put obstacles in your way,
and brutal people threaten you,
you will feel that I'm near you
even when you know I'm far away.

If we meet in our dreams, know that they are real,
if we meet when life is hard, know that life is good.
If you see a white flash in the black sky
know that it is me who came to you ahead of everything.

You Know ...

You know everything.
About heart's storms and rains.
About springs when birds were late,
And that my soul was hurt then.

You know which words healed my pain,
Which songs were lullabies to the twilight,
What autumn flowers faded early,
When I didn't come to you the next day.

You know how the soul sings in summer,
How the fire of fate burns in the heart,
You immediately grasped a young man's state,
How I could almost combust in that instant.

You know how fate tossed me about,
(Like mountains I shake before finding peace.)
Under what flood I was, but dared to look at the sky,
What words I repeated to myself again and again,

You know,
All what my soul craves,
It is known to you – how can I find peace,
What prayer I read in the morning,
What book I read in the evening.

You know everything, spoiled girl,
I couldn't complain to another heart, only yours.
What dreams I have every night,
How they were interpreted.

You know,
Secrets no one knows,
Mysteries I can't solve myself,
Signs that no one saw,
Poems not included in any of my books.

You know,
All facts about everything,
You know the reasons my songs are sad,
… But maybe it is my fault
That knowing everything,
You haven't got a clue how much I need you.

It Is a Mystery

It is a mystery that one can't be tired of someone in a
                                        hundred years,
not be tired of breathing one's breath;
August's night became a young adult
like your tender fresh thoughts ...

Who will solve the riddle of a shy mind?
Who will see its hidden birthmark?
Look, this eighteen-year-old night is lost in its thoughts,
like one of your reflective moments.

Eighteen-year-old night,
how tender you are.
How spoiled was your heart's friend.
Enjoying the last rain of summer,
smelling the very last flower,

you soared in the air like birds,
I was admiring you silently.
... August's night became a young adult.
like an eighteen-year-old song.

Waiting

I'll be back by the autumn – that was my promise
to you and friends, but I haven't kept my word.
My heart is reaching out to you,
but life carries me in a different direction.

The steppe burned out while waiting for the autumn.
What a pity, winding roads can't lead me to you,
birds are circling around the house
in the middle of nowhere, unable to leave it.

Sky flashes momentarily in your rainy eyes,
you come again to the window,
looking again at the road,
unable to draw the curtain …

Where Is Your Summer, My Leaf?

A summer song not sang
brings so much anguish – we know that too well.
Each feeling has its own colour:
green, red, pale,
yellow, black and white –
I kept all of them in my heart for years.
But among all those colours
I couldn't find one
that was a true reflection of you.
My leaf, the Sun is laughing in your eyes.
I cannot leave you, cannot say goodbye.
Who knew you would stay with the summer,
who knew I would meet the autumn alone?

Translated by Rose Kudabayeva